intimate ENCOUNTERS

A Practical Guide to Discovering the Secrets of a Really Great Marriage

David & Teresa Ferguson
Chris & Holly Thurman
and Terri Ferguson

with Carole Gift Page

THOMAS NELSON PUBLISHERS
Nashville

Published in Nashville, Tennessee, by Janet Thoma Books, a division of Thomas Nelson, Inc., and distributed in Canada by Word Communications, Ltd., Richmond, British Columbia, and in the United Kingdom by Word (UK), Ltd., Milton Keynes, England.

Printed in the United States of America
97 96 95   —5 4 3

ISBN: 0-8407-7793-0

FOREWORD

Friendship, fellowship and great sex are part of God's blueprint for an abundant, intimate marriage! Drawing from the believer's intimate relationship with Christ, these pages provide the practical tools couples need to experience freedom from painful emotions, unhealthy thinking, and self-defeating behaviors. Challenging biblical insights are presented to guide couples into vulnerability, mutual giving and affectionate caring—the keys to an intimate marriage.

As you journey through these pages, you'll make discoveries about yourself, your partner, and your marriage. Sometimes the discoveries may be challenging as fears are faced and hurts healed. Sometimes the discoveries will prompt new levels of closeness as sharing deepens and care is communicated. The principles presented will lead you along a Christ-centered journey of genuine change as trust builds and giving to one another increases.

This resource offers something for every relationship:

—practical help to make good marriages even better
—preparation for a future marriage
—hope and healing for troubled relationships

Congratulations to the Ferguson-Thurman team!

This workbook and the companion book, *The Pursuit of Intimacy* are on the "cutting edge" of marriage enrichment and ministry. May God richly bless your journey through these pages as you share together "Intimate Encounters" with Him and with one another.

—Josh McDowell

This book is dedicated to the Lord's ministry through the

Center for Marriage & Family Intimacy
P.O. Box 201808
Austin, Texas 78720

and their commitment to fortify—from a
biblical perspective—homes, churches,
and cities through ministry to marriages and families.

*"The land is still ours, because we
have sought the LORD our God."*
—2 Chronicles 14:7 (NASB)

CONTENTS

Foreword   *iii*
Acknowledgments   *vi*
Let's Get Started!   *vii*
How to Use This Workbook   *ix*

1. Assess Your Marriage Intimacy   *1*
2. What Do We Really Need from Each Other?   *9*
3. What's Filling Your Emotional Cup?   *17*
4. Heal Hurts Through Confession and Forgiveness   *29*
5. Blend Four Ingredients for Marital Closeness   *38*
6. Be Free from Fear   *50*
7. Study Your Family Tree   *64*
8. Be Free for Emotional Closeness   *77*
9. Be Free from Marital Games   *93*
10. Understand the Pain and Potential of Intimacy Needs   *113*
11. Leave Your Father and Mother   *126*
12. Blessed Are Those Who Mourn   *143*
13. Break Free from Unhealthy Thinking   *157*
14. Establish a Vision for Your Marriage and Family   *183*
15. Walk Together Through the Stages of Marriage Intimacy   *215*
16. Become Friends, Lovers, and Saints Through Intimacy Disciplines   *238*

Appendix I: Principles of Intimacy Therapy   *263*
Appendix II: Implementing a Marriage Intimacy Ministry   *266*

ACKNOWLEDGMENTS

Gratefulness for God's work and healing in our own marriage has prompted within us a deep burden for others. In developing these resources, God has again blessed us through several special couples who have co-labored with us in a commitment to experience God's truth for marriage. Special thanks to Jim & Becky Walter, Brian & Wetonnah McCoy, Lewis & Lacy Alexander, Dennis & Jan Gallaher, Donnie & Carolyn Dixon, Rick & Ada Ferguson, Bruce & Simonne Maginnis, and Don & Mary McMinn.

It has been a special joy to work on this project with our daughter, Terri. Her insight, creativity, and resourcefulness are what make the material come alive in discussion and group settings. We can always count on encouragement and support from our daughter, Robin, and son-in-law, Ike. Our son, Eric, provides fun times of diversion and opportunities to enjoy life.

Thanks also to Janet Thoma for her encouragement and support from the very beginning of this project. Finally, many thanks to Carole Gift Page, for her creative input to see real live couples experience the impact of Intimacy Therapy.

David & Teresa Ferguson

Our heartfelt thanks go to David and Teresa Ferguson for allowing us to join them in their efforts to help couples find true intimacy in their marriages. We have learned a great deal from what they have taught us and modeled in their own marriage.

Our deepest thanks go to our Heavenly Father. He brought us together when we didn't have the foggiest idea of what a good marriage was all about and has patiently moved us in the direction of being able to truly love one another. We are thankful for all the many ways He has helped us to grow as husband and wife, and look forward to how He will continue that process.

Chris and Holly Thurman

Donna, Lorri, Debbie, and Cynthia have encouraged and supported me throughout this project, from contract to finished product. Each of them has a unique place in my life, but they all have contributed a very special gift—laughter. I am deeply grateful for their friendship.

We all owe many thanks to Betty Z. She kept her sense of humor in what must have seemed like an endless stream of typing and revisions. As always, she kept it and us together!

Terri Ferguson

LET'S GET STARTED!

Imagine your courtship and marriage have been captured on videotape. If you rewound to the beginning, what would you see?

Perhaps it was the turbulent '60s. You met at a protest march or in the peace corps and married with the Vietnam War shadowing your ecstasy. Or perhaps you married in the introspective '70s. In the midst of Watergate, returning MIAs, and a resigning President, you fell in love to the strains of Simon & Garfunkel and planned a life that would be safe, sane, and secure.

Maybe your decade was the ambitious, opulent '80s. Influenced by a society venerating affluence, prestige, and the good life, you planned a lavish wedding, established dual careers, bought a luxury condo in an exclusive neighborhood, and sent your children to the best schools. Or perhaps you were married in the austere, recession-riddled '90s, as the singles scene discovered love wasn't "free" anymore; in fact, it could cost you your life. Married only a few months or years, you still feel like newlyweds. And yet so much has happened—the breakup of the Soviet Union, the Persian Gulf War, the crumbling of the Berlin wall.

Which decade was it for you? What does your videotape reveal about *your* marriage?

Fundamentally, it doesn't matter in which decade you were married. Your hopes, desires, and expectations were similar to those of every couple in every decade. You were in love. You had found the person of your dreams, and marriage offered the chance to fulfill all your secret yearnings and wishes. No matter how disappointing your childhood had been, no matter how crazy the world might be, you would create the kind of family you always knew you were meant to have. At last—a perfect marriage with abundant harmony, contentment, and intimacy. Your home would be a place of refuge and solace, where each person would be loved and accepted unconditionally. It was the Great American Dream. Only better. Because you knew you had it within you to make it come true.

Now let's fast-forward to the middle of the tape. You've been married a few years, maybe even a few decades, and chances are most of the dreams you started with have been tempered by a bitter dose of reality, if not shattered by disillusionment. Marriage isn't what you expected. Your house of refuge has turned into an armed camp; perhaps you play out the Cold War every night in your bedroom or maintain an uneasy truce for the sake of the children.

You expected unconditional love; you've got manipulation and games; you anticipated undying sympathy; you've got a mate who knows your weaknesses and where to twist the knife. Tenderness and intimacy remain as elusive as a rainbow. Remember being a child and chasing rainbows? Just when you thought you'd reached one, it wasn't really there at all. It was just a mirage.

And now you're afraid your marriage is a rainbow too—lovely in concept, but just an illusion. Surely, this isn't what falling in love was meant to be.

Well, if this isn't it, what is?

What is real intimacy? Is it a rainbow lovely from a distance that disappears when you think you've found it? Is it an illusion? Or can genuine love and intimacy be captured and nurtured in a marriage relationship?

As therapists and as married couples with over forty years of marital experience, we—David and Teresa Ferguson and Chris and Holly Thurman—can give an enthusiastic, unequivocal YES! Yes, you can experience a tender, nurturing intimacy God planned from the beginning for the two of you. Pursuing intimacy doesn't mean chasing rainbows. Intimacy can be an ongoing, day-to-day reality in your marriage.

HOW TO USE THIS WORKBOOK

If you have picked up this workbook, you undoubtedly have a desire to see changes take place in your relationship with your spouse, or you may personally desire to learn how to have a successful relationship.

This workbook, and the principles of Intimacy Therapy™ as outlined in the appendix, are designed to be used by individuals, couples, and groups who want to learn how to make their marriage relationship more intimate, nurturing, and caring.

In this workbook, we have devised practical techniques and exercises to help you develop closeness in your marriage as you and your partner learn to meet each other's needs. We suggest you read *The Pursuit of Intimacy* to see how we walked Jimmy and Marla Carlton through the ten "action verbs" of Intimacy Therapy. They'll join us in this workbook, too, as we show you how to adopt the intimacy ingredients and block the robbers of intimacy. We'll also show you how to think straight, forgive each other, and reject the games couples play. Only after you leave your childhood home and mourn your childhood hurts will you truly understand who you are. Then you'll be ready to practice intimacy disciplines and maintain intimacy over your life cycle. Don't worry. We'll lead you step by step, hand in hand. But you must take the first step. Begin now. It will be an exhilarating journey as you find out what falling in love was meant to be.

Set aside a time each week to work on the exercises alone. All exercises are for individual work unless indicated. With this in mind, you may want to purchase two workbooks—one for each spouse. The exercises you do throughout the week will prepare you for the "Marriage Staff Meetings." These Staff Meetings are designed to give you and your partner a chance to share and discuss your individual work.

If you find yourself doing this workbook alone, we suggest you find someone to walk this path with you—someone to encourage you along the way and give feedback and support. Your work will be most effective if it is done within the context of a group or with a counselor, pastor, or trusted same sex journey mate. As you and your selected partner(s) travel through these exercises, we trust the insights you gain will provide you with the necessary tools to enhance and enrich future relationships.

If you and your partner have chosen to take this journey toward marital intimacy together, you may find one partner's pace differing from the other's. While the exercises are written in a 16-week format, they should be done in an amount of time fitting both partners' needs. It's better to go slowly and gain the full benefit from the exercises than to rush through them just for the sake of completion. Try to find a comfortable pace for both partners.

Near the end of each chapter we have included an opportunity for Scripture Journaling. These exercises will help you focus on God's presence and availability as a source of hope and encourage you to look to Him as the Divine Healer in your relationships.

As part of several chapters in the workbook, you will find symbols indicating the activity is a "Lifestyle Discipline." We consider these the key elements in a successful marriage. You will want to take special note of Lifestyle Discipline exercises and include them as a regular part of your marriage journey after completing this workbook.

For those of you who will be meeting with others in a marriage intimacy class, support group, or mentor relationship, watch for the gray boxes later in each chapter that contain ideas and discussion questions for groups. These boxes will be especially helpful for group leaders.

We have included the following commitment sheet to help clarify what will be expected of you as you complete the workbook exercises. Each spouse should carefully read the items on the facing page and discuss them, if necessary, before signing.

COMMITMENT SHEET

1. *I will set aside time each week to complete the individual exercises in this workbook, with honesty and sincerity.*

2. *I will "prioritize" time in my schedule for Marriage Staff Meetings with my partner.*

3. *I will participate in both the giving and receiving of support and care.*

4. *I will acknowledge and respect any differences in our stages of growth and will refrain from making comparisons with my spouse.*

5. *I will focus on my thoughts, feelings, and actions as I seek to be accountable to God as the Divine Author of marriage.*

6. *I will be open and willing for God to show me how I can relate more intimately with Him, and how I can meet needs in my spouse's life.*

_____   _____
Name   Date

_____   _____
Name   Date

PERSONAL GOALS

Take a few minutes to think about what you want to accomplish with this workbook. Then jot down what changes you hope for in each of the following categories:

Yourself   Children

_____

_____

_____

Marriage   Relationship with God

_____

_____

_____

Relationship with parents   Relationship with in-laws

_____

_____

_____

HOW TO USE THIS GUIDE IN A GROUP:

The majority of exercises in this workbook are designed to be done on your own or with your partner. However, you can gain a great deal by discussing what you've written with others and interacting with couples with similar interests. To help you do that, gray boxes like the one below will be scattered throughout the workbook. They will provide activities that will be useful in a group setting, as well as discussion questions that will help you discuss pertinent issues and maintain your own comfortable level of vulnerability.

Appendix II for group leaders includes some ground rules you will probably want to establish for your meetings. There is a complete "Group Member Commitment Sheet" available in the appendix. However, here are a few recommendations to consider right away:

In a group setting, talk only about yourself, your feelings, and your thoughts, not those of your spouse.

No one has to participate in a discussion or answer a question aloud unless he or she wants to do so.

Always maintain confidentiality (names, words, actions, observations, and impressions are not to be repeated outside the group).

Avoid giving advice. Instead, look for opportunities to give mutual support and care.

Though this workbook is designed with a 16-week format in mind, feel free to adjust the schedule to meet the needs of the group. The purpose of the workbook is to experience the objectives, not just to complete the pages.

———— For Group Discussion ————

In the first meeting you may want to allow time for group members to get to know one another. It may be appropriate to plan some kind of icebreaker activity. (Each couple might tell how they met, an interesting detail about their wedding day, or some other unusual fact about themselves.) You will also want to spend time going over the purpose for the group and ground rules for group discussion.

Ask the entire group to brainstorm about any common misconceptions about marriage. Point out that misconceptions may develop as the result of societal messages, family messages, personal experiences, and the diverse and sometimes contrary expectations of men and women, among other reasons.

A fulfilling marriage is an intimate marriage. Discuss how the group members define intimacy. Let each person have a chance to tell the following:

- What made you decide to work through this workbook and group discussion?
- What changes do you hope for in yourself after working through this workbook?

Ask group members to complete Chapter One before the next group meeting. You may also want to go over the Group Member Commitment Sheet before concluding the meeting.

Chapter One

■ —— ■ —— ■

ASSESS YOUR
MARRIAGE INTIMACY

In our Preface we invited you to think of your marriage as a videotape and "rewind" through the magic of memory to the decade in which you were married. Now we urge you to zero in on that once-in-a-lifetime event—your wedding day.

It may have been the most hectic day of your life. Or the most romantic. Or the most terrifying. Or all of these. And more. Much, much more. Your emotions may have careened from panic to ecstasy to anxiety and back again. And the questions no doubt pummeled your brain like swarming bees. *Will the ceremony go off without a hitch? Have I forgotten anything crucial? Am I really ready to spend a lifetime with this person?*

This last question may have come to mind as you said your vows. The minister or official who performed your ceremony no doubt reminded you of the significance of this moment and of the permanence of your commitment. He probably included in his remarks a reference to the three areas of intimacy we will be discussing in this workbook. You and your spouse may have pledged to "love, honor, and cherish" each other. That's the dimension of *emotional* intimacy (the soul, or your "self-consciousness"). You promised to "forsake all others." This refers to *physical* intimacy (the body, or your "world-consciousness"). And you made a commitment to "what God has joined together." That's *spiritual* intimacy (the spirit, or your "God-consciousness"). There you have it.

1

Your marriage vows suggest "oneness" in three parts—body, soul, and spirit.

Think about these three areas for a moment. In which area(s) of intimacy do you think God would want us to become intimate first? What would the world's perspective be on this order? (Actually, our society often focuses on *one* dimension to the complete exclusion of the other two!)

The essential truth is that God intended for us to develop intimacy with our mate in *each* of these three areas. It is the only way we can establish a balanced, fulfilled marriage.

Are you open to nurturing an emotional intimacy with your spouse? A spiritual intimacy? A physical intimacy?

For the relationships in your marriage or family to be knit closely together, you must share yourselves with one another. "Closeness" doesn't just happen because we have the same last name or live under the same roof. Becoming one in marriage involves the freedom to share all of yourself with your spouse—spirit, soul, and body.

To survive and flourish, your marriage needs nourishment and attention in each of these dimensions. Just as you need air, food, and water to live, so your marriage has essential nourishment needs. A growing, healthy, and balanced marital relationship is one where each partner is enjoying an abundance of intimacy in all three realms—body, soul, and spirit. This means that as the two of you "become one flesh" (Gen. 2:24), you become "best friends" growing together in spiritual fellowship and sexual closeness.

You may know many couples who excel in one of these areas but lag behind in the other two. Rudy and Marisa are newlywed lovebirds who can't keep their hands off each other. They bill and coo and whisper sweet nothings, but one wonders if they'll have anything to say to each other once the novelty of sex wears off.

Glen and Shawna seem like they've been best friends forever, but they act more like brother and sister than husband and wife. Have they forgotten the passions of their youth or did they never give their passions a chance to heat up in the first place?

Cliff and Phyllis are so involved in their church work they have no time for fun and recreation. They teach Sunday school, sing in the choir, and hold positions on every committee. No one has ever seen them together without a Bible or hymnbook between them; all their conversation revolves around the Lord's work. Surely God is pleased. Or is He? Wasn't it

His idea to have *three* dimensions in a relationship? Somehow, in spite of their "spirituality," Cliff and Phyllis have forgotten two of those three vital dimensions of marriage God has ordained.

How about you and your partner? Is your marriage lopsided because you're expending all of your energies in only one or, at most, two dimensions of your relationship?

During the next few minutes we encourage you and your partner to give responses that will help you assess your level of intimacy in each of these three areas—body, soul, and spirit.

Start by silently asking yourselves these questions:

- What does it mean to be physically intimate with my partner?
- What does it mean to be a friend to my spouse?
- What would a spiritual dimension to our relationship involve?

WHERE ARE WE?

After you've taken a few minutes to reflect on your relationship with your spouse, indicate your perception of your degree of intimacy in the three areas of spirit, soul, and body. Place an X on the scale below to signify your view of the relationship.

1. The spiritual dimension of our relationship is

_____

Lacking in   Very
Intimacy   Intimate

What aspect of your spiritual relationship would you most like to see changed or improved in your marriage? _____

_____

_____

2. The emotional or friendship dimension of our relationship is

_____

Lacking in   Very
Intimacy   Intimate

What aspects of being a friend to your spouse would you most like to see changed or improved in your marriage?_____

_____

_____

3. The physical dimension of our relationship is

_____

Lacking in   Very
Intimacy   Intimate

What aspects of your physical closeness would you most like
to see changed or improved in your marriage? _____

_____

_____

What aspects of being a friend to your spouse would you most like to see changed or improved in your marriage?

As part of your relationship assessment, complete the following Marital Intimacy Inventory. Carefully read each of the fifteen (15) questions below and circle the number from 1 to 5 that is most representative of your response.

MARITAL INTIMACY INVENTORY

	Strongly Disagree	Disagree	Generally Agree	Agree	Strongly Agree
1. My spouse is supportive and encouraging of my personal spiritual growth.	1	2	3	4	5
2. We seem to be good at giving one another undivided attention when listening or talking.	1	2	3	4	5
3. When I'm sharing my feelings, my spouse values them and is sensitive to provide understanding reassurance.	1	2	3	4	5
4. We seem to prioritize frequent times of quality talking and having dates together.	1	2	3	4	5

	Strongly Disagree	Disagree	Generally Agree	Agree	Strongly Agree
5. My spouse is attentive and sensitive to my needs in the area of sexual foreplay.	1	2	3	4	5
6. We seem to practice honest confession followed by genuine forgiveness when one of us has hurt the other.	1	2	3	4	5
7. My spouse is good at sharing appreciation and verbalizing love.	1	2	3	4	5
8. Verbalizing my needs and desires concerning our relationship to my spouse would be normal for me.	1	2	3	4	5
9. I'm comfortable communicating my sexual desires and preferences to my spouse.	1	2	3	4	5
10. We seem to frequently recount the good times and blessings we have enjoyed as a couple.	1	2	3	4	5
11. My spouse and I often tend to agree in many of the important issues concerning values and beliefs.	1	2	3	4	5
12. I remember special times when my spouse and I shared strong emotions, like grief, sadness, joy, or brokenness.	1	2	3	4	5
13. I'm very satisfied with my spouse's sensitivity in meeting my sexual needs.	1	2	3	4	5
14. As a couple, our spiritual closeness through prayer or sharing Scripture insights is quite good.	1	2	3	4	5
15. I am satisfied with my spouse's frequency of initiating sexual times together.	1	2	3	4	5

Interpreting Your Score

Add your responses for Questions #1, #6, #10, #11, and #14, and chart your score here:

Spiritual Scale _____
0   25

Add your responses for Questions #2, #3, #7, #8, and #12, and chart your score here:

Emotional Scale _____
0   25

Add your responses for Questions #4, #5, #9, #13, and #15, and chart your score here:

Physical Scale _____
0   25

Did any new insights or questions come to mind as you completed this inventory? _____

_____

Summarize your impressions or feelings about the inventory results here: _____

_____

_____

_____

Scripture Journaling—Isaiah 58:11

The LORD will guide you always;/ he will satisfy your needs in a sun-scorched land/ and will strengthen your frame./ You will be like a well-watered garden,/ like a spring whose waters never fail. (NIV)

Isaiah 58:11 promises the Lord will continually guide you. Reflect on God's promise of provision and strength. Spend some time telling God your desires for your marriage. Ask for His guidance and strength. Write your thoughts and prayers to God here.

_____

_____

_____

_____

MARRIAGE STAFF MEETING

Set aside half an hour of quiet time together with your spouse. Spend this time discussing only the issues related to this workbook; save discussions about the children, finances, or household concerns for a later time.

We suggest the husband take the initiative and begin sharing his perceptions in each of the areas of intimacy. He shares the questions, insights, or summary statements about the inventory exercise, and his final scores for the inventory questions. The wife then shares the same information. Each partner also shares the specific area in each dimension they would like to see improved. Be sure to let each partner share his or her responses without interruption or comments.

Make this first session an information gathering session. Gather information by listening attentively to your spouse. Make eye contact and be sure your mind is free from distractions as he or she is talking. End your time together by holding hands, thanking each other for having the courage to vulnerably share responses, and, if you feel comfortable, say a silent prayer, thanking God for your partner and asking for His guidance in your marriage.

Here are some examples of what you might communicate to your spouse:

"Honey, when I was doing these exercises, I kept seeing the word *verbalize*. I think I've started to realize how important it is to communicate what I'm thinking to you. Maybe that's a good place for me to start."

"Sweetheart, for the emotional part of our marriage, here's the area I'd like to work on. I know it would mean a lot to you if I supported your decisions when you're disciplining the kids. I'm going to make a real effort to do that."

Encourage all couples who have completed Chapter One to answer the following:

After completing the inventory, the thing I realized about myself was

_____

_____

After the first Marriage Staff Meeting, one positive impression I had was

_____

_____

Make a mental note of the couples who did not complete Chapter One and visit with them privately after the meeting. Bring them into the discussion at appropriate times.

Have each group member turn to the results of their inventory questions. Explain that God intended for the marriage relationship to contain oneness in three areas. God wants our marriage to look like an equilateral triangle—with a spiritual base and the emotional and physical intimacy forming the other two sides.

Give each person a rubber band and ask them to manipulate it in such a way that it represents how their relationship started. Ask them: Which dimension formed the base of the relationship when you were first married? How did the other two sides look?

Ask participants to also show their current perception of their marriage. How do they see the relationship now?

Give each person a chance to explain his/her rubber band "creations." Participants may want to actually refer to their scores on page 6. These scores do give some indication as to their perception of strength or weakness in their marriage. Ask for group feedback and discussion.

Lifestyle Disciplines

Marriage Staff Meetings are included so that you and your partner will begin to prioritize your time together. Just as any successful business cannot be run without scheduled times for feedback and organization, a successful marriage requires the same commitment to communication. Begin the habit now of scheduling times to be with your partner. Agree on specific dates and put them on the family calendar or in your daily planner. Make these times a priority. Start incorporating this discipline into your lifestyle today!

Chapter Two

———— ∎ ————

WHAT DO WE REALLY NEED FROM EACH OTHER?

Jimmy Carlton was taught early in life to keep his needs and feelings to himself. "Keep a stiff upper lip," was his father's favorite phrase. His mother echoed that sentiment with the stern admonition, "Big boys don't cry." When Jimmy fell down and cut his knee, he knew better than to run home blubbering. If he held the tears back and assured his mother it didn't hurt when she applied the stinging red iodine, she would reward him with an approving smile.

Pride and self-reliance were what counted in Jimmy's family. When Jimmy told the neighbors his father had lost his job and had to go on welfare, he was spanked soundly for revealing family secrets and making people feel sorry for him. When good-hearted neighbors offered Jimmy food or secondhand clothes, he was forced to return them because his mother didn't want people looking down their nose at his family. "We don't need anyone. We can manage on our own," she assured the teary-eyed little boy. So Jimmy learned early that pride was everything, and to protect it, he must keep his guard up and never reveal his needs or vulnerabilities.

Is it any wonder, when Jimmy married Marla, she accused him of being distant, unapproachable, and unfeeling? The vulnerable little boy was locked deep inside a fortress of self-preservation built stone by stone by parents who thought they were doing the right thing.

When, through counseling, Marla Carlton began to understand the way Jimmy had been raised, she made a conscious effort to show him unconditional love. As she urged him in a non-threatening manner to reveal his feelings and needs, he allowed some of his defenses to fall away. As he experienced the satisfaction of shared intimacy with his wife, he found it easier to be himself and make his needs known. His natural instinct is still to close up emotionally and be self-sufficient, but now that he knows why he's that way, he has the motivation to become more open and vulnerable, for himself and for his family. Now, when his own son, Jeff, comes to him with a scraped knee, he manages to offer comfort without saying, "Big boys don't cry."

Perhaps your family didn't discourage expressing needs the way Jimmy's family did. But chances are you still find it a little uncomfortable to admit you have needs. The truth is, we all have needs. We were born with them, and we won't outgrow them. Just as we need oxygen, food, and water to survive, so God created us with certain emotional needs. We need acceptance, affection, appreciation, approval, attention, encouragement, respect, and security. We call these "intimacy needs." Contrary to what Jimmy's family taught, it is not wrong or selfish or weak to experience these needs. It's normal. It's what being human is all about.

The truth is, we all have needs.

Our intimacy needs are powerful motivators of our behavior. We are driven by these needs, and they determine how we relate to our Creator and other human beings. The challenge is to receive from God's abundant provision rather than respond out of our self-centeredness.

Since God created us with these intimacy needs, He has also provided the means to meet them. Sometimes He meets our needs Himself; sometimes He involves other people. Perhaps you felt His comfort and security during a loved one's illness; you may have sensed His peace again and again in the midst of life's inevitable turbulence.

Can you think of a time when God met your needs directly? Write about your experience here. *(For instance: When my mother died, God comforted me; When I felt rejected by my peer group, God made me feel loved; When I lost that promotion, God encouraged me.)*

_____

_____

_____

_____

_____

God created us with intimacy needs and has provided the means to meet these needs

The other part of God's design is to meet our needs through other people—a grandmother's hugs and kisses, a parent's words of endearment, a friend's encouragement. God also meets our needs through the church (the Body of Christ) and, of course, through the marriage relationship.

Can you think of times when God involved another person(s) to meet your needs (aside from your spouse)? Look at the list of eight intimacy needs that follow and make a list of the people God has used in your life. Feel free to include examples from past as well as current relationships. For example:

- *Rev. Lawrence—God used his comments after the service to encourage me about the way to handle things with the kids;*
- *Karen—She's been so patient with me these last few days as I've worked late each evening. I've seen God's love through her acceptance;*
- *Mr. Kingsley, my boss—He expressed his appreciation for my overtime work and approval of the job I'm doing on the Northridge project.*

Person   **How God Has Involved Him/Her to Meet My Needs**

_____

_____

_____

_____

_____

_____

Learning to meet each other's needs is vital to a healthy, thriving marriage. Take another look at the eight intimacy needs listed below and:

1. mark three (3) in the "Myself" column that are the most important for you to receive from your spouse.
2. mark three (3) in the "Spouse" column that you think your spouse would consider particularly important to receive from you.

Myself	Eight Commonly Identified Intimacy Needs	Spouse
☐	• **ACCEPTANCE**—deliberate and ready reception with a favorable positive response—Rom. 15:7	☐
☐	• **AFFECTION**—communicating care and closeness through physical touch and loving words —Rom. 16:16	☐
☐	• **APPRECIATION (Praise)**—communicating personal gratefulness with words and feelings—1 Cor. 11:2	☐
☐	• **APPROVAL**—expressed commendation; thinking and speaking well of—Rom. 14:18	☐
☐	• **ATTENTION (Care)**—taking thought of another and conveying appropriate interest and support; entering into another's "world"—Acts 27:3	☐
☐	• **ENCOURAGEMENT**—urging forward and positively persuading toward a goal—1 Thess. 5:11; Heb. 10:24	☐
☐	• **RESPECT (Honor)**—valuing and regarding highly; conveying great worth—Rom. 12:10	☐
☐	• **SECURITY (Peace)**—confidence of harmony in relationships; freedom from harm—2 Thess. 3:16	☐

Think now about the three needs you consider most important in your relationship with your spouse. Which needs have gone unmet? Which of these do you need most right now? Once you have decided what those needs are, spend some time identifying how you would most like those needs to be met. Be specific. Read the examples below before responding.

My Needs	How My Spouse Can Meet Them
To feel loved, cherished	Call me unexpectedly just to say you love me, prepare me for sex, hold and kiss me as you leave in the morning.
To feel supported, believed in	Pray with me even silently when I'm in a crisis; see my potential in specific situations and praise me in front of the kids.
To feel comforted when down	Hold me and sometimes just let me cry, feel my hurt and gently reassure me that you care and love me.

My Needs	How My Spouse Can Meet Them
To feel prioritized	Talk for a few minutes each evening and enter into conversation about my day; plan, initiate and enjoy fun times, dates, and surprises.
To feel free to be myself, to be accepted	Allow me to make mistakes with the kids and not criticize me in front of them; avoid teasing me about my shortcomings—protect me instead; give me ten times more appreciation than you do constructive criticism.

Now write down your own three main needs and give examples of how your partner could meet them. Use the space below.

1. NEED:_____

_____

_____

2. NEED:_____

_____

_____

3. NEED:_____

_____

_____

SELECTING THE RIGHT MARITAL "STROKES"

Another phase of your discovery into your intimacy needs will be revealed as you consider the positive "strokes" given in a marriage. A couple's mutual giving plays a significant role in their happiness.

Suppose a husband smiles and tells his wife, "You look great." He gives her a little hug and adds, "I love you." A few minutes later he says, "By the way, thanks for picking up my shirts from the cleaners." His statements "You look great" and "I love you," as well as his smile and the hug, are unconditional strokes—strokes he's giving his wife just for *being*. She didn't have to do anything to earn them. His comment, "Thanks for picking up my shirts," is a conditional stroke—a stroke he gives his wife for *doing*.

Note also that this husband gave his wife three *verbal* strokes: "You look great," "I love you," and "Thanks for picking up my shirts." He also gave her two *nonverbal* strokes: The smile and the hug. The hug was a *physical* stroke.

Some spouses list physical strokes as the kind they want most. Others like to be told "I love you" (a verbal, unconditional stroke). Some mates revel in conditional strokes, such as, "Your dinner was delicious," or "You did a great job trimming the tree."

Unfortunately, many spouses are not aware of the best way to demonstrate love to their mate.

To identify what you and your spouse most enjoy, check the items that appeal to your mate in Column 1, and the ones that appeal to you in Column 2. Check only four items in each column.

Mate	Myself	
☐	☐	Holding hands
☐	☐	Going for a walk
☐	☐	An unexpected hug
☐	☐	Finding a love note
☐	☐	Receiving a surprise gift
☐	☐	Being served a favorite meal
☐	☐	Being told "I love you"
☐	☐	Helping with the kids
☐	☐	Being approached sexually
☐	☐	Receiving compliments on my looks
☐	☐	Taking a shower together
☐	☐	A surprise "date"
☐	☐	Getting a back rub or massage
☐	☐	Having dinner out
☐	☐	Being praised for achievements
☐	☐	Having a quiet conversation

After you and your spouse complete your lists, share them with each other during your next Marriage Staff Meeting. It's important for each of you to understand what makes your partner feel loved and cared for. Pay careful attention to and respectfully consider both sets of answers.

It is important to understand what makes your partner feel loved and cared for.

Scripture Journaling—Ephesians 3:20

Now to Him who is able to do immeasurably more than all we ask or imagine, according to his power that is at work within us. (NIV)

Write a letter to God expressing your needs, feelings, and desires for your marriage. Let Him know what you want and what you can only imagine for your marriage. Sit quietly and give Him the opportunity to show you how He can make an immeasurable difference in your life and in your home. Write down your thoughts as they occur to you. Be transparently honest. Don't "edit" your feelings to make them conform to some standard you think they should meet.

Dear God,

When it comes to my marriage, my deepest desire is that (For instance: *My husband would be the spiritual leader in our home; my wife would occasionally take the initiative sexually; we would come to feel as cherished and in love as when we first married.*) _____

_____

_____

_____

_____

_____

_____

I pray these things in Jesus' name . . . Amen.

MARRIAGE STAFF MEETING

Set aside an hour with your spouse. Each share your three most important needs and how you would like them to be met. You might want to exchange written lists, but be sure to do so without demands or expectations for your partner.

You will also want to share your responses to the Marital Strokes exercises. Take note of how accurately (or inaccurately!) you predicted each other's responses. If your mate's responses surprised you, spend a little time reflecting on the possible reasons for this.

During the next few weeks, resolve to look for opportunities to meet your spouse's needs. View this as an adventure to be pursued, not as a duty to be fulfilled. Catch the excitement and anticipation of pleasing your mate and being pleased in ways neither of you had considered before. Close your Staff Meeting by holding hands and praying silently together.

———— For Group Discussion ————

Divide the couples into groups. Assign each group a portion of the eight intimacy needs listed in this chapter. Have each group make a collage of the ways these needs could be met. You may want to do this activity "graffiti-style," using black markers on blank paper, or cut and paste pictures and words from magazines and newspapers.

Spend some time discussing the possibly new concept of "Intimacy Needs." Ask the group these questions:

- Did you realize you have these needs?
- Do we ever outgrow these intimacy needs?
- How does it make you feel when you think about having these needs? Weak? Guilty? Selfish? Embarrassed? Why?
- What attitude should we have about our needs?

Ask the couples to share the collages they've made. Did they get any new ideas about how to meet needs? Have any attitudes changed? What do the other group members see in the collages?

Encourage each couple to share their experiences during their Marriage Staff Meeting this past week. Invite them to answer these questions:

- How similar were your key needs and marital strokes?
- How well did you know what your spouse really wanted?
- Were you able to meet any of your spouse's needs this week? How did that feel?
- Did you experience "receiving" from your spouse this week? How did that feel?

You might want to close the session by asking if the group can see ways they can meet one another's needs.

- How could we help each other identify needs?
- What can we do to better care for one another?

Chapter Three

■

WHAT'S FILLING YOUR EMOTIONAL CUP?

Perhaps you've noticed. Conflicts in your marriage are inevitable. The wedded bliss you expected never materialized. The truth is, the demands of marital closeness and the imperfections of our humanity inevitably bring hurt, disappointment, and anger. If these hurts aren't properly resolved, they'll accumulate and congeal into bitterness and resentment.

As negative feelings smolder and seethe inside you, they crowd out positive feelings of love, joy, peace, and romance. You begin to wonder if you and your spouse will ever recapture those wonderful feelings you experienced during your courtship.

Conflicts in marriage are unavoidable.

To better understand how our unhealed hurts work against us, imagine that you have a cup inside you that holds your emotions. This is the concept of "emotional capacity." In other words, you can hold only so much emotion before some of it spills out. (You do, in fact, have a portion of your brain that "handles" emotion.) A cup filled with positive emotions will overflow with love, joy, and peace—the fruits of the Spirit. But a cup filled with unhealthy emotions such as bitterness, resentment, anger, guilt, fear, and anxiety will cause symptoms of stress and prevent you from feeling positive emotions.

EMOTIONAL CAPACITY

Symptoms of a "Full Cup"

Escape into ...Work, Drugs, Infidelity, Pornography, Etc.

Loss of Energy, Concentration

Sleep/Appetite Disturbance

Depressed Mood

Impatience, Criticism Quick Temper, Controlling Behaviors

Physical Side Effects

Loss of Positive Emotions like Joy, Love, Affection, Romance

Positive Emotions

Stress

Anxiety

Fear. . . Insecurities

Condemnation . . . Shame

True Guilt . . . Often from Retaliation

Anger—Bitterness Hurt

Biblical References

Manage
- Phil. 4:4-9

Cast Upon Christ
- 1 Peter 5:7

Displace or "Cast Out" - 1 John 4:18-19

Truth Sets Free
- John 8:32; Rom. 8:1

Confess - 1 John 1:9; James 5:16

Forgive
- Eph. 4:31-32

Unhealthy Accumulations of Emotion

You Can Only Hold So Much Emotion

To help you see how your emotional cup relates to your everyday relationships, complete the following exercises. Read each scenario and write down the emotions you imagine are filling each person's emotional cup.

Scenario #1:

It was an ordinary Monday evening. Jay sat in the living room watching the football game on TV. Laura was in the kitchen finishing the dishes. The phone rang, and Laura heard her husband answer it. She could tell from his conversation that it must be Kevin, his old college buddy.

"Hey, man, you're gonna be in town next weekend? That's great!" Jay exclaimed. "Listen, we'd be glad to have you stay with us. Naw, Laura doesn't mind. Sure, I'm sure! No, we don't have plans—nothing important as your visit. Tell you what. I'll get tickets for the game next weekend. It'll be a blast! See you Friday!"

Laura dried her good china, her eyes riveted on the theater tickets on the refrigerator door. They were good only for next weekend—and Jay had promised to take her. It was to have been a romantic weekend just for the two of them! Instead, she would end up playing dutiful little housemaid while her husband and his best buddy pursued their fun and games!

What emotions do you suppose are filling Laura's cup right now? What do you think she's feeling? What does she need? Why?

_____

_____

_____

_____

_____

_____

Scenario #2:

Larry had taken off work early and made special arrangements for a luxury suite in a resort hotel. He wanted this weekend to be absolutely memorable for his wife and himself. After all, it was their tenth anniversary. But Larry and Paula's "get-away weekend" was getting off to a rough start. The weather forecaster's "partly cloudy" had turned into a torrential rain, and now as they headed down the interstate, it was impossible even to see the exit signs.

He glanced over at Paula. "Darling, maybe you'd better check the map, just in case."

Paula's irritation was thinly disguised as she reached toward the glove compartment. "Honey, why didn't you get directions before we started? I hate getting lost in this kind of weather. And you know how lousy your sense of direction is. What if we have car trouble or something? Did you ask the resort office what activities they have available if it's raining? Oh, Larry, I just know our weekend's going to be miserable!"

What do you think is filling Larry's emotional cup at this moment? What is he feeling? Needing? Why?

_____

_____

_____

_____

_____

Scenario #3:

During the premarital counseling session with their minister, Tracy and Bryan were asked to give some information about their family background. Reverend Hinson asked Bryan to go first.

"My folks were really terrific," said Bryan. "Especially my dad. He used to take me hunting and fishing and camping. He was never too busy for me. I hope someday I can be that kind of father to my—"

Suddenly they heard an audible sigh from Tracy. She fished in her purse for a Kleenex and blew her nose.

Reverend Hinson turned to her and said, "Tracy, would you like to tell us how your father showed his affection and appreciation?"

Tracy fought back tears, but managed to reply, "My dad never showed me any attention. He was always too busy. I don't know to this day if he loves me or not. My mom says he does, but I've never felt it. It hurts so much because my dad's the most important man in my life—and he always will be!"

What do you think is going on in Bryan's mind as he hears Tracy's remarks about her father? What is he feeling? What does he need at this moment?

_____

_____

_____

_____

_____

_____

What emotions are apparent in Tracy's cup? What is she needing at this moment? Explain.

_____

_____

_____

_____

_____

Think a few moments about the answers you put down for each of these scenarios. Chances are your comments included some of the following observations: If Jay had told his buddy Kevin he already had plans with his wife for the weekend, Laura would have felt cared for and secure, knowing her husband considered her first. Moreover, Jay would have shown his respect for Laura if he had told Kevin he'd have to check with his wife before inviting Kevin to stay.

Larry would have felt close to his wife if she had appreciated his efforts to give her a special weekend instead of fretting about the rain, the right route, the road, and the resort. Paula didn't realize she was sealing the fate on their "miserable" weekend by her own nagging complaints.

And what about Tracy and Bryan? No doubt Bryan's heart sank when he heard Tracy say her father would always be the most important man in her life. How could Bryan possibly compete against that? And yet, if he dared make the effort, perhaps he could help heal Tracy's wounded heart by cherishing her the way her father never had. But would his own hurt feelings allow him to take the risk?

We identify with these couples, don't we?—because we've all experienced emotional needs that went unmet, and the result was disappointment, pain, and loss. The principle we can draw for our relationships is jarringly simple: When our basic emotional needs are met, we experience intimacy; when our needs are unmet, we experience hurt and loss.

But there's another dimension as well. The pain we feel from unmet needs is often masked by anger. Our hurt feelings leave us violated, saddened, and vulnerable to more pain. So, in order to protect ourselves, we raise up anger as our defense.

For many of us, anger is so automatic we never consciously experience the hurt feelings that prompted the anger. Because it is painful focusing inward on our hurts, we hide our vulnerability and loss by turning outward and becoming angry at others. But be assured, where there's anger, hurt lies beneath it!

When our basic emotional needs are met, we experience intimacy; when our needs are unmet, we experience hurt and loss.

Anger can take many forms—impatience, a quick temper, depression, jealousy, or suspicion. Some of us display our anger in passive-aggressive forms—procrastination, silence, sarcasm, or avoidance.

Our unmet needs produce not only hurt and anger, but also fear. If you are rejected by your spouse, you feel not only a present hurt but also a fear of future rejection. If you are ridiculed over your performance, you feel the pain deeply now, which produces a fear of future failures as well.

Fear, like anger, can take several forms—withdrawal (avoiding situations that might expose you to new hurt); perfectionism (a perfect performance will reduce your chance of failure and hurt); control (you minimize chances for pain by being in charge); and addictions (trying to numb the pain and fear).

Often the final blow to this cycle results when we retaliate against others. As we cause pain for others, we experience guilt. As our own selfishness, criticism, or hurtful words produce feelings of guilt, the sad equation becomes "Unmet Need → Hurt → Anger → Fear → Guilt."

As our emotional cup overflows with these negative feelings, and we leave these emotional issues unresolved, we experience symptoms which often become the focus of marital conflict. Read through the following list and mark the symptoms you see in yourself and in your mate.

_____ addiction to alcohol or drugs
_____ too much or too little sleep
_____ struggles with eating (anorexia, bulimia, or compulsive overeating)

_____ low sexual desire
_____ persistent physical complaints (headaches, stomachaches, high blood pressure)

_____ obsessive behaviors	_____ uncontrollable temper
_____ chronic fatigue/burnout	_____ depression or anxiety
_____ "escaping" into activity	_____ chronic low self-esteem
_____ attempting to control others or situations	_____ loss of romance, love, hope, or joy
_____ feeling guilty while relaxing	

Your hope for resolving these struggles lies in emptying out the negative feelings you've accumulated in your emotional cup. Take a few minutes to think about what happens when you and your spouse experience conflicts. What particular issues or topics do you find yourselves clashing over? List them here:

The conflicts my spouse and I face in our marriage usually involve (For instance: _the way I overspend on our credit cards; the way he yells at the kids; his uncontrollable temper; deciding who's going to do the housework when we both work_) _____

_____

_____

_____

_____

The conflicts you've just listed represent a great deal of hurt that both you and your mate are likely carrying around with you every day. Some marriage partners collect their grievances like baseball trading cards and take them out regularly to review and brood on. Many of us, however, carry around a bundle of marital hurts that we've never tried to identify. We have a hard time putting into words what's wrong. We just know we hurt, and we don't know what to do about it.

We just know we hurt, and we don't know what to do about it.

The first step to emptying the negative emotions of a marital relationship is to identify our specific hurts. Plan now to spend some time alone working on the following activities.

We'll get you started with an example demonstrating the chain reaction of negative emotions. Imagine you're lying in bed with your spouse one night and you reach over and give an affectionate squeeze. If your partner responds by sharply pulling away, how do you feel? At first you may feel hurt, embarrassed, rejected, and put down. A second, automatic reaction may be anger and resentment. So now, at the same moment, you are experiencing hurt for yourself and anger at your spouse.

Now what happens? Your need for affection has gone unmet. In fact, you've been rebuffed by the very one you feel should show you love. So what do you do? You might respond by hurling hurtful words ("What's the big idea of pulling away? I just wanted a little affection! Is that too much to ask?") Or you might jump out of bed, storm out of the room, and slam the door behind you. Or perhaps you just roll over and nurse your pain in silence.

Now it's the next night. The two of you go to bed, and again you desire to reach out to your partner and share a little affection. But this time the impulse is short-circuited by a little wave of fear. What if your mate responds the same way again? Two nights of rejection in a row is more than you care to contemplate. Plus, you might be feeling a tad guilty about those angry words you uttered last night. Maybe your spouse is still sore. Maybe you'd better not rock the boat. So you decide against reaching out to your spouse. Instead, you lie there in silence and feel the distance growing between you.

Sound familiar? If so, this cycle of pain and unmet needs has to be broken.

In healthy marriages, couples heal and resolve their inevitable hurts rather than ignore them or retaliate. Which brings us back to our original point: The first step toward breaking the pain cycle is to identify the hurt.

The following worksheets will help you define your hurts as well as your partner's. Prayerfully consider each entry. Keep in mind the needs that have gone unmet for each of you.

The first step toward breaking the pain cycle is to identify the hurt.

HEALING MARITAL HURTS WORKSHEET #1

Think about all the ways in which you have hurt your spouse and your marriage. Think back to your dating days, engagement, and early marriage. Allow God to show you any behaviors that were selfish, critical, insensitive, disrespectful, verbally abusive, unsupportive, ungrateful, unfaithful, rejecting, or unforgiving. Be sure to consider any specific hurtful events, fights, arguments, or "scenes" that may need confession.

Begin this confession list here as you note the ways you have hurt your spouse and your marriage:

I have hurt my spouse and our marriage by (For instance: *I pressured her sexually before marriage; I belittled him in front of the children; I lied about the money I spent; I went out with my friends instead of helping out at home; I used sex to get my own way; I threaten divorce when we are in a fight.*)

_____

_____

_____

_____

_____

_____

_____

_____

_____

Once you've made your list, go back over it and confess each item to God. Keep in mind that true confession names the deed and admits it was wrong, period! Resist the urge to rationalize your own behavior, and especially be careful not to start blaming your spouse for your deeds—or misdeeds! Before making your confession, note the examples below:

Rationalizing/Blaming:

I know I made fun of Donna the other night at the party, but I wouldn't have done it if she hadn't made such a big deal about me burning the steaks.

True Confession:

I hurt Donna the other night when I made fun of her at the dinner party. It was wrong of me to be so insensitive and rejecting.

Rationalizing/Blaming:

I know Andy gets discouraged about his job and about not getting the promotion. I wouldn't harp about it if we had something to show for all those late nights he's spent at the office.

True Confession:

I hurt Andy each time I bring up the fact that he didn't get the promotion we were counting on. It's wrong for me to be unsupportive of him.

HEALING MARITAL HURTS WORKSHEET #2

Identify the ways in which you and your marriage have been hurt by your spouse. You will want to be sure to list these hurts with "feeling" statements. Include behaviors that would be considered selfish, critical, disrespectful, verbally abusive, unsupportive, ungrateful, unfaithful, rejecting, and unforgiving. Be sure to include both past and current hurts.

Before making your list of hurts, note these examples of specifying the hurt feeling and what caused it:

- "I felt hurt and rejected when you pulled away from me the other night in bed."
- "I felt unsupported and unappreciated when you didn't notice the hard work I put into decorating the house for the holidays."
- "I haven't gotten over the fact that you lied to me on the night of our first date."
- "I felt rejected when you went out with the guys the first night we got back from our honeymoon."

Now, following the examples above, list here the ways you and your marriage have been hurt by your spouse:

_____

_____

_____

_____

_____

_____

_____

_____

_____

_____

_____

Scripture Journaling—Ephesians 4:31–32

Get rid of all bitterness, rage and anger, brawling and slander, along with every form of malice. Be kind and compassionate to one another, forgiving each other, just as in Christ God forgave you. (NIV)

Spend some time reflecting on what it means to "get rid of" your bitterness and anger. What would you like to tell God at this time?

I would like to tell God (For instance: *Forgiving is easier said than done; that I need supernatural help from Him to help me forgive; that I need to remember forgiving is an act of the will and not just a change in my feelings.*) _____

_____

_____

_____

_____

_____

_____

MARRIAGE STAFF MEETING

Set aside thirty minutes this week with your spouse. Devote this time to increasing your *understanding* of your partner's emotional hurts. You will focus on dialogue and confession at your next meeting. Each of you will bring your "Healing Emotional Hurts" worksheets with you. Take the first few minutes to pray silently for God to use this activity to bring healing in your marriage. Pray for receptivity and openness for both you and your spouse.

Exchange your list of hurts. Both partners should read silently the hurts of their spouse. Then, after carefully going over your partner's list of hurts, you may want to briefly discuss any entries that are unclear. Avoid in-depth discussion and rationalizing or blaming. Make sure each partner has an understanding of the feelings listed on the worksheet. Return the list and then spend the remainder of the time apart.

During your time apart, add to or revise your confession list showing the ways you have hurt your spouse. Spend this time considering every aspect of your partner's list of hurts. Try to see your partner's viewpoint as well as your own. Throughout the coming week, allow God the opportunity to show you new insights into how you have hurt your spouse.

——— For Group Discussion ———

Begin the group session by discussing the three marital vignettes. Ask for feedback from both the male and female perspective.

- How would you feel if you were Jay? Laura?
- What thoughts would be going through your head?
- What emotions would be filling your emotional cup?
- What needs were going unmet?

Answer these same questions for Larry and Paula. And Tracy and Bryan.

Ask participants to identify possible **"Hurt—Anger—Fear"** cycles that might result from these marital vignettes. What could each of these three couples have done differently?

After reflecting on the concept of emotional capacity, ask group members to share symptoms they see in their own life and answer the following questions. Leaders should share first, helping to create an environment of transparency and humility.

- How do the displayed symptoms play a role in hurting my spouse? (For instance: *My escaping into work hurts my partner.*)
- What feelings might my spouse experience as a result of my negative symptoms? (For instance: *My escaping into work must make my spouse feel lonely and abandoned.*)
- What feelings do you have about your role in hurting your spouse? (For instance: *I regret that I've hurt my partner.*)

Close the session with a prayer for each couple. Ask for God's healing and restoration during their upcoming time of confession.

Chapter Four

——— ■ ———

HEAL HURTS THROUGH CONFESSION AND FORGIVENESS

In counseling Jimmy and Marla Carlton, David Ferguson discovered some of the needs each had brought to their marriage and hurts that resulted when those needs weren't met by their partner. Jimmy, an insurance sales-person who had been a successful country-western singer, nursed a deep resentment over giving up his musical career to stay home with his family. Rather than face his negative feelings, he had retreated emotionally from his wife and children. Marla, once a singer herself and a Lucy look-alike with the red hair to match, had resorted to constant nagging to cover her guilt feelings for making her husband stay home.

But both wrestled with emotional pain that went much deeper than Jimmy's career decision. Jimmy came from a dominant home, Marla from a neglectful one. Growing up fearful of the real world, Marla began to "perform" in various ways to gain the attention she missed from her parents. Lost in the shuffle of brothers and sisters, she suffered from low self-esteem and underlying resentment; fearful she'd never get the attention and feeling of "specialness" she needed, she became demanding and ma-nipulative.

"As a kid, I was just one of the horde, never an individual," Marla confided. "With four brothers and sisters who all fought tooth and nail for center stage, I was constantly clamoring for my parents' attention, and never able to get it. By the time I was grown, I had an insatiable appetite for attention, and nothing has ever been able to satisfy it."

Even though he came from a home in many ways the opposite of Marla's, Jimmy, too, had a deep need for attention and approval. Growing up with excessive rules and a remote father, Jimmy also suffered from low self-esteem and underlying resentment. Fearful he'd never get attention and approval from those he loved, he had "given up," choosing the safer path of self-reliance and avoiding relational closeness. As much as he loathed the cold relationship he had with his father, he was modeling the same behavior for his wife and children. It was a dismaying paradox—and a truth he gradually began to see for himself.

"I could never figure out what I'd done wrong to make my father dislike me," he said, his voice still edged with pain. "It never occurred to me it was my dad's problem, that he didn't know how to show love. I thought there must be something really wrong with me if my own dad didn't want to spend time with me or get to know me. And now—would you believe?—I guess I'm making my own wife and kids feel the same way! How does a guy change? How do you reverse the process or switch courses?"

"It's a process that begins with confession and forgiveness," David Ferguson explained, then added, "How long has it been, Jimmy, since your wife or children heard you apologize for some wrong you've done?"

"I've never apologized," he admitted. "My dad never apologized to anyone for anything; he always said admitting you were wrong was the mark of a weak man. You held your ground even when you knew it was sinking sand. That's how I've been with Marla and Jeff and Anna. I know I've hurt them. But even when I knew I was wrong, I'd just get more stubborn and deny it. I can't imagine what it would be like to tell my family I'm sorry, but I'm beginning to realize that's what I need to do."

The crucial issue is whether we're willing to admit we hurt, have needs, and make mistakes.

David assured the Carltons that since there's no such thing as perfect marriage partners, we must face the fact we will inevitably hurt one another. "We all make mistakes, have weaknesses, and display inconsistencies," he noted. "Knowingly or unknowingly, we fail to meet each other's needs, and these hurts do not simply go away. The crucial issue is whether we're willing to admit we hurt, have needs, and make mistakes. And perhaps most important, will we be open and vulnerable enough to confess our sins and forgive one another?"

In the previous chapter, we discussed how our emotional cup may be filled with negative feelings of hurt, anger, fear, and guilt. If we can empty these painful emotions, many of our symptoms will go away, including such traits as sarcasm, disrespect, critical comments, and temper outbursts.

How does this emptying take place? We empty guilt through confession and we empty anger and bitterness through forgiveness.

I. Accept Responsibility

The first step in this healing process is to accept responsibility for your part in causing the hurts as well as your part in the healing. Look back over your confession list from the previous chapter. What has kept you from taking responsibility and apologizing? Write your answer here:

I have not taken the responsibility of apologizing for hurting my spouse because (For instance: *I'm waiting for him to apologize first; I think her sins are worse than mine; I'm waiting for the right time.*) _____

_____

_____

So then each of us shall give account of himself to God. (Rom. 14:12)

As you review your confession list, choose one of the main hurts you have caused your spouse. Write a letter to your spouse expressing your feelings and commitments. The model below contains the key elements to a good confession. Use it as you write your letter and later, during your Marriage Staff Meeting, as you verbalize your confession.

Dear _____

I realize that (Identify the behavior.) has hurt you. _____

_____

You might feel _____

_____

God considers this behavior _____

_____

I am asking God's forgiveness, and I am asking for your forgiveness.

From this time forward I will (Describe the specific ways your behavior will change.) _____

_____

II. Show Empathy (Your spouse has been hurt. Do you care?)

In order for forgiveness and healing to take place, each partner must come to realize—and feel—the other's pain.

What is one of the deepest hurts on your partner's list of hurts? Take a moment to reflect on how your partner feels or felt (rejected, unimportant, lonely, disrespected, etc.). View the situation through your partner's eyes. Refuse all thoughts that might be considered rationalizing, blaming, or avoiding your responsibility. Do you feel a sense of regret that you played a role in your partner being hurt and feeling rejected, lonely, unimportant, etc.? Write your thoughts and responses to this question here:

For godly sorrow produces repentance leading to salvation, not to be regretted. . . .
(2 Cor. 7:10a)

Yes, I regret the role I played in hurting my spouse, and—(For instance: *I'm sorry I added to his pain by my behavior; I realize how my words put her down; I feel the loneliness he must have felt because of my cold attitude.*) _____

_____

_____

Regardless of your partner's actions, do you have a sense that treating another person like this is wrong? Write your thoughts here:

Yes, I realize treating another person this way is wrong, and I—(For instance: *know I must change my behavior; hope my partner will forgive me; pray God will give me the wisdom to see my spouse through His eyes.*) _____

_____

_____

III. Agree with God

Confession means to "agree with God" about our wrongdoing. What does God say about being selfish, critical, untruthful, disrespectful, etc.? It's sobering, but God says these are the very reason His Son had to die. After completing the activity below, you will have agreed with God that these behaviors are wrong; they are sinful.

If we confess our sins, He is faithful and just to forgive us our sins and to cleanse us from all unrighteousness. (1 John 1:9)

Read and ponder Isaiah 53, which speaks of Christ's suffering for us. Verse 5 says He was wounded for our transgressions; He was bruised for our iniquities. The first important truth of this verse is that God declares our worth through the gift of His Son. The second truth is that our sinful actions are what caused Him to have to die.

Genuine confession affirms both of these truths. As we approach God with a humble spirit, we acknowledge the wrongness of our actions. As we are grateful for His forgiveness, we recognize He chooses to look upon us as His precious children, made worthy by his grace.

Once again read each item of the list of ways you have hurt your spouse. Privately examine the list from God's perspective. Spend some time meditating on the passage from Isaiah 53.

Then begin to agree with God about each entry on the list. For example, "Christ had to die for my abusive words. Christ had to die because of my unfaithfulness to my spouse. My disrespectful attitude is sin and hurts God, as well as my spouse."

Now write down your thoughts here: (For instance: *For the first time I feel the pain my spouse is feeling; I never realized my actions hurt God as much as they hurt my spouse; I feel a new sense of sorrow for my wrong behavior.*)

_____

_____

_____

What impact does this time of meditation and self-examination have on you? Are there any new thoughts that come to mind? Any new attitudes or insights? Write them down here.

During this time of reflection, I have come to realize (For instance: *how my own attitudes and actions have contributed to my marriage problems; that I was taking my anger at my parents out on my spouse; that I need my spouse's forgiveness as much as my spouse needs mine.*)

_____

_____

_____

Second Corinthians 7:10 speaks of a sorrow that leads to repentance. After spending some time reflecting on how your spouse was hurt by your actions and how Christ was hurt by your actions, examine your own heart. Do you feel remorse? Sorrow? Regret? Allow yourself to experience these emotions. When we truly let God impact us with these truths, we experience a godly sorrow that produces a change in our behavior.

Now, with a broken and humble heart, spend time telling God about your sorrow. Confess to Him and ask for His forgiveness. First John 1:9 tells us if we confess (agree) with Him, He is faithful to forgive us and cleanse us.

A possible prayer might be: "God, I have deeply hurt you and my spouse by my *(angry words and unforgiving attitudes)*. These are wrong and I ask You to forgive me. Thank you for doing so. I ask You to change me into the kind of person I need to be." Now write here about your sorrow, sadness, and regret: (Don't be afraid to let yourself be completely open and vulnerable before God. He loves you and understands your pain.)

_____

_____

_____

_____

_____

_____

_____

After spending this time in prayer, what feelings do you have about the promise of God's forgiveness? Be sure to thank Him. It is this sense of gratefulness for God's forgiveness that will help you forgive your spouse. Express your gratefulness to God here: (If this is the first time you've taken this faith step of receiving Christ's forgiveness for your sin, you may want to record the date of your commitment to Him on the lines below.)

I am grateful to God for (For instance: *freeing me of the burden of my guilt; making me feel like a new person inside; reminding me His love covers a multitude of sins.*) _____

_____

_____

Scripture Journaling—James 5:16

Therefore, confess your sins to one another, and pray for one another, so that you may be healed. The effective prayer of a righteous man can accomplish much. (NASB)

Spend some time reflecting on James 5:16. This verse promises that if we confess to one another we will be healed. Your next staff meeting will be difficult, but the promise of healing will be worth your efforts. Tell God what you are feeling about the staff meeting. What do you need from Him? Write your feelings and needs here:

God, when I think about the upcoming staff meeting, I have mixed emotions, including (*fear, reluctance, anxiety, anticipation, hope, etc.*),

_____

and I really need You to (For instance: *give me the courage to confess my wrongs; help me have a loving, receptive attitude; help me to genuinely forgive.*)_____

_____

_____

_____ **MARRIAGE STAFF MEETING**

Set aside approximately two hours with your spouse. Each partner should only bring their confession list. We suggest that the husband begin this exercise. Both partners confess and verbalize the ways they have hurt their spouse. A possible confession might sound something like this: "I've seen that I've hurt you deeply by my sarcastic words and selfishness. I have been wrong. I will be respectful with my words and will be more considerate of your needs. Will you forgive me?"

Using the words, "I was wrong," is much better than simply saying, "I'm sorry," since *wrong* conveys more ownership and responsibility for the hurt. Acknowledge your wrongs without any explanation, excuses, or rationalization for your actions. As you finish confessing and sharing, end your confession with a request for forgiveness. Ask your partner directly, "Will you forgive me?" This question demonstrates a great deal of vulnerability and humility. The question also provides the listening spouse with the opportunity to choose forgiveness.

A word to the spouse being asked to forgive: Be careful not to judge the sincerity of your spouse's confession. Keep in mind that forgiveness is a choice you make as an act of your will. It doesn't necessarily mean your feelings have completely changed. In fact, the question is not, "Do you *feel* like forgiving?" but *"Will* you?" When you make the choice to forgive, reach over and touch your spouse, and verbalize your forgiveness by actually saying, "I forgive you." Your partner needs to hear the words to receive your forgiveness, just as you need to say them in order to seal your decision to forgive. Each entry on the confession list will need to be confessed *and* forgiven.

Both partners may also want to ask, "Are there other major hurts I've not seen that need my apology? Please share them with me so I can confess them now and seek your forgiveness."

After each partner gives and receives forgiveness, tear up the lists and throw them away. You may even want to burn or bury them to symbolize putting them completely behind you. Read James 5:16 aloud together, and end your meeting with prayer.

Now that anger and guilt have been emptied from your emotional cups, the two of you will find more capacity to enjoy each other. This is a good time to schedule an activity during the next few days that you both enjoy. Do something fun together. You may want to take turns choosing how this time is spent.

——— For Group Discussion ———

Group leaders may want to open this session by discussing the parable of "the log and the splinter" in Matthew 7:1-5. How is this parable applicable to the forgiveness/confession process between spouses? Which is easier to see? How your spouse has hurt you, or how you have hurt your spouse? How do you go about removing the log from your own eye?

In Ephesians 4:31, the admonition to "put away" anger, wrath, and bitterness actually means to "turn loose of." The group leader may want to demonstrate this concept by having members participate in this symbolic activity (if space permits): Divide members into two teams, give them a rope, and ask them to play a game of tug-of-war. As the two sides struggle against each other, ask them to identify the most efficient way to end the game. Is it by pulling harder? By adding more players to your team? Or is it to simply turn loose of the rope?

In applying this tug-of-war exercise to marriage, what are some of the ways you "pull harder," "add more ammunition," or "get other people on your side"? What benefits do you see of turning loose of the struggle through confession and forgiveness?

End the group time by discussing the following questions:

- After reflecting on Isaiah 53, what feelings did this chapter evoke in you?
- What were your feelings after the confession/forgiveness exercise?
- What makes a good confession?
- Since godly sorrow brings repentance or change, name one area of change you are anticipating God will make in your life.
- What changes/commitments will you make in your marriage to keep this forgiveness process up to date?
- How can you and your spouse practically follow the Scriptural admonition of Ephesians 4:26, not to let the sun go down on your anger?
- Be particularly sensitive to individuals making a first-time commitment to Christ, offering additional guidance.

Chapter Five

———■———

BLEND FOUR INGREDIENTS FOR MARITAL CLOSENESS

When they married, Jimmy and Marla Carlton bought into the myth many couples believe. A marriage works, or it doesn't. You click, or you don't. You naturally love each other, or if the loving stops, you call it quits and find someone else more compatible to love. No wonder the divorce courts are jammed!

Genuine, enduring love isn't just a feeling. Feelings change; they can be as fickle as the wind. If you plan to build a lifelong relationship on how you feel today, chances are you'll never make it.

Genuine enduring love isn't just a feeling.

If feelings aren't the key, then what is?

Think a moment about your favorite dessert. Let's suppose it's chocolate cream pie. How can you get a slice? Loving pie, desiring it, or even wishing for it isn't enough. Someone must gather the right ingredients, follow the correct recipe, and make the pie. In a very real sense, it's the same way with your marriage. To develop love that lasts a lifetime, you must create genuine intimacy by blending together the proper ingredients in a recipe for marital closeness.

You may argue, "But I thought intimacy just happens. When you find the *right* person, bingo!—you've got intimacy."

Wrong.

Intimacy isn't merely magic or romance or a castle in Spain. It's not Cinderella and Prince Charming, a full moon, or a thousand violins. Intimacy develops when couples share experiences that draw them together. Intimacy has to be worked at. Some couples mistakenly believe that only poor marriages must be worked at. Wrong again. The *best* marriages are those that are worked at.

Intimacy develops when couples share experiences that draw them together.

To nurture the spiritual, emotional, and physical closeness we've mentioned earlier (the three dimensions of your spirit, soul, and body), you and your spouse will need to plan the experiences you will share.

What do these three dimensions of intimacy look like in a marriage?

Spiritual intimacy may involve couples praying together, working on a mission project, or discussing the devotional readings they've shared throughout the week.

Emotional intimacy, or friendship between spouses, would include sharing your lifelong dreams (no matter how outlandish!), feeling the freedom to express your emotions, and developing common interests.

Physical intimacy involves caring touches, affectionate embraces, tender words, and a passionate union.

How do couples develop these three dimensions in their marriage? By blending these four basic ingredients for marital closeness:

I. AFFECTIONATE CARING says, "I Care About You"

Caring involves reassuring your partner and showing fondness, concern, and attentiveness. You show you care about your spouse when you

- give your undivided attention when he/she is talking.
- give priority time to be affectionate with each other.
- promise to pray for your partner the morning of a difficult day at work.

Think about your relationship with your spouse and complete the following:

I feel cared about when (For instance: *my partner spends time listening to me; we cuddle together in the morning; my partner calls to say he's thinking of me or praying for me.*)_____

_____

_____

I also feel cared about when _____

_____

Unfortunately, caring can be hindered by anger, bitterness, or resentment. Which of these feelings (anger, bitterness, or resentment) have kept you from caring about your spouse? How? When?

My caring feelings for my spouse have been hindered by (For instance: *anger when my spouse is suspicious of my motives; bitterness when my spouse doesn't seem to appreciate my caring expressions; resentment when my spouse belittles my caring gestures.*)_____

_____

_____

For encouragement resolving anger, memorize
Ephesians 4:31

II. VULNERABLE COMMUNICATION says, "I Trust You"

Trusting is the aspect in a relationship that risks being open about one's feelings, needs, and hurts. You show trust in your spouse when you

- share your hopes about the ministry God has designed for you.
- confide your feelings about your difficult day at work.
- express what is most pleasing to you during physically intimate times with your spouse.

Reflect on your relationship with your spouse and complete the following:

I could be more open with my spouse about (For instance: *the misgivings I have about my job; the fears I have about my attractiveness; what pleases me most when we're making love.*) _____

_____

_____

_____

I could be more vulnerable with my spouse by sharing (For instance: *the things he says that turn me off; how hurt I feel when she isn't supportive; how lonely I feel even when we're together.*)_____

_____

_____

Trust is often hindered by fear. Write about the fears that have kept you from being more open and vulnerable with your spouse.

Sometimes I have not been open or vulnerable with my feelings or needs because I fear (For instance: *that my spouse will ridicule me; I'll look weak or foolish; my spouse will be disappointed in me.*) _____

_____

_____

_____

For help releasing fears, memorize
1 John 4:18–19.

III. JOINT ACCOMPLISHMENT says, "I Need You"

This area of closeness comes from enjoying specific activities together. It might include developing common interests, or setting and completing family or household goals. You experience the intimacy of needing your spouse when you . . .

- both decide to read the Bible through in a year.
- experience the joy and excitement of having a baby.
- work together to repaint the garage.

Think about your relationship with your spouse and complete the following:

Together with my spouse, I would enjoy (For instance: *planning a cruise to Alaska; developing our furniture-refinishing hobby into a small business; remodeling the kitchen*) _____

_____

_____

_____

Together with my spouse, I would also enjoy _____

_____

_____

_____

Keeping in mind that needing your spouse and enjoying your joint accomplishments can be hindered by an attitude of self-sufficiency, finish the following statements:

I find myself resisting sharing my needs with my partner because (For instance: *I fear rejection; I don't want to appear weak.*) _____

_____

_____

_____

I resist sharing some of my needs and feelings with my spouse, because I already "handle them myself," especially _____

_____

_____

_____

For help overcoming self-sufficiency, memorize Galatians 6:2.

IV. MUTUAL GIVING says, "I Love You"

This ingredient is characterized by two people who think more highly of each other than of themselves. The focus is on giving to each other rather than taking. You give love to your spouse when you . . .

- surprise your spouse with breakfast in bed.
- ask how you can be the most help during the holidays.

- make a 30-second phone call just to say, "I love you and I'm looking forward to seeing you tonight."

Reflecting on your relationship with your spouse, complete the following statements:

One way I can give to my spouse is by (For instance: *showing an interest in his pet project; taking her out even when it's not a special occasion; watching the children while he/she goes out with friends.*) _____

_____

_____

One way I can demonstrate how important my spouse is to me is by (For instance: *sincerely praising him/her in front of others; scheduling extra time alone just for the two of us; sending a single rose with a love note.*) _____

_____

_____

Giving is often hindered by selfishness, that is, focusing on your own needs rather than your partner's. Write here about the ways you may tend to be selfish in your relationship with your spouse.

I am sometimes insensitive to my partner's need for (For instance: *time alone, more time together for sexual expression, freedom to pursue his own hobbies.*) _____

_____

_____

I am hindered in giving to my spouse because of my selfishness in (For instance: *wanting my own way; wanting the last word; wanting to be free of my spouse's expectations.*) _____

_____

_____

For help or encouragement addressing selfishness, memorize Philippians 2:3.

Blend Four Ingredients for Marital Closeness **43**

Scripture Journaling—Philippians 4:19

And my God shall supply all your needs according to His riches in glory by Christ Jesus.

This verse promises that our God will meet all our needs according to His glorious riches in Christ Jesus. In the exercise above, you expressed some of your needs. Now tell God your personal needs and express your thoughts about His promise to meet them, realizing that He can be trusted to encourage your spouse to be a part of this mutual "giving" process.

Dear God, I trust You to meet my needs directly through Your bountiful riches or indirectly through the spouse You have given me. Today I feel most needy in the areas of (For instance: *my walk with You; my desire for a more affectionate relationship with my spouse; my exhaustion in trying to handle the kids*) _____

_____

_____

_____

Thank you, Lord, for meeting these needs in marvelous ways I can only imagine. In Jesus' name, Amen.

MARRIAGE STAFF MEETING

The recipe for marital happiness involves blending the four intimacy ingredients—**Caring, Trusting, Needing,** and **Giving** into your marriage relationship. This can only be accomplished by meeting the "intimacy needs" of your spouse.

In the next several chapters, each staff meeting will include exercises that address selected needs of husbands and wives. These practical exercises will help you identify one specific need in your partner's life each week.

As you travel your marriage journey during the next few weeks, our hope is that you will begin to view your partner as **SPECIAL** and someone to **CHERISH.** Notice that several of a woman's key needs form the acronym **SPECIAL** and some of a man's needs form the acronym **CHERISH.** Keep these words in mind each day as you think about your partner's needs.

A woman needs to feel . . .	A man needs to feel . . .
Secure	**C**omforted
Protected	**H**onored
Enjoyed	**E**xalted
Courted	**R**espected
Intimate	**I**ntimate
Appreciated	**S**ecure
Led	**H**appy

Set aside at least two hours with your spouse. Make sure you have read and completed the following activities, as well as the exercises in the chapter above. Share your responses to the four ingredient questions (i.e., "I feel cared about when you notice I'm wearing a new outfit.").

Listen attentively and receptively to your partner (without defensiveness or interruptions). You might also want to share any new insights you discovered regarding the hindrances to the intimacy ingredients. For example, "I realized my selfishness about wanting time alone on the weekends keeps me from enjoying fun times with you and the kids." Review with one another the four memory verses to help you overcome the hindrances to intimacy.

After this discussion and time of sharing, hold hands and spend some time in prayer. During this prayer, verbalize to God (and your spouse) the things you know God will be working to change in you. Ask God to begin making these changes. Your prayer might sound like this:

"Dear Heavenly Father, I know You want to work in my life to make me more sensitive to JoAnn, and less critical and selfish in our daily life together. I ask You to begin those changes now. Help me to recognize the specific instances where I need to change. I want to be more loving and giving. Amen."

As you complete this time of prayer, one of you may want to read Philippians 3:13. This passage speaks of forgetting what lies behind so that we may press on to what lies ahead.

Now you can begin "pressing on" by meeting the intimacy needs of your spouse.

FOR MEN ONLY

Husbands, you will want to meet your wife's need for security this week. Security may be defined as "freedom from threats of danger or pain;

safe; certain and sure of one's safety." The key issue in meeting a wife's need for security is *a removal of fears*. A wife fearing her husband's work is more important than she is will probably feel insecure. A wife who fears her husband is not totally committed to marriage fidelity or permanence will likely feel threatened or jealous. Countless fears will arise over the course of a marriage relationship, and a loving husband will actively help remove them, thus building a more secure relationship.

Better Understanding This Need

Noted below are several ideas to help deepen your understanding and increase your awareness of your wife's need for security.

Ask your wife to make two lists for you, answering as honestly as possible; then discuss her answers without defensiveness at your next marriage staff meeting.

What I'd Love Your Top Five Priorities to Be:

1. _____
2. _____
3. _____
4. _____
5. _____

What I Often Feel Your Top Five Priorties Are:

1. _____
2. _____
3. _____
4. _____
5. _____

Here are a few statements and questions that may help identify and remove your wife's fears:

- "Darling, I can sense you're feeling fearful, and I want to ease those fears. I want you to know I'm committed to (For instance: *our marriage; our family; being faithful; showing you how much I love you*)."

- "Honey, can you tell me some of the things you've been worrying about lately? I'd like to help you with them."
- "Dear, what can I do to help you feel more secure in our relationship? I really want to help."

Practical Suggestions:

Weekly Marriage Staff Meetings

Schedule time (at least an hour) to talk with your wife each week to discuss plans, schedules, children, family needs, or anything else your wife wishes to discuss. This priority time will help your wife feel more secure and reassured that she and the family are very important to you.

Regular Dates with Your Wife

Just the two of you doing something fun gives your wife something to look forward to. Plan an activity without the children (that's family time) and without friends (that's social time). A husband who initiates such special "dates" helps his wife feel secure in his leadership.

30-Second Phone Calls

"Hi, sweetheart. I was just thinking about you and wanted to call and remind you I love you. I'm looking forward to seeing you tonight." Such calls convey an important emotional message that even though you're busy, you're thinking of her!

FOR WOMEN ONLY

Wives, you will want to meet your husband's need for comfort this week.

Comfort may be defined as "giving loving reassurance and nurture to someone who is very special to you." Comfort involves several aspects—one's words, one's actions, plus the atmosphere of a relationship. Words of tenderness, affirmation, and empathy minister comfort; actions which nurture include touching, love notes, and cooking favorite meals. You may create a comforting atmosphere at home through a well-managed household, an enthusiastic welcome home, or by putting your husband's needs above the children's.

Better Understanding This Need

Noted below are several ideas for exploring this need with your husband.

During a private conversation with your husband, ask him to list five specific ways you can better provide comfort to him.

1. _____
2. _____
3. _____
4. _____
5. _____

Here are some questions that will help you identify the best ways to meet your husband's need for comfort.

- Ask about your **Words**—"I want to verbalize how much I care about you. What words would you most like to hear?"
- Ask about your **Actions**—"What kinds of things can I do to be more reassuring and nurturing?"
- Ask about your **Home Atmosphere**—"I want to provide a more comforting, supportive environment at home. What ideas do you have for making our home more comfortable for you?"

Practical Suggestions

Welcome Him Home

Notice your husband each evening when he returns home; go to him, initiate contact with a smile, words, touch. Communicate that you're glad to see him.

Cards and Notes

Leave love notes in unexpected places, such as a lunch box, suitcase, briefcase, or on the bathroom mirror.

Empathize

Give your husband the freedom to feel "down" and to express his frustration, anxiety, or fear; be there for him with sympathetic words and a loving touch.

A group leader may want to congratulate each couple for taking steps this week to develop spiritual, emotional, and physical intimacy in their marriage. Couples may not have been aware of it, but by completing the exercises above they have further developed spiritual intimacy by praying together, physical intimacy by holding hands, and emotional (friendship) intimacy by sharing their needs and feelings with each other.

You may note that the order of **Caring, Trusting, Needing,** and **Giving** tends to flow from one to the other. In other words, "It's hard to trust if I don't sense that you care. It's hard to let you know I need you if I'm not sure I can trust you. It's hard to be motivated to give if I don't sense you really need me."

Spend some time discussing the four hindrances to the intimacy ingredients—unresolved anger, fear, self-sufficiency, and selfishness. Invite couples to relate which of these they battle most often. Review the four memory verses which help overcome the four hindrances to intimacy.

In future chapters, we will be looking at the impact of childhood experiences on our marriage intimacy. With this in mind, do you see any childhood experiences that may have affected how you handle anger, fear, self-sufficiency, or selfishness? Encourage couples to share some of these experiences. Ask them to share whether they knew adults who battled some of these same hindrances.

Also during each group session, ask members to relate some of the ways in which they have met the intimacy needs of their spouse (remember the specific husband/wife needs through the acronyms SPECIAL and CHERISH). Ask each husband to give examples of how he met his wife's need for security. Ask each wife to give examples of how she met her husband's need for comfort.

Ask each spouse to reflect on how it felt to "receive." Did they identify gratefulness, appreciation, care, or love? If they seem ready, ask members to verbalize their appreciation to their giving partner.

Encourage group members to express their appreciation during the week when they see their spouse giving to meet their intimacy needs. Expressing appreciation helps reinforce the giving habit!

Chapter Six

■

BE FREE FROM FEAR

Imagine you're at the checkout stand in your local grocery store, and your Wheaties, Diet Pepsi, cauliflower, and extra lean ground beef are happily moving along the conveyer belt to be bagged. The clerk smiles and asks about your day. You are right in the middle of lamenting your latest misadventure at work when the clerk yells out, "Hey, Joe, give me a price on these Wheaties, willya?"

You feel a trifle miffed that your story was cut short and that the clerk obviously wasn't really interested in your day after all, but by the time you arrive home you've forgotten the incident. You greet your husband with a kiss, go to the kitchen, and start frying some of that ground beef for his favorite spaghetti dinner. As you busy yourself at the stove, you begin telling your husband about a misadventure at work. But right in the middle of your story he cuts you off with a question: "Hey, did you pick up my suit at the cleaners? I gotta have it for tomorrow, you know."

Immediately you feel that same irritation you felt when the clerk cut you off, but this time the feeling spreads quickly to a deep sense of hurt. Why do you feel so much more wounded this time? What makes the difference? The *relational closeness* between you and your mate.

The reason your spouse's lack of interest hurts you more than the indifference of a casual acquaintance is that you care more about your spouse's concern, support, and attention. You need his loving involvement in your life. That's why the closest relationships have the highest risk for disappointment, hurt, and rejection.

In marriage relationships, imperfect and needy people are thrust together in close physical proximity, making marital hurts inevitable. Since a conflict-free marriage is impossible, a more realistic goal is to learn to express your needs and handle your conflicts productively.

The closest relationships have the highest risk for disappointment, hurt, and rejection.

As we've discussed in previous chapters, experiencing hurt or emotional pain is an indication of unmet needs. What do we do when our needs go unmet? When we're hurt? How couples deal with these intimacy needs spells the difference between a healthy versus an unhealthy relationship.

We've all heard plenty in recent years about unhealthy relationships. The terms blaze across magazine and book covers and are bandied about in social circles like favorite recipes: **Codependent . . . Dysfunctional . . . Abusive!** We live in a day when people are preoccupied, if not obsessed, with problem relationships. And even though volumes have been written on these subjects, great confusion remains. We ask ourselves:

- Did I grow up in a dysfunctional family?
- Am I codependent on my spouse?
- Are my children being emotionally abused by an alcoholic parent?

Such labels as *codependent*, *dysfunctional*, and *abusive*, whatever they actually describe, stand in sharp contrast to our goal of intimate relationships. So, in order to avoid problems and build closeness, we need to consider some of the key issues in establishing healthy relationships.

In healthy relationships, we look to God as our source of help.

In healthy relationships, we look to God as our source of help, allowing Him to involve people in meeting our needs as He desires. In healthy relationships, we are willing to "entrust" our partner to God so He may accomplish His work in that person's life. Rather than nagging, criticizing, or demanding, we allow God to prompt unselfish behaviors and loving attitudes in our partner.

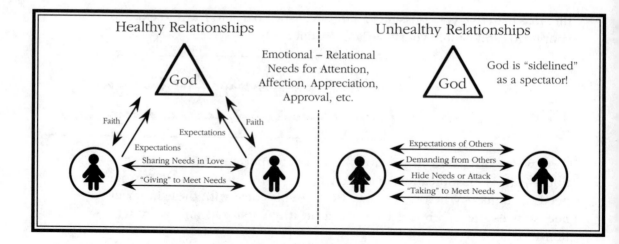

Sharing the truth in love is also pivotal in a healthy relationship. Partners who verbalize their feelings in a loving manner will deepen trust in the relationship. Equally important is a focus on mutually giving to each other rather than selfishly taking.

I. Expectations from God versus Demands of Other People

Needs, needs, needs! Relationships are built around needs. A popular song claims, "People who need people are the happiest people in the world." And it's true. We need others. They need us. And when we meet one another's deepest needs, we experience that elusive emotion known as love.

But the question is: Who are you expecting to meet your needs? In your marriage, each of you has genuine, God-given needs. If your relationship is healthy, each of you will give your needs to God and trust Him to meet them, without making demands of how or when or through whom. By contrast, in an unhealthy relationship, a couple may expect their partner to meet all their intimacy needs. These expectations may become demanding and manipulative, and may result in anger when needs go unmet.

Identify one area of need you often expect your spouse to meet and are usually disappointed (For instance: *affection? attention? comfort?* etc.)

_____

When we meet one another's deepest needs we experience love.

_____

Describe a specific time when you were disappointed (For instance: *I was disappointed when John forgot my birthday. I was hurt last night when Ruth pretended to be asleep. I was disappointed by Tom's lack of interest in my project.*) _____

_____

_____

_____

_____

When you are disappointed, how do you retaliate? (By giving your partner the silent treatment? By showing a critical attitude? By ignoring your partner's needs? By doing something to hurt your partner in return?) Describe a time when you demonstrated this behavior:_____

_____

_____

_____

_____

_____

Each of the types of retaliation mentioned above is a sign of misplaced expectations. When we wrongly direct expectations toward our spouse and are then disappointed, we retaliate. In healthy marriages, partners direct their needs and disappointments to God for His provision.

Take a minute to reflect on the passage in John 10:10. This Scripture explains that Christ came so that we could have *abundant* life. God wants to provide us with this abundant life. Will you choose to trust Him for this provision? You may want to express your decision to God now in this prayer of faith:

"Dear Heavenly Father, I seem to always find myself needing more *(acceptance, attention, appreciation, etc.)*_____
from my spouse. These needs are God-given and important to me. I know You have planned an abundant life for me, so I trust You to provide for my needs, in the best way You see fit. Please empower me as I resist the tendency to retaliate, and comfort me in my disappointment. Thank you, Lord. Amen."

II. In Healthy Relationships, Couples Are Open About Needs.

While we should ultimately direct our expectations toward God, communicating needs to your partner is a crucial first step in trusting God.

Many times, God desires to involve others in our lives to meet our needs, but we have to tell them what our needs are. In so doing, we face our fears of being let down, and trust in God's faithfulness. Be assured that God will meet your needs, either through your spouse, or directly through His provision and comfort.

Often we fall into one of two extremes: "Hiding" or "Hurling."

1) Some of us "hide" our needs. We expect others to read our minds. We think it doesn't count if we have to tell our partner what we need. We say, "No, nothing's the matter. I'm fine," when, of course, we are not fine at all.

2) Others "hurl" their needs at their partner like fiery darts. Sure, they are verbalizing their needs, but not in a loving way. They say, "You just don't care about what I want. It's always the same. The kids are more important to you than I am!"

When you are feeling hurt, do you tend to *hide* your needs or *hurl* them? Check one.

_____ I hide them   _____ I hurl them

Write your thoughts about that practice here. Include some specific examples (For instance: *If I don't get my way, I scream at my spouse. I go to my room and pout. I nag my spouse until he gives in.*)_____

_____

_____

_____

Which of the two extremes does your spouse tend to use most often? Check one.

_____ he/she hides them   _____ he/she hurls them

What thoughts do you have about the combination of your personalities? Write them here (For instance: *It's hard to communicate when one of us hides and the other hurls. It gets awfully noisy when we both hurl. We never solve our problems because we both hide our needs.*) _____

_____

_____

_____

Ephesians 4:15 instructs us to share the truth, but to do so in love. Here's what healthy communication about your needs might sound like:

My needs	How my spouse can meet them
to receive affection	It's very important to me to hear the words, "I love you."
to receive support	Honey, would you go with me to the family reunion? I could really use your support.
to receive attention	I've missed our time alone together. Can we plan a date for this weekend?

Practice identifying your needs and how you will verbalize them to your spouse in the space below. Be sure to state them in a way that is free from accusation and blame.

My needs	How my spouse can meet them

1. _____

2. _____

3. _____

III. Mutual Giving

Mutual giving is the third key to healthy relationships. The focus is on two people *giving* to meet the important emotional needs of the other rather than *taking* from each other.

In contrast, unhealthy relationships can be described as two "emotionally bankrupt" people trying desperately to take from each other. Look what happens when two such partners join forces in marriage. Bob and Sally come from broken homes; they've both been married before and have been deeply wounded by messy divorces. Each is looking for someone to heal the hurts of their childhood as well as the agonizing pain of previous splintered relationships. Bob wants the ideal woman—the nurturing mother he never had and the devoted, supportive wife he expected to find in his first marriage. He's carrying so many needs around he could use a U-Haul trailer.

Unfortunately, Sally is just as needy. Going from an abusive home into an abusive marriage, Sally traded one set of crises for another. She, too, wonders if she'll ever find a man who will take care of her in a way that will make her feel happy and whole. But her "love tank" is so empty, it would take an ocean to fill it. And Bob doesn't have a drop to spare.

It doesn't take a psychologist to see that Bob and Sally will have major problems in their marriage. They're both out for all they can get, never thinking about what they have to offer their partner. They're like ticks on a dog, with the disastrous attitude, "I'm here to take from you." But, as author Larry Crabb in his book *Marriage Builder: A Blueprint for Couples and Counselors* (Grand Rapids: Zondervan, 1992) would describe it, what we find in such a marriage is that we have "two ticks and no dog!"

Christ offers a counterbalance to such self-destructive relationships. In Luke 19, His relationship with Zacchaeus gives us a good example of mutual giving—giving that was unconditional, regardless of the other person's behavior. Zacchaeus was a tax collector by occupation. By all accounts in the Gospels, he was probably guilty of stealing, lying, and deceit. Because of his unpopular position and apparent misdeeds, he must have felt lonely and rejected by his peers. He may even have felt fearful and insecure because of his small stature. In *short* (pun intended), Zacchaeus needed acceptance and understanding.

How did Christ treat Zacchaeus? Did He focus on his negative behaviors? Tell him to get his act together? Did He say, "I'll love you if . . . ?" No, Christ looked beneath surface behaviors and ministered to his emotional needs. Christ asked Zacchaeus to have dinner with Him. In fact, He said (paraphrased, of course), "Hey, Zack, I'm coming to your house and staying a spell!" Christ's desire to eat and fellowship with Zacchaeus on his own home turf met the man's need for acceptance and understanding.

After his visit with Jesus, was there a change in Zacchaeus? Definitely! The Gospel of Luke reports that after the two met for dinner, Zacchaeus declared he would give half of his possessions to the poor, and anyone whom he had cheated would receive four times as much. Experiencing Christ's unconditional *giving* changed Zacchaeus' behavior.

Think about the negative behaviors you sometimes observe in your spouse. Isn't it possible that underneath the negative behaviors, there might be genuine needs that haven't been met? Make a list below of your spouse's behaviors and specific needs that might be related to them. For example, a behavior might be "an uncontrolled temper" and the unmet need behind it could be "a need for security, to feel adequate in all of his circumstances." Or, an insecure spouse's habit of "criticizing others" might cover a need for "attention and admiration."

Behavior I See in My Spouse	Possible Unmet Needs in My Spouse

Now, reflect on what you've written about your spouse's behaviors and the needs that might have prompted them. Can you identify some ways you can give to your spouse to help meet these needs? Write your thoughts here (For instance: *When my spouse gets angry and upset over circumstances, I can assure him of my love and loyalty in spite of circumstances. Recognizing my spouse may criticize others because she needs attention, I will watch for opportunities to praise her and express my genuine admiration.*): _____

_____

_____

Now that you've identified some possible ways you can give to your spouse, you may want to verbalize your commitment to God in this prayer of faith:

"Dear Heavenly Father, make me sensitive to my partner's needs and help me be a part of Your plan to meet these needs. I especially want to be available to meet his/her need for_____

_____ .

Keep reminding me of how You give to me unconditionally and prompt me to give in the same way to my spouse. Amen."

Scripture Journaling—Philippians 2:3–4

Do nothing from selfishness or empty conceit, but with humility of mind let each of you regard one another as more important than himself; do not merely look out for your own personal interests, but also for the interests of others. (NASB)

Contemplate these verses and examine your own heart. How often do you act out of selfishness or regard yourself as more important than others? In a society that says, "Me first," do you find it difficult to put another's interests ahead of your own? What would you like to tell God about your own interests? Ask Him to make you more sensitive to your partner's interests as well. Write your prayer here.

Dear God, when I think about my own interests and the interests of others, I realize_____

_____

_____

_____

Set aside approximately one hour with your spouse. Each of you will want to have completed this exercise before the staff meeting.

THANKS/WISH LIST

Begin by listing at least six areas of genuine thankfulness you have about your relationship and marriage partner. Be specific. Look particularly for things you may take for granted. (For example: *"I'm grateful for your hard work as a provider for our family." "I'm thankful for your loyalty and faithfulness to our marriage commitment." "I'm thankful for the way you show you care with words and affection." "I appreciate your sensitivity to others' feelings."*)

Thanks List

1. _____
2. _____
3. _____
4. _____
5. _____
6. _____

Now, list up to six wishes you'd like to see concerning improvements and changes in your marriage. Keep in mind the needs you identified earlier and how you might communicate them in a loving manner. (For example: *"I'm hoping you can become more comfortable initiating affection." "I'd like for us to use respectful words when speaking to one another." "I wish we could avoid criticizing each other in front of others, especially the children." "I'd like to spend a few minutes talking with you alone each day."*)

Wish List

1. _____
2. _____
3. _____
4. _____

5. _____

6. _____

Be positive, hopeful, and encouraging, using such phrases as: *It would be important to me if . . .; It would mean a lot to me if . . .; I'm looking forward to the time when. . . .*

Share your lists with each other privately and in an unhurried fashion. Discuss any item that either spouse feels is important. Show interest in your spouse's responses, be open and genuine with your own, and demonstrate good eye contact.

Make no further mention of your wishes during the next month. To do so might be considered nagging or demanding. Do focus on giving your partner his or her "Wishes." Additionally, look for opportunities to appreciate your spouse for those items on your "Thanks" list and for any efforts to meet your "Wishes." Express your thanks privately, through special notes, and even when you're in the company of others.

FOR MEN ONLY

Secure

Protected

E

C

I

A

L

You will want to meet your wife's need for protection this week. Protecting your wife specifically addresses her areas of vulnerability. She needs to feel your protection as a safe umbrella under which she can take refuge and find support. Two major areas of vulnerability would be the pressure of family finances and the pressure of raising children. Other sensitive areas might include weight, shyness, education, job skills, or appearance. In whatever ways your wife feels vulnerable and insecure, protect her!

Better Understanding This Need:

List below five of the recurring topics of marital conflict in your home and then identify an underlying vulnerability that may need protecting. Discuss these with your wife when appropriate.

Conflict Topic	Possible Vulnerability
Examples: sexual frequency	*wife fears being "used"*
husband works too much	*wife overwhelmed with*
	child-raising duties

1. _____   _____

2. _____   _____

3. _____   _____

4. _____   _____

5. _____   _____

Speaking with love and reassurance to put her at ease, ask your wife about her vulnerabilities. You might say something like this: "Sweetheart, I want to better protect you from highly stressful times and feelings. Can you share with me how I can meet some of these needs for you?" Be sensitive to the things that overwhelm your wife—too little money, too many people, too many kids, too little private time, too many meetings, and so forth. Become her umbrella of protection, shielding her as much as possible from these pressures in her life.

Practical Suggestions:

Encourage Times of Escape.

Lovingly suggest and then support your wife in occasionally escaping from her overwhelming world into something fun, such as lunch with friends, reading a book, window-shopping, or a drive in the country.

Develop and Follow an Agreed-upon Family Budget.

Get outside help if you need to create a family financial plan.

Set Family Goals.

Discuss and write down goals for family outings, household chores, discipline plans for the kids, etc.

Eliminate Critical Teasing.

Review times when you might have teased your wife about her weight, her cooking, appearance, habits, or any area where she's especially sensitive. Instead of teasing, start protecting!

Cherish

Honor

E

R

I

S

H

You will want to meet your husband's need for honor this week. Honoring your husband means valuing him as an especially meaningful person in your life. It means seeing him as your personal hero. It also includes honoring his wishes as you are sensitive to pleasing him. You honor his decisions as you free him to lovingly protect you.

Better Understanding This Need:

List below five areas of strength, or positive character qualities you see in your husband. (For instance: *He's good at discerning other people's motives. He's very gentle with the children. He has a knack for knowing how to save money.*)

1. _____
2. _____
3. _____
4. _____
5. _____

Now practice communicating your appreciation for these five qualities. Tell your husband verbally when you're alone, publicly when you're with others, and by writing special notes.

Ask about his *wishes*, saying something like this: "Honey, I want to honor you more as my husband. Would you share with me some of your wishes I could help fulfill?"

Talk about his *decisions*, saying something like: "I've come to realize how much I value your leadership, and I want to be more sensitive about not criticizing or undermining your decisions. Will you share with me some decision areas in which you'd appreciate more of my support?"

Practical Suggestions:

Make Him King for a Day.

Schedule a surprise day for giving just to him—perhaps breakfast in bed, a special card or gift, a favorite outing, inviting close friends over, or simply spending quiet time together.

Brag About Your Husband.

Emphasize his strengths and communicate your appreciation. Don't compare him to other men, such as co-workers, fathers, brothers, or pastors.

Don't Sweat the Small Stuff!

Back off and let him make decisions and even mistakes; let him miss an exit off the expressway, or pick a restaurant with a long waiting line. Let him verbalize "wild" ideas without shooting them down.

Explore Your Passive-Aggressiveness.

What are some things you know he enjoys but withhold from him when you're angry? What are some of the things you say "innocently," knowing they'll serve as barbs to irritate him? What are some of the subtle little things you do to "ruffle his feathers"? Take steps to put away your anger so you'll be free to show him unconditional love.

——— *For Group Discussion* ———

Let each group member share his or her retaliation method of choice, saying something like this: "When I am disappointed or hurt that my spouse is not meeting important needs, I usually retaliate by_____."

Study Romans 8:31–32, as an encouragement to turn one's expectations toward God. Invite discussion on how this verse gives us hope.

Also review the account of Adam and Eve's responses in Genesis 3. Notice that there were two interesting patterns of dealing with conflict—**hiding and hurling.**

Hiding—Genesis 3:10   Hurling—Genesis 3:12–13

Discuss the tendencies to hide and hurl. Invite members to share their thoughts about having two "hiders" in a marriage. Two "hurlers." One of each.

Ask the women to express how they have received protection from their husbands this week. And ask the men how they have been honored by their wives.

Allow each member to talk about how he/she felt during the Thanks/Wish List exercise. Ask: "In what specific ways do you plan to be more giving to your spouse?"

Close the session by going around and having all members share with the group how they would complete one of the following statements:

- "It really means a lot to me when my spouse _____."
- "I feel loved by my spouse when _____."

Finally, ask each couple to give another response to these statements. But this time, have couples face each other, hold hands, look each other in the eye, and express their appreciation for each other in front of the group. After each partner hears this affirmation, encourage him or her to verbally acknowledge and "receive" the affirmation. This exercise will help couples solidify their commitment to speak the truth in love and truly appreciate one another.

Chapter Seven

———————— ◼ ————————

STUDY YOUR FAMILY TREE

It's time to get personal. Perhaps uncomfortably personal. It's time for you to examine your own unresolved childhood issues—those incidents from your past that have colored who and what you are today.

Pause a moment now and reflect on your childhood memories. They may be as faded as old, yellowed snapshots. Perhaps you've buried your memories so deep nothing comes to mind. You say, "I can't remember my childhood. It's a blank." But it's not. It happened. It happened to you.

When you grew up and left your childhood home, you didn't go empty-handed. You packed your emotional bags with all the "stuff" your family gave you—good and bad. When you married, the first thing you unpacked was this same old familiar stuff; it fit like a glove; you could wear it like an old shoe; it was comfortable and predictable. By following your parents' example (whatever it was), you found you could slip into the same rut and maneuver through your marriage on automatic pilot.

In your bag of "stuff," you also brought with you all the unmet needs of your childhood. Your parents hadn't fulfilled them, but surely your spouse would. What else was marriage for? So you dumped your bag of needs at your spouse's feet and said, "Meet these and we'll have a happy marriage." The only thing you hadn't anticipated was that your mate would have a bag of stuff as big as yours to unload at your feet. Now what? You're both stuck with each other's useless stuff.

Before long, your patience wears thin and you stop being polite. After all, how much "stuff" can you accumulate in one little house before you're up to your neck in, well, *stuff*? Disillusionment sets in as you realize your mate isn't going to meet your needs any better than your parents did. Might as well pack up your "stuff" and move on until you find someone who will. Or if, by chance, your partner hurts you in the same ways your parents did—rejecting you when you wanted acceptance, neglecting you when you needed attention, or demanding a perfect performance when you yearned for unconditional love—then you feel truly betrayed and all you want is O-U-T!

One of the most destructive items your parents may have heaped in your bag of "stuff" is the pressure to perform in order to be loved. Both marriage and family life suffer dramatically from this terribly unfair pressure. Expecting another person to perform in certain ways to merit acceptance, affection, approval, and love is a key ingredient in unhealthy relationships.

Performance pressure can be displayed in marriage relationships in two primary ways. Expecting or demanding that a spouse meet relationship needs or perform a certain way conveys the message, "In order to be loved by my spouse, I have to _____." In a similar, but more subtle way, we also may withhold giving to our spouse because he/she doesn't perform to our expectations. How would you finish these sentences?

Love becomes conditional when I withhold affection because my spouse has not (For instance: *behaved romantically; taken me out as he promised; agreed with me on an important issue*) _____

_____

_____

I sometimes feel performance pressure concerning (For instance: *love-making; keeping up the house; advancing in my career*)_____

_____

_____

I sometimes find myself pressuring my spouse about (For instance: *getting a raise; helping more around the house; spending more time in the bedroom*) _____

_____

_____

Some of my common "pressure tactics" include (For instance: *nagging and complaining; becoming remote and withdrawn; saying "no" to sex*)

_____

_____

In family relationships, the pressure to perform begins early. A child who desperately wants to please his/her parents may go to any lengths to gain acceptance, approval, and attention. This child unknowingly begins to believe that performing equals love.

In families, the pressure to perform begins early.

Performance pressure is also contagious. If I feel I must perform, then you must also perform. If Mom and Dad operate on a performance equals love basis, they will most likely expect the same performance mind-set in their children.

The most obvious home environment that contributes to performance pressure is the highly demanding one. The demands might come through constant criticism, perfectionism, comparisons, unattainable expectations, endless rules, or social pressure. The demands might be communicated through verbal put-downs, sarcasm, temper rages, and harsh discipline. Demands can also be communicated through silent rejection, emotional withdrawal, or withholding affection.

When Jimmy Carlton was asked about performance pressure in his family, he confided that he was brought up in a very demanding home. "My dad made me feel that if I didn't toe the line I was in a heap o' trouble. I thought life was one long list of rules and regulations. Man, my life was one long performance! I still find myself hearing my dad's voice in my head telling me what I should or shouldn't do. It's like his voice became my conscience. I'm just starting to realize I can turn that voice off if I want to."

Marla Carlton said she experienced performance pressures when she was growing up, too, but her home didn't offer the rigid, militaristic atmosphere Jimmy faced. "Our home was just the opposite—a madhouse, everybody doing his own thing, keeping his own hours, setting his own rules. My parents didn't believe in rules or maybe they were just too lazy to enforce them. They didn't try to run my life; they ignored me. I practically had to stand on my head to make them notice me. Sometimes I just wished they would take enough interest in what I was doing to say, "You can't do that," or, "You can't go there," or, "You've got to be home by ten." I had to muddle along and set my own rules by trial and error. And I constantly had to compete with my brothers and sisters for bits and pieces of my parents' attention. The child giving the best performance won out— and it usually wasn't me. I think that's why I became a singer when I grew up. I couldn't stop performing, trying to get *somebody's* attention!"

What about you? Did you grow up in a demanding home like Jimmy

Carlton's? Or a neglectful home like Marla's? Did you feel the pressure to perform to gain love and acceptance? You may be saying you're not quite sure your home fit either description. Read through the list below. Performance pressure/demands might look like any of these:

- a parent's consistent focus on a child's lowest grade in school
- a parent constantly asking, "Is that the best you can do?"
- emphasis on what's not done, not complete, and not sufficient rather than simply praising the child's progress
- verbal put-downs that attack the child's worth or character
- derogatory nicknames
- comparisons with others who are seemingly more perfect
- not tolerating normal emotional expressions of hurt, sadness, and anger
- any form of abuse—physical, emotional, or sexual
- expectations to be just like Dad or just like Mom
- pressure *not* to cause problems for your parents like a rebellious sibling did

After reading through the list above, write your answers to each of the following statements:

Growing up in my family, I sometimes felt like I needed to measure up to (For instance: *Mom's expectations for the way I looked; Dad's plans for my academic achievements; fulfilling certain roles as a woman/ man*) _____

_____

_____

When I was growing up, I received praise for (For instance: *good grades; my appearance; playing sports; my honesty; my willingness to help around the house*) _____

_____

_____

Now look at your list. Are most of the things you were praised for as a child related to things you *did*, or was the praise focused on *who you are as a person*? Write down any thoughts you may have about this.

_____

_____

_____

_____

Did this contribute to a feeling of obligation or pressure to perform? _____ Yes _____ No   Explain your answer.

_____

_____

Looking back at your childhood now, are there any messages you received from your parents that seem inappropriate? (For example: *Real men don't cry. Nice girls don't have sex. Being fat is unacceptable, even weak. I must always be the best. Children should be seen and not heard.*)

List your inappropriate messages here: _____

_____

_____

Write about any ways that these messages may have affected your marriage. (For example: *I've always believed that real men don't ever show emotion, especially sadness or fear. I realize now that this has caused me to be insensitive to my wife.*)

_____

_____

_____

A less obvious home environment that brings performance pressure is the neglectful home, such as Marla's. In this environment, parents are under-involved in meaningful ways with their children. The neglect may be present in several situations: alcoholic or workaholic homes, or parents who are preoccupied, distant, or emotionally closed. In each case the message to other family members is the same: "You're just not very important to me!"

As a result, family members set out to earn their rightful recognition through performing in order to gain approval. A child might seek attention through academics, athletics, popularity, or from disruptive behavior. The message is always, "Notice me . . . I'm important!"

Think back again to your childhood. Were there needs that went unmet because of under-involved parents? Are there things that you missed growing up? (For example: *I missed having my mom's attention when I was growing up. Her depression kept her in bed so much of the time. I remember always having to take care of things around the house.*) Write here about any experiences you may have had with under-involved parents.

_____

_____

_____

Finish the following statements as they apply to you:

Now that I think about it, it really was disappointing and hurtful that (For instance: *Mom didn't ever come to any of my games. I'd look in the crowd every week to see if she was there. She always promised but never came.*) _____

_____

_____

I tried to get attention or to be noticed when I (For instance: *played hookey from school; stole my grandmother's car; tried out for drill team; joined every club at school.*)_____

_____

_____

Scripture Journaling—Lamentations 3:22–23

Because of the LORD's great love we are not consumed, for his compassions never fail. They are new every morning; great is your faithfulness. (NIV)

Step back and look at your responses to the exercises above. Some of your answers undoubtedly provoked some painful feelings. In light of your responses, how are you feeling about God right now? Perhaps you realize that, as a child, your perception of God was greatly influenced by the role models in your home—your parents or other caregivers. If your father was stern and demanding, you likely picture God the same way; if your mother expected you to win her approval by constantly performing, you may be caught in the performance trap now in your relationship with God. You may have been telling yourself, *God can't be trusted! He's too busy to care about me; He's distant and uninvolved in my life.* What thoughts do you have after reading the Scripture passage in Lamentations? Can you grasp the truth that God loves you unconditionally, that you don't have to perform to earn His love? Write your thoughts and feelings here:

_____

_____

_____

_____

MARRIAGE STAFF MEETING

Before coming to the Marriage Staff Meeting, each spouse should complete the Childhood Questionnaire below. Then, during your staff meeting, share your responses with your partner. Be gentle, attentive, full of empathy and understanding.

CHILDHOOD QUESTIONNAIRE

Drawing from your memories of childhood, list one-word or one-phrase descriptions for each of your parents (both strengths and weaknesses).

FATHER

Strengths

(For example: *hard working, easy to talk to, honest*)

_____

_____

_____

_____

_____

Weaknesses

(For example: *lots of anger, perfectionistic, rigid*)

_____

_____

_____

_____

MOTHER

Strengths

_____

_____

_____

_____

Weaknesses

_____

_____

_____

_____

What things did you most like about yourself when you were a child? (For instance: *I liked that I was so creative. I liked being the best swimmer in my neighborhood. I liked the way I could talk easily with adults.*) _____

_____

_____

What things did you like least about yourself when you were a child?

(For instance: *I felt like a klutz around my friends. I was afraid to stand up for myself. I didn't get good grades like the other kids.*) _____

_____

_____

When you were a child, how would Mom:

praise you? _____

criticize you?_____

When you were a child, how would Dad:

praise you? _____

criticize you?_____

As you grew up, how did you know that Mom loved you? (For instance: *She would hug me and tell me she loved me.*) _____

_____

_____

As you grew up, how did you know that Dad loved you? (For instance: *He would buy me things—clothes and toys and stuff.*)_____

_____

_____

How did Mom and Dad deal with conflict between themselves?

Dad would _____

Mom would_____

How did Mom and Dad handle conflict with you?

Dad would _____

Mom would_____

How did you know your parents loved each other as you were growing up? How did they show it? (For instance: *They hugged and kissed a lot. They spoke kindly to each other. They laughed a lot together.*) _____

_____

_____

Indicate either "Mom," "Dad," "both," or "neither" next to the following phrases to help describe your home life as a child:

- Family leader _____
- Main disciplinarian _____
- Quick temper _____

- Comfortable giving affection to me _____
- Hard to please _____
- Parent I felt closest to _____

Check the following phrases that best describe your thoughts about your childhood:

_____ Our family *appeared* normal to everyone else.

_____ I was cared about because of the things I did.

_____ I was loved for who I was—my character.

_____ I was kind of an outsider, an observer to the rest of the family.

_____ Our home was demanding, performance-based, lots of rules.

_____ I often felt alone.

_____ I always felt like we "walked on egg shells" around our house.

_____ I seemed to always be the "adult," even when my parents were around.

_____ It was always important for me to please everyone.

_____ I'm not sure anyone knew the "real" me.

Now that you are an adult and have observed other families, what do you think was missing in yours? (For instance: *I realize now my mom was overly controlling. My parents didn't make me feel very secure. We could have used a lot more joy and laughter around my house.*) _____

_____

_____

How did you feel as you were completing the questions above?

_____

_____

Do you think your experiences as a child may be affecting how you relate to your spouse? In what ways? (For instance: *I resist my wife's suggestions because they remind me of my controlling mother. I need a lot of attention from my husband because I didn't get it from my dad.*)

_____

_____

When you have finished this exercise, be sure to set aside plenty of time to discuss your responses with your spouse during a staff meeting. Listen carefully and responsively to all that your partner says.

Secure

Protected

Enjoyed

C

I

A

L

This week you will want to meet your wife's need to be enjoyed. She needs to sense that you enjoy her company and look forward to spending time with her. As you enjoy your wife, you'll experience the blessing of true friendship in marriage. How is this accomplished? Two ways: 1) Include your wife in things you enjoy and 2) involve yourself in things she enjoys. *Enjoying* someone means spending time together as well as putting that special person above other activities.

Better Understanding This Need:

For this activity, both partners list several activities they would enjoy doing together and then trade lists. Make plans to do at least one item on each list in the next two weeks.

Husband's List	**Wife's List**

The things I would enjoy doing together are:

1. _____   1. _____

2. _____   2. _____

3. _____   3. _____

4. _____   4. _____

5. _____   5. _____

Talk about common interests, saying something like, "Can you think of some common interests you would like us to pursue?" (For instance: *develop a hobby; enjoy a sport; attend cultural events; complete a project together.*)

Communicate your enjoyment, saying something like, "I'm not sure if

I've ever told you, but I enjoy just being with you. Your friendship is very important to me."

Discuss friendship, saying something like, "What are some ways you could think of to help deepen our friendship?"

Practical Suggestions:

Return to some "first loves."

Recall some of the activities you enjoyed during courtship that were particularly meaningful to your wife. Surprise her by repeating history!

Stop excluding your wife.

Review your hobbies and pastimes to make sure your wife is not being excluded. Ask her to play golf or go hunting or fishing with you.

Stop avoiding your wife's enjoyable activities.

Think about the things she likes to do and join her, whether it's shopping, gardening, jogging, sightseeing, or antique hunting.

FOR WOMEN ONLY

Comforted

Honored

Exalted

R

I

S

H

This week you will want to meet your husband's need to be exalted. This means building your husband up, rather than hindering him by playing his "holy spirit." Exalting him results in his coming to trust implicitly that you're lovingly working for his good and supportive of his needs. A helpmate has a particular ministry through her words in building up her spouse.

Better Understanding This Need:

Below is a checklist of common family situations. In each scenario note which one best describes your response.

SITUATION	HINDER	HELPMATE
1. Husband late for dinner.	"Well, Dad's late again. We can never depend on him!"	"Dad must have had a really hard day. Let's plan a special welcome home."
2. Child says, "Dad told me, 'No.'"	"I'm sorry he said no. Don't worry. I'll talk him into it."	"Respecting Dad's decision shows us you're growing up."
3. Husband makes an obvious mistake.	Publicly—"Really, dear, I wish you hadn't done that!"	Privately—"I need to share my feelings and concerns with you about _____."
4. Group of women complaining about their husbands.	Join in the criticism and focus on your husband's faults.	Resist temptation to criticize and focus on your husband's strengths instead.

- Ask about your husband's needs, saying something like, "I genuinely want to be a good helpmate to you. Can you think of ways I can better meet your needs?"
- Talk about trust, saying something like, "What changes can I make so you're better able to trust me?"

Practical Suggestions:

Private Praise

Focus on your husband's character strengths (diligence, honesty, sensitivity, and so forth), and during a quiet time move toward him, touch him, meet his gaze, and verbalize your appreciation and love.

Public Praise

Look for opportunities to tell the children, family members, in-laws, business associates, church friends, and others about your husband's strengths.

Journal of Gratefulness

For one month keep a written record of how God blesses you through your husband. Enter the date, how you were blessed, and how you showed your appreciation. This focus on blessings will help you overcome a critical attitude, and showing your appreciation will encourage and affirm your husband.

Discuss how each group member felt performance pressures in his/her family. Invite responses to these questions:

How did you try to be accepted or noticed by your family?

How easy was it to remember things about your childhood?

Was it easy or hard to put your memories into words?

What did you learn about yourself from writing down your responses in the Childhood Exercise?

As the group leader, during this discussion time, you will want to be especially alert to members' feelings, tone of voice, and body language.

Let group members report any observations about how their childhood may be affecting their marriage relationship. Ask for group feedback.

Some individuals may want to try an exercise of family sculpting. Family sculpting is a physical representation of an individual's perception of family relationships. It requires an individual's vulnerable sharing and sensitive group feedback.

Ask one group member to think about the way their family members relate to each other. Have this person arrange selected group members to show a physical representation of family relationships. Two people may be standing back to back with their arms crossed, to show anger and avoidance. Another member in the family may be leaning, to depict the need for constant support. Be sure to have the "sculptor" put himself or herself in the family sculpture.

When the sculpture is complete, have the group give feedback. Let them share observations about the sculpture and the individual's placement of each member. Let the individual tell how it felt to do this activity and how it felt to grow up in this environment.

The goal of family sculpting is to gain new insight into family dynamics. We do not suggest it be used to "punch emotional buttons" or to vent strong feelings. Ultimately, it will be important for members to express sadness over painful experiences, and to receive comfort from a caring support group.

Close the session by asking everyone who feels comfortable to give a one-sentence prayer, asking for God's continued healing for marriages and individuals.

Chapter Eight

——— ■ ———

BE FREE FOR EMOTIONAL CLOSENESS

You've seen the headlines blazing that our schools are in crisis; you've heard our educators bemoan the fact that Johnny can't read, can't spell, can't do his math. But one headline you won't see, because few recognize the problem: Johnny can't *feel!*

We're all programmed from an early age to focus on achievement, not emotional development. Young children are praised for learning to tie their shoes, but who helps them identify times when they're sad, angry, or happy? School-age children begin the treadmill of activities—Scouts, dance, sports, piano—but when do they learn to deal with the rejections and disappointments that inevitably accompany these activities?

And what happens when we grow up? Since most of us enter marriage without an adequate "feeling vocabulary," or much experience in emotional sharing, is it any wonder our marriages lack closeness?

Think about it. You probably married with hopes of developing a deep emotional closeness, only to find that neither you nor your partner knew exactly how to achieve such a relationship. Frustrated by the lack of intimacy, one or both of you (perhaps unconsciously) began seeking a way to escape. At some point you woke up one morning to find that you and your partner had drifted apart into very separate worlds. One or both of you may be absorbed by the demands of the office or workplace; you may have escaped into the role of "super parent"; or you may be consumed by an endless onslaught of activities. Busy work. Anything to keep you from feeling the pain of your relationship.

Have we described you? Or have you and your partner discovered different "escape" techniques? What are yours? Put them into words by finishing the sentences below.

I often find myself absorbed with (For instance: *my friends; TV; my hobbies; church functions and meetings*) _____

_____

It seems like my spouse is often preoccupied with (For instance: *sports; classes; clubs; traveling*) _____

_____

Some of the ways we cope or get by in marriage, rather than get close, are (For instance: *we talk only about necessary things—schedules, bills, the kids—never about us or how we're really feeling*): _____

_____

A lack of intimacy in marriage is painful for any couple, but the hurt can be even more severe for couples with religious expectations. If you married anticipating a close spiritual walk with your partner and the relationship falls short, guilt gnaws at you. You feel inadequate. You think, *God expects me to "think more highly of others," but I'm putting my career above my family's needs. God commands me to love others, but I'm harboring resentments toward my mate.* Describe some of your feelings by completing the sentences below.

I'm troubled over the inconsistency I see within myself concerning ___

_____

_____

I know God wants my marriage to be _____ and He wants me to _____

_____

I want God to change me in the following ways: _____

_____

_____

Take a moment to write your prayer to God. Tell Him your desires, your feelings, and your willingness to change.

Dear God, _____

_____

_____

_____

_____

Because many of us missed the opportunity to develop a feeling vocabulary as children and therefore entered marriage with little experience in the art of intimacy, we must develop new skills in this area. Developing the skill of emotional responding can help end our "coping" lifestyles and help us experience the joy of intimacy in our relationships.

We must develop a feeling vocabulary.

Simply stated, emotional responding means when emotion is expressed by one partner, an emotional response is given in return. Emotion needs emotion—not logic, facts, criticism, complaints, or excuses. Let's look at some examples of unproductive responses, or what many refer to as a "communication gap":

One spouse shares emotion

"Honey, I was disappointed and hurt that we didn't get to go on the date we had planned."

And in return, she may receive:

1. Logic or reasoning

"I wouldn't have made plans for a date if I'd known this business trip was going to come up."

"I couldn't have gone anywhere with this sore throat. That's just the way things worked out."

This first partner may also receive:

2. Criticism

"You sure are being sensitive this week. I didn't think this date was going to be such a big deal!"

"I wouldn't have canceled our plans if you hadn't been so impulsive and spent the money we'd been saving."

Or she may receive:

3. Complaints

"Well, I'm hurt too. We could have spent last weekend together, but you went to your sister's instead."

"Yeah, I know you're disappointed, but I wish you'd told me about the dinner party before you told them we could go."

Sometimes a spouse simply gets a response of:

4. Neglect

"Can't we just drop it! I really don't want to discuss it anymore!"

(Or a complete lack of recognition)

"I think I'll go pull those weeds I've been meaning to get to."

Do any of these four responses sound familiar? Each one misses the mark when it comes to developing intimacy with your spouse. How would you feel after receiving a response of criticism or neglect?

If my spouse responded by criticizing or neglecting me, I would feel

_____

_____

How do you think your partner would feel after sharing some hurt and receiving a response of complaints or logical reasoning?

If I responded to my partner's hurt with complaints or logical reasoning, my partner might feel_____

_____

The first step in closing this communication gap is to be able to recognize these unproductive responses. Here's your chance to practice. After reading each of the examples below, circle which type of unhealthy response is being given.

The first step in closing the communication gap is to recognize unproductive responses to your mate's emotions.

1. You and your partner were supposed to have a quiet dinner alone, but you've kept her waiting for over an hour. When you finally arrive, your first words are, "I'm sorry, hon. The traffic was terrible. I just couldn't get away, and I didn't even have time to stop and call you."

This response is: Facts/Reasons   Criticism   Complaint   Neglect

2. After you and your partner have finished the evening meal, he/she says, "I'm feeling really upset about not seeing you any more than I do." You answer, "Yeah, well, let's get dressed so we can be on time for the kids' game tonight."

This response is: Facts/Reasons   Criticism   Complaint   Neglect

3. You walk in the front door to find your partner sitting alone in the living room, obviously upset. You respond sharply, "What's wrong with you now?"

This response is: Facts/Reasons   Criticism   Complaint   Neglect

4. As you pick your spouse up from work one Friday, he/she announces, "I'm worn out and discouraged about my day." Your response is, "Yeah, I know what you mean. You wouldn't believe how bad *I* had it today!"

This response is: Facts/Reasons   Criticism   Complaint   Neglect

To achieve emotional closeness in marriage, we must begin to avoid these types of responses. They miss the mark and leave us feeling empty, hurt, and alone.

For emotional closeness to take place, two people have to be emotional, communicating with feelings. But, since many of us don't have the vocabulary or experience to communicate with emotion, we must begin to develop our own feeling vocabulary.

Spend some time alone reading the story of the Prodigal Son found in Luke 15:11–32. Read it several times, paying close attention to the characters and their feelings. Use the "feeling faces" on the following pages to help you identify all the possible responses to this difficult family crisis. See the story through each character's eyes, then ask yourself, "How would I feel if I were this person in this situation?"

What do you think the father of the two sons felt as he watched his younger son gather his belongings and leave home, perhaps forever (verse 13)? Write down your feelings as if you were this father. (For instance: *My heart wrenches when I think I may never look upon my son again. My soul is tortured. It is so painful to remember him as a baby, so loving and trusting. I am worried over what will become of him.*)

_____

_____

_____

_____ *Be Free for Emotional Closeness*   **81**

Emotions . . . How Do You Feel?

 Afraid

 Angry

 Anxious

 Apologetic

 Ashamed

 Bored

 Confused

 Depressed

 Disappointed

 Disgusted

 Embarrassed

 Enraged

 Frustrated

 Grateful

 Grieving

 Guilty

 Happy

 Hopeful

Hurt

 Insecure

 Insignificant

 Jealous

 Joyful

Lonely

 Loved

 Misunderstood

 Nervous

 Overwhelmed

Pressured

 Regretful

 Rejected

 Relieved

 Resentful

 Sad

Sympathetic

Unappreciated

 Unimportant

 Unloved

 Used

Violated

 Vulnerable

Worried

How did the son feel after spending all his money and finding himself destitute in a foreign country, forced to grovel and eat scraps left for pigs (verses 14–16)? Write your answer as if you were this son. (For instance: *I had such big dreams and now I've lost everything. I feel disillusioned, sick, regretful, frightened, vulnerable, ashamed, alone.*) _____

_____

_____

_____

How did the father feel when, at long last, he spotted his wayward son, dusty and disheveled, making his way up the winding road, returning home (verse 20)? (For instance: *I feel overjoyed, thrilled, and excited. I am filled with gratitude and overcome with love for my son!*) _____

_____

_____

_____

How did the older son feel when he heard the news of his brother's homecoming (verses 25–30)? Answer as if you were this son. (For instance: *I'm jealous. I admit it. I feel hurt and angry. Ignored, unimportant, resentful.*) _____

_____

_____

_____

As you emotionally stepped into the hearts of each of these characters and articulated their feelings, we assume the story of the Prodigal Son became significantly more real to you. Did you notice that each character felt a variety of emotions? Viewing your own life situations with this same sensitivity to the complexity and varied nuances of emotion will not only enhance your marital life, but also give you a more healthy personal perspective as well.

Now that you've had practice looking at a situation and identifying feelings, let's go back to our previous marital examples. We recognize that if we are to avoid responding with facts, criticism, complaints, or neglect, we need to be able to identify the right way to respond.

Remembering that emotion needs emotion, write out new responses to these examples that would be caring and sensitive to your partner's feelings. The first step is to see the situation through your partner's eyes. What are his/her feelings, and how can you respond in a caring, supportive way? We've given you one possible answer for each situation; you come up with another.

See the situation through your partner's eyes.

1. You kept your spouse waiting over an hour. You might say, "Darling, I'm genuinely sorry for being late. I know I disappointed you. Will you forgive me?"

Now write out your own response: _____

_____

_____

2. Your spouse shares, "I'm feeling upset over not seeing more of you." You reply, "Honey, tell me how I've hurt you. I want to understand what you're feeling."

Now write out your own response: _____

_____

_____

3. You enter the house and find your spouse visibly upset. You say, "It makes me sad to see you hurting. Can you tell me about it? Maybe I can help."

Now write out your own response: _____

_____

_____

4. Your spouse tells you, "I'm just worn out . . ." You answer, "Sweetheart, I care about you and want to be there for you. How can I help you feel better?"

Now write out your own response: _____

_____

_____

During the next few days, practice identifying the emotions you feel throughout your day. Then, before you go to bed each night, take time with your spouse to recount the day's events, being sure to use your new "feeling vocabulary" to express your feelings about those events. Your spouse will have the opportunity to respond to you emotionally— carefully avoiding responding with facts, criticism, complaints, or neglect. Then switch places, and respond emotionally as your spouse expresses his/her feelings about the day's events. Take turns exchanging emotion for emotion this week.

Scripture Journaling—Philippians 3:10

That I may know Him and the power of His resurrection, and the fellowship of His sufferings, being conformed to His death.

There is only one way we can reach the place where we can truly comfort one another. We must enter into the fellowship of Christ's sufferings, as Philippians 3:10 suggests.

Dr. David Ferguson struggled with this passage for nearly a year, trying to understand it. How did one enter the fellowship of Christ's suffering? It sounded almost mystical. Was it merely a poetic phrase? Or did those words possess an underlying truth that could transform a person's life?

One Sunday morning David spoke in a church on the death of John the Baptist. When the disciples told Jesus of John's death, Jesus withdrew to a place where He could be alone with His Father, grieve His deep loss, and receive the Father's comfort.

To help you begin your emotional responding journey, use key phrases. "It hurts me that you ended up feeling rejected (lonely, etc). . . because I care about you. . . . I love you."

After the message that morning, while David was driving home, he began to cry. Even as he maneuvered his vehicle through noonday traffic, he couldn't stop the tears. He wondered, *Who am I crying for? Who am I hurting for?* As he struggled to understand the reason for his tears, it dawned on him that maybe he was crying for Jesus.

During the next few weeks David read the passage in John 14 about the upper room, where Jesus tells his disciples, "Let not your heart be troubled . . . in My Father's house are many mansions . . . I go to prepare a place for you . . . I am the way, the truth, and the life. No one comes to the Father except through Me."

After Jesus' profound and moving statements, Philip looks blankly at Him and says, "Show us the Father, and it is sufficient for us."

Jesus answers out of an anguished heart: "Have I been with you so long, and yet you have not known Me, Philip?"

For the first time, as David read those words, he felt an emotional reaction. He explains, "I felt what Jesus must have felt when He spoke those words. After all He had said and done, after all the close times He had shared with His disciples, they still didn't have the foggiest notion of who He was. I can identify with that. I can feel His hurt. I can embrace a Savior who hurts like I hurt."

In the same upper room, Jesus offers the bread and wine as His body and blood. He says, take. Eat. Drink all of it. This is my body that is broken for you. This is my blood that is shed for you.

"Think about this powerful moment," David urges. "Jesus offers His own body to be broken for His disciples. His own blood to be shed. What love! What vulnerability! And how do His disciples respond? They begin to quarrel among themselves over which is the greatest (Luke 22:24). Can you feel that—what the God-man Jesus must feel at that moment? He has just laid bare His soul, and those who claim to love Him are too consumed with their own importance to notice!"

Later, in the garden of Gethsemane Jesus makes himself vulnerable to his disciples again, revealing His pain and neediness: "My soul is exceedingly sorrowful, even to death. Stay here and watch with Me" (Matt. 26:38). He needs those He loves beside Him, supporting Him in His torment, but His disciples grow weary and fall asleep.

Three times Jesus goes off to pray and returns to wake His disciples, entreating, "Could you not watch with Me one hour?" (Matt. 26:40.)

"Do you feel Jesus' pain?" asks David. "His disappointment? His loneliness? This isn't a sermon on prayer; this is a hurting Savior going through the agonizing loneliness of dealing with His own pain. And no one remains awake to console Him!

"Can you weep with Jesus? Can your heart break for Him? Do you feel His anguish wrench your own emotions? This is part of knowing the fellowship of His sufferings. Feel His humanness, and find in Him the Great High Priest who understands your need.

"My challenge to Christian audiences is often this," David continues. "We may never be sensitive to our spouse, or to a lost world, until we can hurt for our Savior. If we can't hurt for Him, how can we hurt for other people? If I can't feel sorrow for Him who has always loved me, how can I feel compassion for someone who hurts or rejects me?

"God wants to do a work of freedom in our emotions. When we hurt, we don't need facts, logic, or reasons. We need emotion. We need someone to love and console us. When your wife is crying and upset, she doesn't want to hear, 'What's wrong with you now?' She needs you to enter into her pain. When your husband is in misery over a lost job, he doesn't need advice; he needs your comfort and compassion. We are part of the Body of Christ; we are to weep with those who weep."

Spend some time now picturing yourself standing in the crowd on the hill of Golgotha as Christ was crucified. Describe the sights and sounds and smells that would assail you in those moments. What would you feel as you looked upon Christ's sufferings? What emotions would you like to share with Him? What would you desire to tell Him about this experience? Write your feelings below and share them with Christ in your own prayer time.

Dear Christ, when I think about the way You suffered for me on the cross, I feel _____

_____

_____

_____ MARRIAGE STAFF MEETING

The last exercise to further develop your awareness of feelings should be discussed in this week's Marriage Staff Meeting. Read the list of emotions below. Circle any of the feelings you would consider commonplace for you during your childhood:

angry	depressed	hurt	guilty	joyful	excited
content	hopeful	scared	insecure	frustrated	bitter
happy	calm	enthusiastic	secure	significant	lonely
hostile	fearful	relaxed	shameful	elated	sad
satisfied	unimportant				

During the Marriage Staff Meeting, take turns talking about two or three sad or hurtful emotions each of you circled. Take the opportunity to share specific times when you felt these emotions as a child. Each of you should also express care and concern for your partner's feelings. This exercise will give you both a chance to practice identifying your feelings and responding emotionally.

As your partner shares his/her feelings, you will need to pay close attention to words, body language, and verbal cues. These times of sharing may be difficult for your spouse, so you will want to give lots of eye contact, reassuring touches, and support with your own emotional words that say, "I care," and "I love you."

End the Marriage Staff Meeting by scheduling a time in the next two weeks for you and your partner to go out alone on a date.

Lifestyle Discipline

The habit of "dating" your spouse again needs to be a lifestyle discipline. This date is NOT family time, NOT church fellowship time, NOT time to discuss the family budget or family concerns, NOT even a time for double dates. This is the time when you and your partner do something you both enjoy—alone.

As you develop this habit of dating your partner, you will always want to have at least one date scheduled for the near future, since looking forward to the date is part of what makes the event enjoyable. You will find that these dates will provide the most conducive environment for responding emotionally to your mate. The emotional distance will begin to disappear as you purposefully spend time relating to your spouse in an emotional way. So set that date now—and enjoy!

FOR MEN ONLY

Secure

Protected

Enjoyed

Courted

I

A

L

This week you will want to meet your wife's need to be courted. Courting your wife means treating her special, so she feels valued as a person— a person of unmeasurable worth. Courting your wife includes planning special evenings out, giving her unexpected gifts or flowers, and behaving with the manners and politeness of a gentleman. Courting means you take the initiative!

Better Understanding This Need:

Courting your wife means giving her your undivided attention when she's talking, instead of reading the newspaper or watching television.

Courting your wife means planning ahead by making dinner reservations, giving her special touches and love pats, using good manners and engaging in intimate conversation with her, instead of arguing over where to go for dinner because no plans have been made, or making polite conversation over a perfunctory meal and then hurrying home.

Courting your wife means making a 30 second phone call just to say, "I love you and was thinking about you."

During private moments with your wife, ask her, "From your point of view, how could we improve the romance in our marriage?"

Talk about your leadership role, asking your wife, "What areas of our relationship would benefit from more of my leadership?"

Practical Suggestions:

Reminisce about your courtship.

Talk about your first date, your early romance, fun times you spent together, your favorite songs, or your honeymoon romance.

"Capture" your wife for an overnight date.

Plan a surprise picnic for two; take a carriage ride or a drive to the country or beach; or spend a night in the bridal suite at a local hotel.

Send flowers or gifts occasionally.

Slip a love note in her purse; shop for a personal gift; surprise her at the office or home with flowers.

Update your manners.

Return to opening doors and helping with chairs; review your personal hygiene, table manners, and social etiquette; eliminate off-color jokes and crude language.

FOR WOMEN ONLY

Comfort

Honor

Exalt

Respect

I

S

H

This week you will want to meet your husband's need to be respected. Respect is communicated when a wife is supportive of her husband's leadership and decisions. Respect is fostered as a wife allows God to prompt her husband to meet significant needs in her life. Respect is conveyed in a variety of settings—at home, work, church, and social activities.

Better Understanding This Need:

List below six important roles your husband fills at home, at work, at church, and in the community.

1. _____   4. _____
2. _____   5. _____
3. _____   6. _____

Now review this list and think about opportunities you have to show your husband respect in each of these areas. Then consider changes you might need to make. Write your thoughts here: (For instance: *In my husband's role as father, I have the opportunity of showing respect for the way he disciplines the children. I need to change my attitude and the words I say, so I don't come across as taking the children's side against him.*) _____

_____

_____

During a private time with your husband, ask him, "Please share with me ways I can better communicate my respect for your leadership and decisions."

Resist self-reliance. Ask yourself, "What things do I need from my husband? Encouragement? Appreciation? Affection?" Now verbalize those needs to him and thank him for specific times he has recently fulfilled these needs.

Practical Suggestions:

Give feedback privately.

If you have a question or concern about your husband's decision, lovingly discuss it with him in private.

Appreciate his leadership.

Make positive comments about his leadership in different areas. Be specific. For example: "Darling, I'm glad you make sure we have family devotions even though our busy schedules make it hard to get together." "Dear, I'm glad you help us stick to a budget. Otherwise, we never could have afforded a second car."

Consider spoken and unspoken requests.

Give sensitive attention to your husband's spoken desires, but be aware also of those that are unspoken. Be attuned to underlying attitudes, facial expressions, and body language.

"Brag on" your husband in front of the family.

Your children provide the best audience; they love to hear you praise Dad's strengths and positive characteristics.

─────── *For Group Discussion* ───────

Group leaders may want to begin this session by introducing activities that further develop the participants' feeling vocabulary. Two possible activities include:

1. Using the "feeling faces," ask group members to pantomime selected feelings as other members identify the feeling name. Begin with common feelings (angry, anxious, bored) and move toward more challenging ones (depressed, contented, helpful, misunderstood).

2. Give each group member a lunch sack and markers or pens. Ask them to think about the events of the past week. On the inside of the sack they are to list the feelings they had about the week's events, that is, words or phrases describing how they felt "inside"—stressed, anxious, angry, lonely, etc. On the outside of the sack, group members are to list phrases that describe what others might have observed about them on the outside—smiling, worried, angry, frowning, perspiring, etc. If your group is especially ambitious, you might invite them to draw their own "feeling faces"—one inside the sack to show their "inside" feelings, and another on the outside of the sack to show how they came across to the world at large. Use this activity to discuss how, sometimes, the emotions we feel inside are different from what we let the rest of the world see. Discuss what problems this might cause—in your marriage, in your family, in your community.

Ask group members to discuss their experiences with emotional responding. Encourage them to share examples of unproductive responses group members may have observed this week (allow only those examples observed outside their marriage relationship). Discuss what kinds of unproductive responses were noticed and what feelings were likely to result.

Invite examples of positive emotional responses. Ask the group, "How did it feel to have your feelings acknowledged during the sharing of childhood experiences (in the last Marriage Staff Meeting), and during the evening times of sharing with your spouse? How did it feel to have emotion given in return?"

Discuss the ingredients that are often included in emotional responding: understanding, empathy, gentleness, reassurance, and confession. Review the benefits of emotional responding and its positive effects on the marriage relationship.

Close this session by checking with each couple about their plans for a special date together. If members seem a bit reluctant or embarrassed about scheduling actual dates with their mates, you may want to include a brainstorming session for discovering creative dating opportunities in your local community. Then, challenge each couple to "make a date" with each other and write it on their calendar before leaving the meeting.

Chapter Nine

— ■ —

BE FREE FROM MARITAL GAMES

Suppose you could take a quantum leap from the twentieth century back to the Garden of Eden. What would you find? The local inhabitants would be Adam and Eve, the first married couple, living in their lush garden condo just a stone's throw from the Tree of Knowledge. If you could peer through their garden window and eavesdrop, what would you hear them saying? Well, that would depend on whether you arrived before or after the "Fall."

If you arrived before Adam and Eve committed that first sin, you would notice that they walked with God in the Garden, communicating freely and openly with Him and each other. Their relationship—like everything else in the Garden—would be good, a mutual blessing, just as God designed it to be. With nothing to hide, the man and woman could be completely transparent and loving with each other. Imagine such a relationship!

If you arrived after Adam and Eve succumbed to Satan's lies, you would discover quite a different scene. Setting the example for hundreds of generations to come, Adam would angrily blame the woman for leading him into sin. "The woman whom You gave to be with me, she gave me of the tree, and I ate" (Gen. 3:12). And rather than confessing, Eve would resort to blame as well: "The serpent deceived me, and I ate" (Gen. 3:13).

Adam and Eve's behavior after sin entered their hearts reveals a universal pattern in marriage that replays itself in each new generation. Our deep need for attention, acceptance, and approval is a tremendous driving force. But, rather than reveal our true needs and feelings to God and our partner, we often find it easier to play emotional games. In the previous chapter, we discussed the unproductive responses of criticism, complaint, and offering facts or logic. When these unproductive responses are not stopped, they form patterns of behavior we call "marital games."

For example, suppose you're feeling a little lonely and ignored. You need comfort and affection from your spouse, so you fix a special candlelight dinner, hoping to recapture some lost romance. But your spouse arrives home late from work, and now both the dinner and your mood have grown cold. You may spend the rest of the evening sulking, until, at last, your partner apologizes. True, you've finally managed to get some attention, but you had to use manipulative tactics to get it.

Playing marital games creates negative emotions.

Why put a stop to marital games? First, because the hurts from unmet needs and the guilt from such manipulation keep your emotional cup filled with negative emotions. As we discussed in previous chapters, the opportunity for an abundant life and marriage is available only when our emotional cup is free from unresolved hurt, anger, guilt, and fear. Playing marital games only creates more of these negative emotions.

The second tragedy of playing marital games is that if we have to play a game to get a need met, it doesn't really satisfy. In the example above, what you really needed was an attentive partner offering you comforting words and a reassuring touch. When your partner didn't "give," you set out to "take" what you needed by sulking, that is, behaving in a way that would force your partner to respond the way you desired. Playing games always involves *taking* from your spouse, but real marriage intimacy is built on freely *giving* to each other.

Review the twelve statements below and indicate any that sound like statements you, your spouse, or both of you might make. Check the appropriate boxes:

Myself	Spouse	Both	Neither	
☐	☐	☐	☐	1. Sure, dear, I'll do it later.
☐	☐	☐	☐	2. Nothing's the matter. I'm fine!
☐	☐	☐	☐	3. I wouldn't have done that if . . .
☐	☐	☐	☐	4. Never mind, I don't feel like going now.
☐	☐	☐	☐	5. You think *you've* had a bad day!
☐	☐	☐	☐	6. I still don't feel you care.

Myself	Spouse	Both	Neither	
☐	☐	☐	☐	7. Yes, I'll help you *after* . . .
☐	☐	☐	☐	8. Don't worry about it. I'll get over it.
☐	☐	☐	☐	9. I'd do more of what you wanted if you would only . . .
☐	☐	☐	☐	10. Just forget it! I wouldn't enjoy it now anyway!
☐	☐	☐	☐	11. I know what you mean about being upset. Let me tell you what happened to *me* today!
☐	☐	☐	☐	12. If only you would _____, then I would feel happy.

The twelve questions above correspond to six Marital Games:

1. Complainer vs. Procrastinator
   (Questions #1 and 7 above)
2. Nothing's Wrong Game
   (Questions #2 and 8 above)
3. Blame Game
   (Questions #3 and 9 above)
4. Performer vs. Yes, But
   (Questions #4 and 10 above)
5. Outdone vs. Sweet Martyr
   (Questions #5 and 11 above)
6. Frustrated vs. Never Enough
   (Questions #6 and 12 above)

Which of the games above sound most like you? Your spouse?

Each of the games is explained below. Spend time reading the explanations carefully, and then determine if you see yourself in any of the examples. Pay special attention to the guidelines for stopping the marital games.

I. Complainer versus Procrastinator

This game typically begins with one partner making a request. The spouse agrees to the request, but doesn't follow through. After asking over and over with no results, the first spouse becomes the Complainer, while the other postpones fulfilling the request and becomes the Procrastinator.

Example:

Complainer: "Honey, can you help with the light bulb outside? It's too high for me to reach."

Procrastinator: "Sure, after I finish this TV show."

Complainer: "Dan, I thought you were going to change that light bulb for me."

Procrastinator: "I said I'll do it in just a minute!"

Complainer: "Well, I can't count on you for anything!"

Procrastinator: "I'd help out more around here if
you weren't such a nag!"

Both the Procrastinator and the Complainer should address their underlying emotional needs:

The Complainer may really be needing attention from his/her spouse. He or she may also be carrying around unhealed hurts over not feeling "special" in childhood.

The Procrastinator may need to feel needed or appreciated. He or she may also harbor unhealed anger over excessive control or complaining by parents in his/her childhood home.

Can you see yourself in the example above? Which role do you play? Procrastinator or Complainer? _____

What are your real needs when you engage in similar conversations with your partner? _____

_____

Are you willing to accept responsibility for stopping this marital game? Check one. _____ Yes _____ No

You may be asking, "How do I put an end to the Complainer versus Procrastinator game?" Either partner may disengage by taking the steps listed below.

The Complainer can disengage in the following ways:

1. When requesting assistance from your spouse, gently clarify your time requirements. For example: "Dan, would you check the car this week, before I make my trip to Chicago next weekend?"

2. If your spouse agrees, but then doesn't follow through, lovingly point out that the job hasn't been done and give a final time frame: "Dan, I can take my car to the shop on Thursday if you can't fit it into your schedule tomorrow."

3. If your spouse still doesn't follow through, then implement another plan:

- Do the task yourself (but without bitterness and resentment)
- Hire someone else to do the task (but without bitterness)
- Let the task go undone, especially if the consequences will affect your spouse as well

The Procrastinator can disengage in the following ways:

1. Finish the task you committed yourself to doing, or . . .

2. Honestly share your intentions to leave the task undone:

- "Listen, hon, I don't think I'll be able to get to the car before this weekend."
- "Let's plan to hire someone to look at the car."
- "I want to do it, but I need to resolve my anger so I can."

Think about the most frequent situation in which you find yourself and your partner engaged in this game. Are you the Complainer or the Procrastinator? What specific steps will you take to stop this game? Write out your plans here: _____

_____

_____

_____

II. Nothing's Wrong Game

A classic way of drawing attention to unmet needs without being vulnerable is the "Nothing's Wrong" game. These persons convey by facial expression, body language, attitude, or behavior that something IS wrong. When their partner asks about it, they coldly reply, "Nothing," thus inviting further questioning and their partner's full attention. Unsuspecting partners are now "hooked" into prying information out of their reluctant spouse. This game often erupts into a full-fledged quarrel if the "hooked" spouse begins to feel he or she is being used, or if the "Nothing's Wrong" spouse is ignored.

The "Nothing's Wrong" game may sound like this:

"Hooked" Spouse: "What's wrong, hon? You're not upset, are you?"

"Nothing's Wrong" Spouse: (With a downcast look) "No, nothing's the matter. I'm perfectly fine."

"Hooked" Spouse: "Are you sure? You're not angry with me?"

"Nothing's Wrong" Spouse: (While slamming drawers) "Didn't I say everything's fine? I'll survive!"

Both partners playing this game should address their underlying emotional needs:

"Nothing's Wrong" spouses, who likely have a deep need for attention or support, find playing this game is much less emotionally risky than asking their mate to set aside time to talk, or vulnerably sharing their real needs. They may have missed someone being sensitive to their hurts and needs as a child, and, since they play this game on their own terms, it serves as a means of controlling their partner.

"Hooked" spouses may lack an awareness of their own needs, and therefore be oblivious to their partner's needs. They also may nurse considerable anger from previous games. Because they, too, may have missed having someone concerned about their needs as a child, they remain insensitive to their spouse's needs, or wait for dramatic cries for help.

Can you see yourself in the example above? Which role do you play?
_____ "Nothing's Wrong" Spouse   _____ "Hooked" Spouse

What emotional needs are you trying to communicate when you have similar conversations with your mate?_____

_____

Are you willing to accept responsibility for doing your part to stop this game? _____ Yes   _____ No

How do you put an end to the "Nothing's Wrong" game?
The "Nothing's Wrong" spouse can disengage in the following ways:

1. Think carefully about your real need. (For example: *support with the kids, time alone with your spouse, appreciation for a job well done, empathy because of a rough day*)

2. Choose the right time to express your need. (For example: *privately, after your spouse has had a chance to relax, or after the kids have gone to bed*)

3. Lovingly express your need. (For example: *"Now that you've relaxed a little, I need a few minutes to visit with you. I've had a rough day and need to tell you about it. I could really use some comfort and support."*)

The "Hooked" spouse can disengage in the following ways:

1. Let your partner know when you've sensed the game has begun, saying something like, "Your tone of voice sure tells me something is going on."

2. Express your support and availability: "When you're ready to talk, let me know. I'd sure like to support you in whatever is troubling you."

3. Listen attentively and respond lovingly. Give your spouse your undivided attention, lots of eye contact, comfort, and reassurance.

Take a moment to imagine a similar conversation between you and your spouse. Which role are you playing? Now, recreate the same situation, except this time do your part to stop the marital game. What are the specific steps you will take? Write them down here:_____

_____

_____

III. The Blame Game

This game most commonly has two players. It is played in order to avoid personal responsibility for one's own actions. By diverting attention to your partner's behavior, rationalizing your own becomes much easier. Blaming or accusing responses may sound like this:

- "If it weren't for all your nagging, I'd come home earlier!"
- "If it weren't for all the nights I was left alone, I wouldn't have had an affair."
- "I wouldn't say such hurtful things if you wouldn't provoke me."
- "I'd spend more time with the kids if you wouldn't put me down in front of them."

Both players of the Blame Game should address their underlying emotional needs:

Both players usually have tremendous unmet relational needs—a need for acceptance, respect, and approval. Unhealed hurts block emotional sharing. Each may fear being hurt again, so the focus is on criticizing each other's behavior.

Avoiding personal responsibility is often a learned behavior from childhood, and may stem from a lack of empathy or appropriate apologies in the family of origin. These individuals may have come from homes where parents were under-involved, critical, or hard to please.

Can you see yourself in the statements above? What blaming statements have you made? Write them here: _____

_____

_____

What real needs are behind these statements? _____

_____

_____

Are you willing to do your part to stop this game?

_____ Yes _____ No

How do you disengage from the Blame Game?

_____

The "Blamer" can disengage in the following ways:

1. Allow yourself to sense your accountability to God.
2. Assume responsibility for your own behavior and attitudes.
3. Express your confession and regret to God and your spouse.

For help accepting responsibility for your own actions read Romans 14:10, 1 John 1:9, and James 5:16.

The "Blamed" partner can disengage in the following ways:

1. Receive any criticism your partner gives as an opportunity to assess your accountability with God.

2. Express to your partner an appropriate response to the criticism, such as, "Sweetheart, as for my part in the argument, I see where I said some hurtful things to you, and I regret that. It was wrong of me. Will you forgive me?"

3. Express the truth of your needs in a loving way, such as: "Honey, I care so much about our relationship, it hurts me when I'm criticized in front of the kids. I feel shamed and disrespected. I'd appreciate you considering my feelings about this."

Reflect again on the blaming statements you communicate to your spouse. How can you assume responsibility for your own behavior? Write your answer here: _____

_____

_____

How can you communicate your need next time instead of making an accusation? _____

_____

_____

Reflect on any blaming statements that have been directed toward you. Is there any part of the statement that God may be using to change you? Write about it here: _____

_____

_____

What might your partner need from you during the situations where blaming might occur? _____

_____

_____

IV. Performer versus Yes, But

This game is common among couples who engage in power struggles. One partner may give a suggestion and the other quickly shoots it down. This game is often played by couples who are anxious about being close; they use the game to avoid intimacy. The "Performer vs. Yes, But" game may sound like this:

Yes, But: "I wish we could go out to dinner together sometime."

Performer: "Okay, let's plan on going out this Friday."

Yes, But: "Oh, I'm always so tired on Friday."

Performer: "We'll go on Saturday then."

Yes, But: "It's so hard to get baby-sitters on Saturdays."

Performer: "I can arrange for my sister to keep the kids."

Yes, But: "I feel guilty asking her since we don't pay her."

Performer: "I can ask Jennifer from across the street."

Yes, But: "I don't think she's very responsible. Let's just forget it!"

Both the Performer and the "Yes, But" player need to address their underlying emotional issues:

Performers often have unresolved hurts and keep playing this game out of a need for acceptance, approval, and appreciation.

"Yes, But" players often feel such a magnitude of unmet needs that they don't really expect someone to lovingly give to them. They may also be experiencing substantial pain from unmet needs in their childhood home.

Do you see yourself in either of these roles. Which one?

_____ Performer   _____ "Yes, But"

What needs do you have a difficult time expressing?_____

_____

_____

What do you really need from your spouse when you engage in similar conversations? _____

_____

_____

Are you willing to accept the responsibility for doing your part to stop this marital game? _____ Yes   _____ No

How do you go about putting an end to this game?

The Performer can disengage in the following ways:

1. Lovingly reassure your spouse concerning your desire to address the situation, saying something like, "I really would like us to go out together."

2. Present a maximum of three options: "We can go out Friday or Saturday, and I'll be glad to arrange for the sitter. If you're worried about not paying my sister to sit, we could trade off and watch her kids some other time."

3. Gently point out that your spouse is now free to decide and is responsible for his/her own decision: "Those are several options for how we could go out together. You think about it and let me know when you've decided which you prefer."

The "Yes, But" player can disengage in the following ways:

1. Listen to the suggestions offered and think about them.
2. Either pick one of the suggestions or offer one of your own.
3. ENJOY one of the suggested ideas, rather than focus on the negative—what you don't have or what won't work.

After you have determined what role you play in this game, spend some time planning what you will do differently the next time a similar situation occurs. What will your responses be? Write them here: _____

_____

_____

What decisions will you make to avoid this game?_____

_____

_____

V. Outdone versus Sweet Martyr

This game is often initiated by the spouse who is overwhelmed by his/her own neediness. Almost every conversation is turned back toward Sweet Martyr's needs, while the hapless partner is "outdone" in every way as his/her own needs, hurts, and desires are minimized or ignored. Sweet Martyrs ask about their partner's needs only to be polite, while still remaining self-absorbed. Here's an example:

Sweet Martyr:	"Well, how was your day, dear?"
Outdone:	"It was terrible. One of the worst I've had lately."
Sweet Martyr:	"Really? It was the pits for me too. I worked my fingers to the bone around here. Did you notice how clean the house is?"

Or this:

Sweet Martyr:	"You look tired, dear. Do you need some rest?"
Outdone:	"I'm really wiped out. I think I'll relax for a few minutes before we go out."
Sweet Martyr:	"I know what you mean. I'm exhausted too. Would you mind handing me a pillow?"

Both the Sweet Martyr and the Outdone player need to address their underlying emotional needs:

Sweet Martyrs undoubtedly feel a multitude of unmet needs in spite of their spouse's giving, and they are quick to call attention to these needs at every opportunity—perhaps out of a fear their needs will never be noticed. Sweet Martyrs may have had plenty of material possessions as a child; but their emotional needs for attention, empathy, and unconditional approval may have gone unmet.

Outdone partners are likely to grow weary and increasingly frustrated in their attempts to meet their partner's needs, and may even begin experiencing passive-aggressive tendencies. Outdone partners may have learned to minimize their own needs as a child and entered marriage hoping for a change—an unlikely event as long as Sweet Martyr holds the reins.

In which role do you see yourself most clearly?

_____ Outdone _____ Sweet Martyr

As the Outdone partner, what needs of your own have you been minimizing? _____

As the Sweet Martyr, what needs are you hoping to have met? _____

_____

What changes would you like to make in your relationship? _____

_____

Are you willing to accept responsibility for doing your part to stop this game? _____ Yes _____ No

What steps can you take to end the "Outdone versus Sweet Martyr" game?

_____

Be Free from Marital Games **103**

The Sweet Martyr can disengage in the following ways:

1. Express a wish or desire to your spouse in a loving way. For example, "I've been wanting us to spend more quality time together. Can we make plans for an evening out?" Then show your appreciation for the response you receive.

2. Give undivided attention to learning about your partner's needs, saying something like, "Come sit down and tell me about your day, sweetheart."

3. Give liberally to help meet your partner's needs, offering comforting responses, such as, "It sounds like you really had a rough day, honey. How can I help you feel better?"

The Outdone partner can disengage in the following ways:

1. Be gently assertive when you hear the "Sweet Martyr" game begin, by saying, "I appreciate your asking me about my day, but it hurts when I sense that you're not genuinely interested."

2. Express your needs in a loving way: "Can we sit down so I can tell you about my day? I really need your understanding."

3. Be available and give to meet your partner's needs: "Now that I've told you about my day, sweetheart, I'd like to hear about yours. What do you need from me right now?"

Make plans now for the next time this situation occurs. What will you do differently?_____

_____

_____

As the Sweet Martyr, begin now to think about ways to become more sensitive to your partner. Write them here:_____

_____

_____

As the Outdone player, practice communicating assertively. What will you tell your partner when this situation occurs again? Write your response here: _____

_____

_____

VI. Frustrated versus Never Enough

The Never Enough game begins with the message, "If you'll only do this for me, . . . I'll be satisfied." But the Never Enough partner is not satisfied, he or she always finds something else to complain about, and always sees the cup as "half empty."

For example:

Never Enough:	"I wish we had more money to fix up the house."
Frustrated:	"My overtime schedule starts next week. We'll be able to buy some things then."
Never Enough:	"I don't like you spending so much time at work. You're gone enough as it is!"
Frustrated:	"If I cut back my hours, I can't bring in the money we need."
Never Enough:	"See what I mean? We have no money for nice things and no time to enjoy life!"

Or:

Never Enough:	"I can't decide what sounds good for dinner."
Frustrated:	"Let's go to Luby's tonight. We usually enjoy that."
Never Enough:	(during dinner) "You know I didn't want to come here. This place is awful!"

Both the Never Enough player and the Frustrated partner need to address their underlying issues.

Never Enough partners may need attention or security, but they seek to meet these needs through their partner's performance. They may fear that their needs will never be met unless they constantly communicate their dissatisfaction. They've often missed a great deal of emotional support as a child and therefore have developed a self-sufficient, performance orientation.

Frustrated partners may continue to play this game out of a need for approval. They may express passive-aggressive anger as a result of never being able to satisfy their spouse. Having possibly missed acceptance and approval as a child, they therefore feel a constant pressure to perform.

Do you see yourself in the Never Enough player or the Frustrated player? Check one.

_____ Never Enough Player   _____ Frustrated Player

What similar conversations have you had with your spouse? Recount one or more here _____

_____

_____

What were you really needing from your spouse? Be specific. _____

_____

_____

Are you willing to do your part to stop this game?

_____ Yes _____ No

How do you go about ending the Never Enough game?
The Never Enough player can disengage in the following ways:

1. Think about the things you already have; list your reasons to be grateful.

2. Express appreciation privately and publicly to your spouse.

3. Think about how your spouse could practically meet three of your top needs (for example, time to talk, schedule a date, offer a hug). Express these needs, and then show your gratitude to your spouse when they are fulfilled.

The Frustrated player can disengage in the following ways:

1. Express your commitment to your spouse, such as: "I'm committed to being supportive and available to you."

2. Express your needs: "It means so much to me when you show how much you appreciate my efforts."

3. Express your appreciation: "Thanks for noticing my help around the house. Your appreciation really motivates me."

As the Never Enough player, what areas of your marriage can you already be grateful for? Write them here: _____

_____

_____

What are your top three needs that you will express to your spouse? ____

_____

_____

How will you lovingly express these needs? _____

_____

_____

How will you verbalize your appreciation as needs are met? Be specific.

_____

_____

As the Frustrated player, think about the last time you and your spouse had a similar conversation. How could you have expressed your commitment to meeting his/her needs? _____

_____

_____

How could you have expressed your own needs and gratitude?_____

_____

_____

Are there other things you would like to do differently next time? Write them here: _____

_____

_____

Scripture Journaling—Psalm 34:8–10

Oh, taste and see that the LORD is good; Blessed is the man who trusts in Him! Oh, fear the LORD, you His saints! There is no want to those who fear Him. The young lions lack and suffer hunger; But those who seek the LORD shall not lack any good thing.

This entire Psalm speaks of God's provision. Our Heavenly Father wants us to "taste and see"—to sample His goodness. He is ready to provide. Have you taken refuge in Him? Does He have your respect? What thoughts do you have regarding God's loving care? What would you like to say to God now? Write your letter to God in the space below.

Dear God,

_____

_____

_____

_____ **MARRIAGE STAFF MEETING**

Spend some time before this staff meeting reflecting on how you will finish the following statements:

Looking back on my family of origin, the game(s) I saw played most often were_____

As you reflect on your childhood, think about the games you saw modeled as you grew up. You may find you have a tendency to repeat the games you observed as a child, or you may react the opposite way. (For example, your parents may have played the Blame Game. Now, as an adult, you have the same tendency toward blaming, or you may try to avoid all conflict by playing the "Nothing's Wrong" game. Discuss these two possibilities with your spouse.) Now circle the correct word in this sentence: I tend to repeat/oppose the games I observed in my family.

After reviewing the games covered in this chapter, I saw myself most clearly in _____

The role that I play most often is _____

When I play the role of _____, I am really needing _____

(Remember, eight of the basic needs we all share are: acceptance, affection, appreciation, approval, attention, encouragement, respect, and security.)

Allow time for both partners to share their new insights into their OWN behavior. (This is not the time to point out observations you've made about your spouse.) Be sure to be a good listener, using frequent eye contact, offering supportive words, and paying attention to your partner's body language. And, of course, remember to respond to emotion with emotion.

LIFESTYLE DISCIPLINE

Developing the habit of vulnerably sharing your needs with your spouse instead of playing marital games will keep intimacy alive in your marriage. In a healthy, intimate relationship, couples communicate about needs and hurts on a consistent basis. As you practice this habit you will begin to look at your own behavior and question, "Why am I saying this to my partner? What am I really needing?" You can then give your partner the opportunity to meet your need in a loving way.

As you continue to be sensitive to this "behavior equals need" connection, you will have the chance to look beneath your partner's behavior and respond to his/her need. This mutual giving is what intimacy is all about. Consistently sharing needs followed with mutual giving will maintain the intimate connection between you and your spouse—and will stop the marital games!

Secure

Protected

Enjoyed

Courted

Intimate

A

L

This week you will want to meet your wife's need for intimacy. Intimacy involves a freedom to share all of yourself—body, soul, and spirit—with your mate. A wife needs a husband who is constantly assessing his ability to "share himself" with his partner, who has the freedom from unhealthy thoughts and behaviors that allows him to give. He's committed to giving, not taking.

Better Understanding This Need:

Noted below is a list of areas which need to be assessed for personal freedom. Review this list and circle those areas which may need your attention. Ask God to bring to your mind specific examples or situations that demonstrate your need for freedom in these areas.

In order for a wife to be secure in marriage intimacy, a husband needs to be free from:

- excessive moodiness
- selfishness
- fears/insecurities
- a focus on taking/not giving
- legalism

- temper outbursts
- childish self-pity
- spiritual pride
- perfectionism
- avoiding emotion

After you have prayerfully considered which of these areas may need to be addressed, make a list of specific examples that come to mind. Spend time with God, asking Him to show you what new freedom He desires for you and what steps you need to take to get there. Next, discuss these insights with your partner, saying, "Honey, I want to work on any areas that might be limiting our closeness. Can I share with you some of the areas I believe I need to work on—and then get your input?" (Share your list above.)

Second, honestly review several areas of communication in your marriage and consider necessary changes. Ask yourself: Do I share these with my wife: (1) my feelings, fears, and dreams? (2) my impressions from the Lord, prayer concerns, and blessings? (3) affection and physical intimacy aimed at pleasing my wife?

Practical Suggestions:

Take time—for talking, relaxing together, dating, and spending occasional weekends away—just the two of you.

Give to your wife's needs—for attention, affection, appreciation, and related needs.

Initiate—times of prayer, gentle touches, verbalized love, quiet closeness, and loving glances.

Focus on your wife's pleasure—in sexual intimacy, considering her desires, preferences, and wishes.

FOR WOMEN ONLY

Comfort

Honor

Exalt

Respect

Intimate

S

H

You will want to meet your husband's need for intimacy this week. Meaning "inner most," intimacy involves vulnerably sharing one's inner thoughts, feelings, and self. A man needs to feel secure in sharing, and confident of his wife's support. Her support might come through listening, empathy, or reassurance. Intimacy is also expressed by physically sharing oneself in sexual closeness.

Better Understanding This Need:

Review the following list of hindrances to intimacy. Each of these areas will inhibit the closeness between you and your husband. Prayerfully consider which areas need your attention. Ask God to show you specific examples or situations that reflect your need for change.

In order for a husband to feel secure in marriage intimacy, a wife needs to be free from:

- criticizing her husband's ideas
- rejecting his affectionate advances
- a lack of interest in her husband's dreams
- little or no interest in sexual initiative
- the tendency to share his confidential secrets
- under-involvement in her husband's interests
- publicly teasing him
- comparing him with others

After reviewing this list, decide which areas need the most attention. Write down the items the Lord brought to mind and the steps for change He would desire for you.

Next, share these insights with your husband, including the areas you plan to work on. Ask for his input, saying, "What changes can I make to improve our marital intimacy?"

Practical Suggestions:

Review your confidentiality. Is your husband secure in knowing his thoughts and feelings will not be revealed to others?

Consider your supportiveness. Can your husband confide in you, knowing you won't be critical or uninterested?

Reassure him of your desire for closeness, of your commitment to meet his needs and your appreciation of his special role in your life.

Listen!!! to his ideas, dreams, interests, fears, joys, hopes, and plans.

Initiate affection by physically touching, verbalizing your love and appreciation, and by slipping him little love notes.

Read *Solomon on Sex* (Nashville: Thomas Nelson, 1977). Take turns reading a chapter of this insightful book by Joseph Dillow; mark special items of interest and then share your ideas.

Plan surprise dates. Men desire to be needed, so plan some unexpected "alone times" when you can show your husband how much you need him.

Begin this group session by asking each couple to act out two of their most "popular" marital games. See if other group members can guess the games being played. Be sure to include in the discussion which of the intimacy needs are going unmet (acceptance, affection, appreciation, approval, attention, encouragement, respect, or security).

As a second part of this activity, practice the disengaging techniques for each of the six games. Replay the same situations already presented, but this time stop the marital games with the proper disengaging technique for each player.

Next, ask individuals to report what games they identified in their family of origin. Discuss ways they have repeated behaviors and ways they have opposed family games. How has this affected their marriage relationship?

Finally, ask group members to complete the following statement privately: "I really feel cared for by my spouse when. . . . " Ask each person to share their response. Invite the group to help identify what intimacy need is being met. Be sure to appreciate the uniqueness of your group members.

After everyone has identified their intimacy need, discuss any connection to their childhood. Have them ask themselves these questions: "Is this need something I missed as a child? Is it something I received as a child, and therefore is it most important to me now?"

Encourage participants to look for opportunities to support other group members during this time of sharing.

Chapter Ten

—■—

UNDERSTAND THE PAIN AND POTENTIAL OF INTIMACY NEEDS

God did a curious thing. He placed Adam in a perfect environment in the Garden of Eden, where all his physical needs were met and there was no such thing as hurt, fear, or guilt (since sin hadn't yet tainted the world). Adam's behavior was innocent and his thinking pure, and the Creator of the universe was his intimate Friend. Yet, amazingly, God recognized that all of Adam's needs were *not* being met, when He declared, "It is not good that man should be alone" (Gen. 2:18).

What could God possibly be talking about? One simple, yet profound fact: He had created human beings with needs that could only be met in the context of human relationships. God wanted us to receive not only *His* divine acceptance and approval, but also the love and acceptance of others. So, He established the institutions of marriage, family, and the church to meet human needs.

Freely you have received, freely give.
Matthew 10:8b

As our needs are met, we experience an overflow of love and gratitude to God that enables us to give freely to others. In principle, God's design for humankind offers us the potential of great joy and fulfillment; but, in the hands of sin-riddled humanity, His plan is often discarded in favor of selfishness and greed. In this chapter, we will take a look at both the pain and the potential of our deepest intimacy needs.

Imagine bringing your newborn baby home from the hospital—a precious little bundle with bright eyes, rosebud lips, creamy smooth skin, and cornsilk hair. From the beginning she loudly lets the world know she has needs—food, water, warmth, care, and protection. Of course, during those 3:00 A.M. feedings, there is no doubt about her need for nourishment. Now, if only she'd realize her need for sleep!

But that tiny baby needs much more than just the basics to sustain life. She has needs that require a distinctly human response. In other words, she needs *you*. When she cries, her little arms flail and seem to gather you in as you approach. Her gaze follows the sound of your voice. Sometimes, she simply wants to be held or rocked or caressed. Without the loving touch of another human being, she might not survive.

As your child grows, you begin to notice a definite connection between her needs, her way of thinking, her feelings, and her behavior. Imagine this same little girl at five years of age. She has just finished drawing her very best picture of a rainbow. She calls from the kitchen table: "Mommy, come look at my rainbow!" This little girl has a need—although it's unconscious—and it motivates her behavior.

What needs do you think she's expressing? Write your answer here:

_____

_____

_____

Now, let's take this commonplace event and play it out two ways. First, imagine that Mother hears her daughter call from the kitchen. She stops what she is doing and joins her child at the table. They spend the next few minutes discussing the beauty of the Crayola rainbow. Mom gives her undivided attention, freely expressing her approval and encouragement. What do you suppose the child *thinks* as she returns to her coloring? She thinks (For instance: *Mommy likes my drawing, she thinks I'm important.*) _____

_____

_____

What do you think the child would be *feeling*? (For instance: *loved, accepted*)_____

_____

_____

How might she behave after this experience? (For instance: *She might give her mom a hug and try drawing another, more challenging picture.*) _____

_____

_____

Now, let's suppose this same mother hears her daughter call, "Mommy, come see my rainbow," and the mother replies, "I can't. I'm too busy. Why don't you go play in your room for awhile?"

What do you imagine the child will think? (For instance: *Mommy's too busy for me.*) _____

_____

_____

What do you think the child is feeling? (For instance: *rejected, unimportant*) _____

_____

_____

How might she behave after this experience? (For instance: *She might scribble all over the rainbow and tear up the picture. She might trudge sullenly to her room.*) _____

_____

_____

Just like the newborn baby and the five-year-old, we have needs that require positive human responses. We don't outgrow our need for food or sleep, nor do we outgrow our need for attention or affection.

So, let's put this in an adult context. Suppose your spouse has gotten very busy with work lately and has been so caught up with his/her daily activities that it has been weeks since you've had time alone together. You might try dropping a few hints about your desire to spend time together; you may even verbalize your need for attention.

After you've confided these feelings, your partner may reply, "Honey, you're right. I really have been busy. I can see how you must have felt neglected. I'm sorry. Let's spend some time alone this Thursday evening. Just the two of us."

What will you think? (For instance: *He/she cares about me and thinks I'm important. He/she loves me and wants to spend time with me.*)

_____

_____

What will you be feeling? (For instance: *relief, loved, secure*)_____

_____

_____

How might you behave? (For instance: *I might offer a hug or kiss to show my appreciation for my spouse's sensitivity. I might express my gratitude for my partner's positive emotional response to my need.*)

_____

_____

In this example, we see the potential for intimacy when our needs are expressed and then met within the marriage relationship. You may also notice that healthy thinking patterns, and positive feelings and behaviors are the result of our needs being met.

Let's contrast the example above with the pain that occurs when our needs go unmet. Again, you let your spouse know about your need for attention, but this time he/she gives a cold, unemotional, uncaring response, such as:

Facts or Logic

"You know I've had this deadline hanging over my head. I just haven't had any extra time these past few weeks. After all, there are only so many hours in the day!"

Criticism

"You know how hard I've been working. I'm just trying to bring in a little extra cash so we can get our head above water. I'll just quit putting in these extra hours if you're going to be so ungrateful!"

After hearing either of these responses, what would you be thinking? (For instance: *My needs aren't important to him/her. I'm not important. He/she doesn't care, doesn't want to be with me.*)_____

_____

_____

How would you feel? (For instance: *rejected, hurt, angry, insecure*)

_____

_____

Describe how you would behave. (For instance: *I might withdraw and isolate myself the rest of the evening in the bedroom. I might yell and scream in anger.*)_____

When personal needs go unmet in marriage, often a cycle of unhealthy thinking, feeling, and behaving begins. Unmet needs produce negative feelings and launch the manipulative games of marriage. Take a look at the diagram below showing the pain and potential of intimacy needs.

Understanding Intimacy Needs

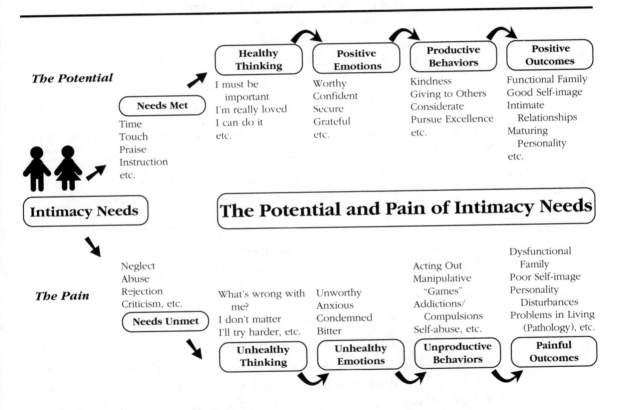

The Potential

Needs Met

Time
Touch
Praise
Instruction
etc.

Intimacy Needs

The Pain

Neglect
Abuse
Rejection
Criticism, etc.

Needs Unmet

Healthy Thinking
I must be important
I'm really loved
I can do it
etc.

Positive Emotions
Worthy
Confident
Secure
Grateful
etc.

Productive Behaviors
Kindness
Giving to Others
Considerate
Pursue Excellence
etc.

Positive Outcomes
Functional Family
Good Self-image
Intimate Relationships
Maturing Personality
etc.

The Potential and Pain of Intimacy Needs

Unhealthy Thinking
What's wrong with me?
I don't matter
I'll try harder, etc.

Unhealthy Emotions
Unworthy
Anxious
Condemned
Bitter

Unproductive Behaviors
Acting Out
Manipulative "Games"
Addictions/ Compulsions
Self-abuse, etc.

Painful Outcomes
Dysfunctional Family
Poor Self-image
Personality Disturbances
Problems in Living (Pathology), etc.

Now, look over this list of the eight most commonly identified intimacy needs. First, mark the three (3) needs you consider the most important for you to receive from your spouse. Next, mark the three (3) needs you think your spouse would consider most important to receive from you.

Myself	Intimacy Needs	Spouse
☐	Acceptance—deliberate and ready reception with a favorable positive response.	☐
☐	Affection—communicating care and closeness through physical touch and loving words.	☐
☐	Appreciation—communicating with words and feelings a personal gratefulness for another.	☐
☐	Approval—expressed commendation; thinking and speaking well of.	☐
☐	Attention—taking thought of another and conveying appropriate interest and support; entering into another's "world."	☐
☐	Encouragement—urging forward and positively persuading toward a goal.	☐
☐	Respect—valuing and regarding highly; conveying great worth.	☐
☐	Security—confidence of harmony in relationships; freedom from harm.	☐

What are the three needs that are most important to you? Write them here: _____

_____

How do you feel when your spouse meets one of these needs? _____

_____

How do you feel when these needs go unmet? _____

_____

What is your behavior like? _____

_____

What are the three needs you think are most important to your spouse? Write them here: _____

_____

What opportunities have you had recently to meet one of these needs? Be specific. _____

_____

If you have noticed evidences of unhealthy thinking patterns or negative feelings or behavior in your spouse lately, what personal need might have gone unmet? (For instance: *I've noticed my wife showing feelings of anxiety. Maybe she needs more security.*) _____

_____

During this next exercise, focus on the personal needs you had as a child and ways they were met or unmet. Look over the list of needs again, and think back over your own childhood experiences.

When I think about my childhood, I remember needing (For instance: *encouragement, affection*) _____

_____ from my mother.

Do you remember a time when it was important for your mother to meet this need and she didn't? Write about it here:_____

_____

_____

When I think about my childhood, I remember needing (For instance: *attention, security*) _____

_____ from my father.

Do you remember a time when it was important for your father to meet this need and he didn't? Write about it here: _____

_____

_____

As a child, it was always important for me to receive _____

_____

When this need was not met, I remember thinking_____

_____

I remember feeling_____

_____

Did your family seem to deny or ignore your needs?
_____ Yes _____ No   If so, write about it here:_____

_____

_____

Did your family tend to blame or criticize you in response to your needs? _____ Yes _____ No   If so, write about it here:_____

_____

_____

What three needs from the list above do you think you missed most during your childhood? Write about it here:_____

_____

_____

_____

Now, compare the three needs you would like to have met by your partner and the three needs you missed from childhood. Are there any similarities? Explain. _____

_____

_____

What thoughts do you have about the two lists of needs? Write them here. _____

_____

_____

Often we enter marriage hoping our spouse will make up for some of what we missed as children. Great hurt can take place in a marriage when these needs from our childhood go unmet within our marriage as well. However, part of the intimate connection between husband and wife is understanding each partner's hurts from childhood and then allowing God to involve you in giving to your partner's unmet needs and healing these wounds.

Scripture Journaling—Psalm 28:6–9

Blessed be the LORD, Because He has heard the voice of my supplications! The LORD is my strength and my shield; My heart trusted in Him, and I am helped; Therefore my heart greatly rejoices, And with my song I will praise Him. The LORD is their strength, And He is the saving refuge of His anointed. Save Your people, And bless Your inheritance; Shepherd them also, And bear them up forever.

In this Psalm, David shows us the benefits of expressing our needs to the Lord (verses 6–7). Can you see his thinking? What is he feeling? What does he decide to do? After he expresses his gratefulness to the Lord, David is able to look to others' needs (verses 8–9).

What do you want the Lord to hear from you? What needs do you have? Tell Him. Express your feelings. Talk to Him from your heart. Do you need His strength? His protection? The tender care of the loving Shepherd? Write your prayer here.

Dear God,

_____

_____

_____

_____

_____

_____

_____

_____

MARRIAGE STAFF MEETING

Set aside one or two hours for this staff meeting. Begin by discussing your responses to the checklist of Eight Intimacy Needs. Each partner should share his/her list of three most important needs.

How well did you guess your partner's needs?

Were you surprised by your partner's response?

Do you find your tendency is to focus on giving your partner what *you* need, rather than on meeting *his/her* needs? Discuss this possibility with your spouse.

Next, spend some time discussing your responses to the "thinking-feeling-behaving" questions found earlier in this chapter. You and your partner will undoubtedly react with different thinking patterns, different feelings, and different behaviors when your needs go unmet. Discuss these differences.

You will notice, however, that the same need can provoke many different responses when it goes unmet. Read together 1 Peter 3:7 and Proverbs 31:27–29, which speak of the need for understanding your mate.

You will also want to discuss the needs you each missed during childhood. Both partners should share their responses to the childhood questions and give their partner the opportunity to show comfort and empathy. Remember to maintain eye contact and offer plenty of reassurance and encouragement as your partner shares.

Close the Marriage Staff Meeting by recalling a time when your partner did meet one of your top three needs. Discuss this experience and how it made you feel.

FOR MEN ONLY

Secure

Protected

Enjoyed

Courted

Intimate

Appreciated

L

You will want to meet your wife's need for appreciation this week. Appreciation is best understood as a process of discovering and expressing your gratefulness for another person in terms of what they do *and* for who they are. Appreciation can be expressed privately as well as publicly. It can be expressed verbally, in writing, or in other creative ways. Discovering how another person blesses you requires getting to know him or her intimately.

Better Understanding This Need:

From the list below select four character qualities your wife possesses. After you've selected them, think of specific events or experiences that reveal or display these attributes.

- Contentment
- Hospitality
- Understanding
- Generosity
- Creativity

- Gratefulness
- Truthfulness
- Discernment
- Self-control
- Loyalty

- Sensitivity
- Diligence
- Patience
- Resourcefulness
- Forgiveness

My wife often demonstrates these four primary qualities:

1. _____

2. _____

3. _____

4. _____

Practical Suggestions:

Share private, verbal praise.

When just the two of you are alone together, say something like this: "Honey, I've been thinking lately of how much I appreciate you for your patience and sensitivity. The other day when you were so tolerant with Josh and his friends, I really admired you. I love you."

Share private, creative praise.

Stick a special note on the bathroom mirror or refrigerator; slip a note in her purse or briefcase.

Share public praise.

When you're around friends or family, express your appreciation for your wife; declare your admiration for her recent accomplishments.

Rediscover areas of appreciation.

Consider some of the reasons you were originally attracted to your spouse. You'll find many of these qualities still exist, but you've just taken them for granted.

Discover new areas of appreciation.

Reflect on your own areas of limitation. Are you shy, impatient, insensitive? Notice and appreciate the fact that your wife probably has many "compensating" qualities that make up for what you lack.

Pray often with thanksgiving.

Thank God for how He has blessed you through your wife. You'll be amazed at the positive attitude that emerges as your negative, critical thoughts fade away.

FOR WOMEN ONLY

Comfort
Honor
Exalt
Respect
Intimate
Secure
H

This week you will want to meet your husband's need to be secure. Security speaks of an inner confidence that is certain and sure. A husband develops this deep confidence in your love as you demonstrate your trust and commitment to him. A wife can deepen security and help eliminate a husband's fears by verbalizing her reassurance, taking an initiative in showing affection, and giving genuine support and sincere praise.

Better Understanding This Need:

Review the list below and check those statements about which it can be truthfully said, "My husband has a deep confidence in:

_____ my speaking only the best about him."

_____ my not comparing him with others."

_____ my not being his conscience or playing Holy Spirit."

_____ my deferring to his leadership."

_____ my genuinely needing him."

_____ my forgiving past hurts."

_____ my support of his decisions."

_____ my lifelong commitment to him and our marriage."

Apologize to your husband for any area above that you were unable to check. Let God show you specific situations that may need to be addressed. Then make amends with your husband.

Practical Suggestions:

Express reassurance and recommitment.

Address any fears your husband may have, saying, for example, "I just want you to know that I am committed to supporting your decisions with the children."

Review his past successes.

Think about the past successes, accomplishments, or wise decisions that your husband has made. Then share your remembrances with him, saying, "I remember how you handled _____. I'm proud you're my husband."

30 second phone calls.

Call and say, "Hi, honey. I was just thinking about you and wanted to call and let you know I love you and I'm looking forward to seeing you tonight."

Initiate affection.

A man's need to be "desirable" to his wife is of major importance to him. A wife diminishes her husband's fears when she occasionally takes the lead in showing affection.

For Group Discussion

Begin this session by asking group members to reflect again on how their family of origin handled needs. Participants may want to imagine themselves as the five-year-old child drawing a picture of the rainbow. Ask members: "How would each parent have handled the situation? Did they ignore needs? Neglect them? Criticize you for expressing your needs?"

Next, ask each group member to draw a diagram that represents this information. Draw a symbol that represents yourself—this should go in the center of the diagram. Now, show how each parent and/or sibling handled the expression of needs. (For example, criticism could be shown with arrows; neglect, by a brick wall.)

Discuss the varied ways family members handle needs. How did you feel when your needs weren't met? How did you feel when your needs were acknowledged? What were your top three needs?"

Next, discuss any similarity between your unmet needs in childhood and your top three marital needs. Discuss: How could the similarities affect a marriage? How do your unmet needs from childhood affect your relationships with your own children?

Close this group session by asking couples to practice meeting their spouse's need for appreciation. Challenge the men to begin the exercise. Each husband will need to hold his wife's hands, look into her eyes, and complete the following statements:

(Wife's name) _____, I appreciate your (For instance: *sensitivity, patience, humor*) _____. It means so much to me when (For instance: *You notice I've had a hard day and give me time to relax before dinner.*) _____

_____

Ask the women to complete the following sentences. They also need to hold their husband's hands and look into his eyes while sharing.

(Husband's name) _____, I remember when you handled (For instance: *the situation with your boss*) _____so well. I'm so proud you're my husband. I appreciate your (For instance: *wisdom, discernment*) _____

_____

After each couple has had a chance to exchange words of appreciation, check with group members to learn how they felt during this exercise.

Chapter Eleven

LEAVE YOUR FATHER AND MOTHER

Mother knows best!" That was the motto of Mike's mom. It could have been emblazoned in lights over the front door. Instead, her words—in fact, her very tone of voice—were imbedded forever in his memory: "Mikey, sweetheart, you must wear your raincoat or you'll get a chill . . . Mike, you play with little Reggie, not Sam. Reggie comes from a fine family; we don't know Sam's kin."

When Mike was seven, his mother bought him a piano and announced, "Mikey, dear, all my life I dreamed of playing the piano. Now you'll have the chance I never had. I'm going to see that you become an accomplished pianist!" It didn't matter to his mom that he hated practicing and would rather have spent his time drawing or making model planes. Hour after hour, he hammered out the scales on those ivories, seething inside that he couldn't follow his own dreams.

Twenty years later, Mike found himself overreacting with rage and frustration to seemingly minor events. When his wife, Sarah, urged him to play a sonata for their guests, he could feel that familiar knot in his stomach—the way he felt when his mom stood over him instructing, "Keep practicing, one, two, three . . ." "Stop nagging me!" he would explode at Sarah. When they were shopping and Sarah picked out a tie for him, he would bitterly accuse her of trying to run his life. And when Sarah suggested they take the toll road instead of the interstate, Mike's rage erupted as if on cue: "Don't tell me how to drive!"

Think about it: Who do you think Mike is really angry with?

Margaret is a forty-year-old woman whose track record with men has never been good. Her third marriage is teetering on the edge of divorce.

She yearns for more affection and attention from her husband, Jack—something she claims she's missed from her previous husbands and her father as well.

With tears, Margaret shared this memory from her childhood: "Night after night, I would sit by the window of my second story bedroom watching for my dad to come home. I knew he was out drinking, and it made me feel sick and panicky inside. I couldn't bear to crawl into bed until I was sure Dad was home too. So, I'd prop my pillow on the windowsill and lay my head down and wait. More often than not, that's where I would wake up in the morning. Now, when my husband is away or we've had a fight, I get that same sick feeling of abandonment in the pit of my stomach. Even though my husband is nothing like my father, I still feel like I'm that needy little girl waiting by the windowsill for her daddy to come home.

"It didn't end there," Margaret continued sadly. "When I was older, time after time my dad would promise to pick me up after school. I'd wait and wait, then finally walk home alone and find him already passed out on the couch. My dad's been dead for years, but his broken promises still haunt me even now. I think somehow my dad jinxed my relationships with men. They always abandon me. In fact, I have this nagging fear that my husband, Jack, is going to leave me for someone else. What am I going to do?"

Did Margaret's dad jinx her relationships? What emotions is Margaret really dealing with here? _____

_____

_____

Nick faced the inevitable pains and disappointments during his childhood and teenage years. He came in fourth in the inter-city track meet; his team lost the "big game" his senior year; and he broke up with his best girl, Tina, after two years of steady dating. His parents always had plenty of advice for him. After each disappointment, they would deliver their usual pep talk, filled with little homilies and clichés: "It's not so bad, honey. At least you got to the finals." "Don't worry, your team will do better next time." "Look at the bright side. You did better than the others." "Give it a little time. Tomorrow's another day. Wait and see. You'll find a girl twice as nice."

Now, Nick's an adult and his marriage has hit a few bumps in the road. It seems every time his wife comes to him for support or comfort in her disappointments, they end up arguing. He's proud of all the helpful advice he gives her, but she claims he's insensitive and unsympathetic.

What do you think is really going on here? _____

_____

_____

_____

Genesis 2:24 gives us a clear picture of God's design for marriage: "For this cause a man shall leave his father and his mother, and shall cleave to his wife; and they shall become one flesh" NASB. The order of events here is crucial—*leaving*, then *cleaving*. In the illustrations above, Mike, Margaret, and Nick all had some leaving to do. They were still tied to their family of origin by unresolved emotional issues and were therefore unable to totally embrace or "cleave" to their spouse. We are never free to cleave until the leaving takes place!

Look back at the examples above. What "leaving" does Mike need to do? _____

_____

What emotions does he still need to deal with? _____

_____

What "leaving" does Margaret need to do? _____

_____

What emotions does she still need to deal with? _____

_____

What "leaving" does Nick need to do?_____

_____

What emotions does he still need to deal with? _____

_____

The purpose of this chapter is to identify some of the possible childhood emotions that might be affecting your marriage relationship today. You will first need to identify the unmet needs from your childhood and the emotions attached to these unmet needs.

We are never free to cleave until the leaving takes place.

The following is an expanded list of intimacy needs. These thirty (30) items represent needs that God Himself designed—needs He desires for us to receive. In this exercise, read each definition carefully. Then ask yourself, "How did my mother meet this need?" If you are able to recall a specific event or circumstance that demonstrates this need being met, put a half circle around the word. (For example: *"Attention"—I remember many times when my mother would read to me as a child; she also came to all of my school events.*)

Next, ask yourself the same question about your father. "How did my father meet this need?" If you can recall a specific event or circumstance that demonstrates this need being met, put a second half circle around the word. (For example: *"Attention"—I remember my dad made it a priority to be at all my basketball games. He would take me on fishing trips, too, just the two of us.*)

If you are unable to think of a specific example of this need being met, mark the word with an X. As you finish this exercise, your list will have complete circles, half circles, and Xs.

You may be asking yourself, "What do I do if my father and mother weren't around during my childhood?" You may have lost one of your biological parents through divorce, death, or adoption. This exercise will be particularly crucial for you. We encourage you to complete the exercise twice. The first time you complete it, go through each of the thirty definitions and ask yourself *how* or *if* your biological parents met these needs. It is extremely important for you to consider how the absence or loss of a parent affected you.

If your parents divorced when you were young and your biological father or mother was not available, we still ask you to complete the exercise first with him or her in mind. The fact that he or she was not available to meet your needs means you have had to endure tremendous loss. You experienced growing up without two biological parents available to meet your needs—to attend school functions, Scouts, fishing or shopping trips, or athletic events. You have had to endure recurring pain over the loss of your parent. It is important for you to grieve this loss.

After you have completed the exercise using your biological parents, complete the exercise again to reflect any other significant caregivers. Ask yourself, "As I was growing up, who showed me attention?" (For example: *grandparents, stepparent, aunt, uncle, nanny, or foster mother, among other possibilities.*)

Again, read each definition carefully and then identify the needs you received from each biological parent. (Complete the exercise twice if you had other significant caregivers.)

1. ACCEPTANCE—deliberate and ready reception with a favorable response—Rom. 15:7

2. **ADMONITION**—constructive guidance in what to avoid; to warn—Rom. 15:14

3. **AFFECTION**—to communicate care and closeness through physical touch and loving words—Rom. 16:16

4. **APPRECIATION**—communication of personal gratefulness for another with words and feeling—1 Cor. 11:2

5. **APPROVAL**—expressed commendation; thinking and speaking well of—Rom. 14:18

6. **ATTENTION**—taking thought of another and conveying appropriate interest and support—1 Cor. 12:25

7. **COMFORT**—giving consolation with tenderness—1 Thess. 4:18

8. **COMPASSION**—suffering with another person in a trial or burden—Heb. 10:34

9. **CONFESSION**—open acknowledgment of wrongs committed, based on inner conviction—James 5:16

10. **DEFERENCE**—yielding or deferring to another for their benefit—Eph. 5:21

11. **DEVOTION**—a firm and dependable foundation of committed care—Rom. 12:10

12. **DISCIPLINE**—reproval and correction when boundaries are crossed and limits exceeded—Prov. 23:13; Rev. 3:19

13. **EDIFICATION**—positively promoting the growth and development of another—Rom. 14:19

14. **ENCOURAGEMENT**—urging forward and positively persuading toward a goal—1 Thess. 5:11; Heb. 10:24

15. **FORGIVENESS**—cancellation or release of wrongs committed and granting instead of unconditional favor—Eph. 4:32

16. **HARMONY**—an environment of pleasant acceptance and secure love—1 Tim. 2:2-3

17. **HOSPITALITY**—open reception of another with a loving heart—1 Peter 4:9

18. **INTIMACY**—deep sharing and communion with another—1 John 1:7

19. **KINDNESS**—pleasant and gracious servanthood—Eph. 4:32

20. **LOVE**—seeking welfare of others and opportunity to do good unto others—John 13:34

21. **PRAYER**—entreating God's attention and favor upon another—James 5:16

22. **RESPECT**—valuing and regarding highly; conveying great worth—Rom. 12:10

23. **SECURITY**—confidence of harmony in relationships; free from harm—Mark 9:50

24. SERVING—giving up oneself in caring ministry to another—Gal. 5:13

25. SUPPORT—coming alongside and gently helping carry a burden—Gal. 6:2

26. SYMPATHY—identifying with another emotionally—1 Peter 3:8

27. TEACHING—constructive and positive instruction in how to live—Col. 3:16

28. TOLERANCE—patient endurance of another's humanness—Eph. 4:2; Col. 3:13

29. TRAINING—modeling God's way of facing life's issues—Luke 6:40

30. UNDERSTANDING—seeking to know and accept another without judging—Rom. 12:16

Now reflect on the activity above, especially noting the half-circles and Xs you made.

How would you summarize what you *missed* from your mother? _____

_____

_____

_____

Are the things you missed from your mother still important to you? How? Be specific. _____

_____

_____

_____

What are some of your needs that were *met* by your mother? _____

_____

_____ _____

_____

Are these needs still important to you? How? _____

_____

_____

How would you summarize what you *missed* from your father? _____

_____

_____

Are the things you missed from your father still important to you? How?

_____

_____

_____

What are some of your needs that were *met* by your father? _____

_____

_____

Are these needs still important to you? How? _____

_____

_____

How would you summarize what you *missed* from other caregivers?
(stepmother/father, adoptive parents, grandparents, etc.) _____

_____

_____

Are the things you missed from them still important to you? How? _____

_____

_____

What were some of your needs that were *met* by these significant caregivers? _____

_____

_____

Are these needs still important to you? How? _____

_____

_____

What feelings do you have about this exercise? How do you feel about
your number of Xs? Your number of circles? _____

_____

_____

Are some of the needs listed above important to you in your marriage
relationship? How? Be specific. _____

_____

_____

_____

When important needs *were* met by parents in childhood, we develop
the expectation that we will receive the same in our marriage. For example, if our parents were affectionate and supportive, we may expect our
partner to be affectionate and supportive in the same ways. Or, we may
go into marriage anticipating that some of the things we missed from our

caregivers will be met by our spouse when we marry. For example, if our parents gave us little attention, we may expect our partner to make up for that deficit. Do you see either of these tendencies in your own marriage? Explain. _____

_____

_____

_____

> *Often, whatever we received from our parents in childhood we expect to receive from our spouse in marriage.*

The next exercise will also help you assess the relationships that were a part of your childhood emotional development. A *genogram* is a pictorial representation of the relationships in your family of origin. For this exercise you will describe the major caregivers and siblings from your childhood (birth—age 18).

First, draw symbols for each of the caregivers who played important roles in your life—squares representing males and circles representing females. (This is not a complete representation of your family tree; however, be sure to include all of the adults who were a part of your nurturing as a child.) Next, draw symbols that represent you and any brothers or sisters (include step-siblings or half-siblings). Birth order is represented from left, oldest, to right, youngest.

To complete your genogram, think about the relationships between family members. Was a relationship *close*, with a lot of sharing and communicating? Was a relationship *distant*, with very little intimacy, emotional contact, or vulnerable communication? Was a relationship *enmeshed*, offering no individuality or separation of emotion and feelings? Enmeshed relationships often involve a child feeling responsible for a parent's feelings or welfare. The child will meet the parent's needs instead of having his or her own needs met. Was a relationship *conflictive*, with frequent arguments or hostility? Was a relationship *estranged* because of silence, rejection, abandonment, or punishment? Draw lines that represent this information, using the key presented in the genogram example on the following page:

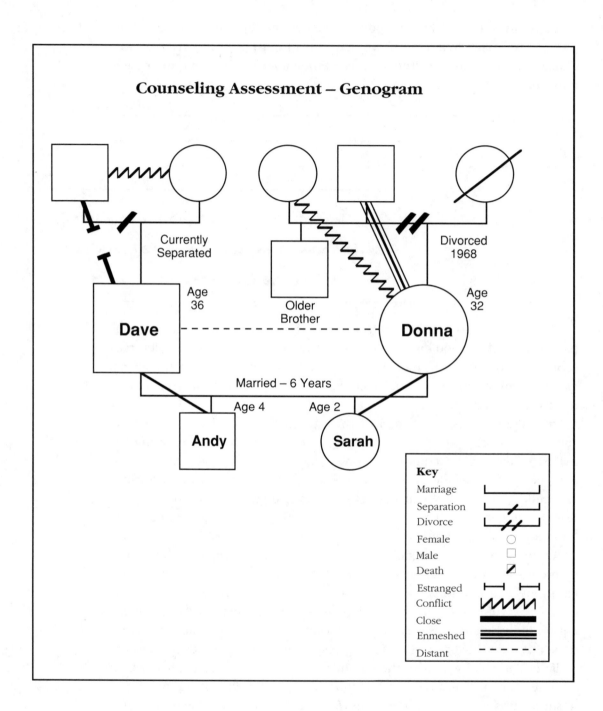

Counseling Assessment – Genogram

Currently
Separated

Divorced
1968

Age
36

Age
32

Older
Brother

Dave

Donna

Married – 6 Years

Age 4

Age 2

Andy

Sarah

Key

Marriage	
Separation	
Divorce	
Female	○
Male	□
Death	
Estranged	
Conflict	
Close	
Enmeshed	
Distant	

Wives, draw your genogram for your family of origin here:

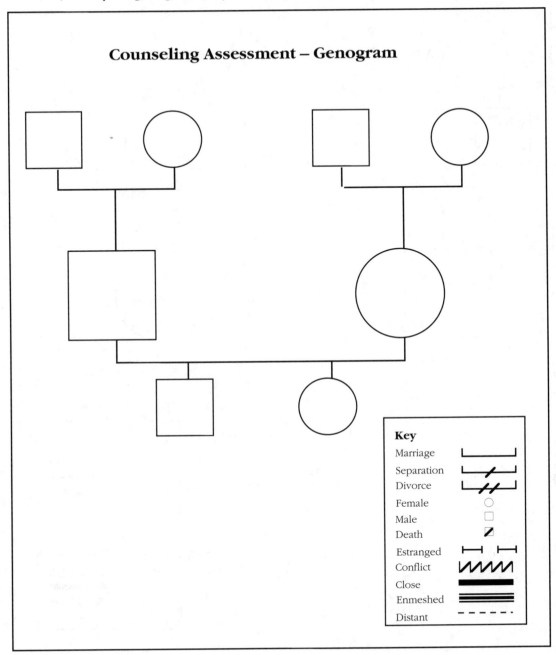

Counseling Assessment – Genogram

Key

Marriage	⎩___⎭
Separation	⎩_/_⎭
Divorce	⎩_//_⎭
Female	○
Male	□
Death	◪
Estranged	⊢ ⊣
Conflict	∿∿∿
Close	▬▬▬
Enmeshed	═══
Distant	– – – –

Husbands, draw your genogram for your family of origin here:

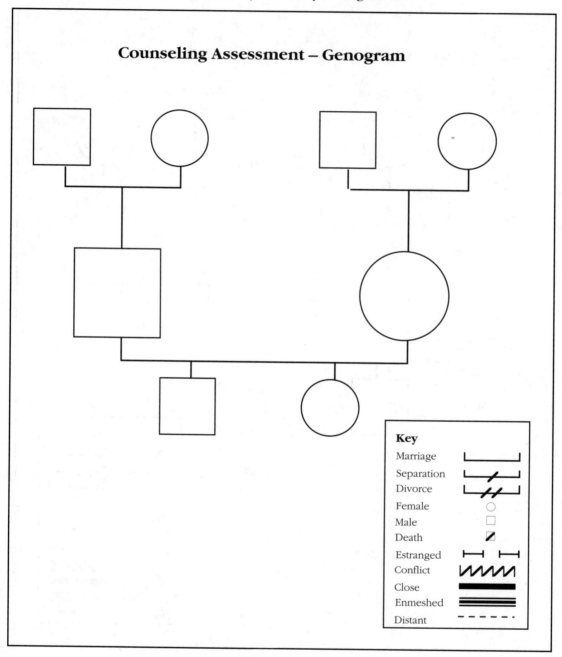

After you have completed your genogram exercise, respond to the following questions:

Who really met your need for attention? (That is, who left their world, entered into yours, and did things with you that you liked to do?) _____

_____

Who gave you affection? (That is, who communicated care and closeness through physical touching and verbalized love?) _____

_____

Who gave you empathy? (That is, who expressed their feelings of hurt and sadness when you hurt, instead of just giving advice or pep talks?)

_____

Who gave you approval? (That is, who expressed their affirmation and appreciation to you?)_____

What was the approval for?_____

Was it for things you did? _____

Or was it for who you were?_____

What feelings do you have about the answers you gave? What thoughts do you have about the genogram exercise?_____

_____

_____

Scripture Journaling—Psalm 147:3

He heals the brokenhearted and binds up their wounds.

Our Lord is the Great Physician. What hurts do you want Him to heal in your own heart? What pain do you need to tell Him about? Do you need relief? Peace? Comfort? Encouragement? Rest? What do you need to say to Christ now?

Dear Christ, I need to tell You _____

_____

_____

_____

_____

_____

_____

Set aside approximately one and a half hours for this staff meeting. Begin by sharing with your spouse the feelings you had during the needs exercise. Express the needs that were met by your mother/father/caregivers. Share the needs that were not met. Give your spouse the opportunity to comfort and reassure you. Also express any insights you may have gained from the genogram exercise, as well as any feelings the exercise prompted.

For example, Marla Carlton was surprised by what her genogram revealed. "I knew I had some hostile feelings toward my parents for not giving me attention when I was little," she confessed, "but I didn't realize those feelings extended to my brothers and sisters as well. I always wondered why we weren't closer. Now I see that part of the problem was my anger. I was holding them at a distance to punish them for getting my parents' attention. Now I know how I can begin mending some fences in my family."

We do offer one word of caution. As you hear your spouse discuss certain painful or traumatic events from his/her past, you may find it easy to feel anger toward your spouse's family. However, at this time, expressing anger at your partner's family will not be helpful. Your partner may have a tendency to defend his/her family, thus shifting the focus away from hurts experienced. As an alternative to expressing your anger, you will want to convey empathy for your spouse and sadness over the pain he/she experienced. (For instance: *"It saddens me to think of you missing out on attention from your family . . . often feeling lonely and afraid; I hurt for you because I care about you, I love you."*)

FOR MEN ONLY

Secure

Protected

Enjoyed

Courted

Intimate

Appreciated

Led

This week you will want to meet your wife's need to be led. Leadership encompasses initiative, direction, and example, as a husband lovingly serves his wife. He is to lead as Christ led—by example and with a motive of serving others. Practically, leadership might include apologizing first, being the first to give, or taking the initiative in finances, goals, or children's discipline. Biblical leadership has nothing to do with demanding or taking, but has everything to do with serving and giving.

Better Understanding This Need:

Review the following areas of leadership and mark the ones that you realize require greater attention on your part. Then prayerfully consider how you can lead more effectively in those areas.

Areas of Needed Leadership

_____ 1. Serving others by giving

_____ 2. Developing family goals

_____ 3. Children's guidance/discipline

_____ 4. Initiating apologies

_____ 5. Spiritual concerns/priorities

_____ 6. Financial pressures/ planning

_____ 7. Entering wife's emotional world

_____ 8. Communicating love/ affection

_____ 9. Sharing compliments/ appreciation

_____ 10. Role-modeling humility/ gentleness

After you have considered your leadership responsibilities in each of these areas, discuss them with your wife to learn her perspective on ways she could benefit from your leadership.

You may also want to review the leadership qualities of Moses, Joseph, Joshua, David, Solomon, and Nehemiah. Look for the character qualities, convictions, initiative, and positive role-modeling of these Old Testament patriarchs.

Practical Suggestions:

Develop goals.

Discuss each of the following areas with your wife: personal, marital, family, financial, professional, social, household, spiritual, and ministry. For each of these areas, determine what you want to see accomplished, how the task will be completed, and when. We will spend more time on goal setting in Chapter 14.

Heal hurts quickly.

Occasional misunderstandings, irritations, and impatient words are inevitable in close relationships. The critical issue is healing the hurts through genuine apologies and forgiveness. Be an example to your family by apologizing to your wife and children as soon as you realize you have hurt them.

Take a stand.

Develop convictions, standards, and disciplines for your personal life. Model these to your family.

FOR WOMEN ONLY

Comfort

Honor

Exalt

Respect

Intimate

Secure

Happy

This week you will want to meet your husband's need to be happy. Happy is the husband who has a wife and not a second mother, a helpmate and not another boss, a "completer" and not a competitor. Become your husband's cheerleader, encouraging him, urging him on, and offering plenty of affirmation. Pamper him with a little extra tender loving care, and he'll bask in the reflected light of your love.

Better Understanding This Need:

Review the two lists below. Prayerfully consider the ways you are meeting your husband's need for happiness and areas that may need improvement. Check each definition that describes you in your marriage relationship with your husband.

A husband's happiness is ENCOURAGED by a wife who is:

___ a consistent cheerleader offering encouragement and support.

___ trusting God to make needed changes in her husband while she continues loving and accepting him unconditionally.

___ appreciative, positive, and grateful.

___ willing to spoil him in little ways.

___ vivacious, sexy, and interested in intimacy with her husband.

A husband's happiness is DISCOURAGED by a wife who is:

___ constantly focused on her own needs, giving little attention to others.

___ insistent on perfection, precision, and her own timing.

___ bossy, nagging, and complaining.

___ always putting her children before her husband.

___ focusing on what she doesn't have and what she can't do.

After you've marked those items in each category you believe describes you, discuss your answers with your husband and invite him to share his perspective on your responses. Ask him to tell you specific ways you could make him happier. Listen openly to his suggestions.

Practical Suggestions:

Become his cheerleader.

Send your husband off each day with expressions of encouragement, gratefulness, and affection. Welcome him home with empathy, understanding, and tenderness. Praise him publicly and privately.

Express your gratitude.

Begin a list of blessings, each day writing down one new way you realize your husband blesses you. When you sense the Lord has truly given you a grateful heart, share your appreciation with your husband.

Pamper him occasionally.

Surprise him with his favorite meal, breakfast in bed, or a few uninterrupted hours to himself. "Capture" him for a surprise date, or plan a passionate evening alone.

—— For Group Discussion ——

Begin this group discussion by giving every member a small Styrofoam cup. Ask members to think back to the "needs exercise" in this chapter and then draw a line on the outside of their cup that represents how well their needs were met during childhood. For example, a line drawn at the top of the cup would indicate that many of their emotional needs were met during childhood. A line drawn near the bottom would suggest that few needs were met.

Have members write on the "full" part of the cup two or three key needs that were met during their childhood. Then have them write on the "empty" part of the cup two or three key needs that went unmet during their childhood.

Give all members an opportunity to show their cup and explain why they marked it as they did. Ask them: "How did it feel to complete the needs exercise? What observations do you have about your needs from childhood? How do you see these met and unmet needs impacting your marriage?"

Group leaders may want to use this week to ask a few participants to complete another family sculpting exercise. Participants may have a new perspective on their family of origin. Again, these activities are not designed to "punch emotional buttons" or to vent strong feelings. This exercise may, however, promote strong emotions. Leaders will want to be sensitive to the needs of individuals as well as the needs of the group.

Think about the way the family members relate to each other, then arrange the participants to show a physical representation. When the sculpture is complete, ask the group to give feedback. Let them share observations about the sculpture and the individual's placement of each member. Be alert to feelings and emotions during this exercise.

The last exercise of this group meeting is designed to give couples practice in sharing empathy. Ask each member to recall some of the crucial needs that went unmet in their partner's childhood. Each member should think about their partner's pain that resulted from these unmet needs. (It may be helpful for group members to imagine how a child would feel in the same situation.)

Go around the room and ask members to verbalize their feelings of empathy about their partner's pain. (For example: "It makes me sad when I think about Teresa missing out on attention from her dad.")

The leader will want to make sure each member understands the exercise and has empathetic caring to share with his/her spouse.

Ask the women to begin the last part of the exercise by holding their husband's hands, looking into his eyes, and saying, "As I think of you growing up and missing out on _____ or being hurt by _____, it makes me very sad. I feel sad because I care about you and love you."

After the women have had their turn, the men will want to share empathy for their wife's unmet needs as well, following this same format.

Group members may wish to rephrase these sentences, but whatever they say, they'll want to be sure they're expressing empathy. Both partners need to hear their spouse's sincere concern and compassion for their unmet needs.

Chapter Twelve

■

BLESSED ARE THOSE WHO MOURN

Most of us think of mourning as something we do when someone close to us dies. We mourn because our loved one has been removed from our lives, leaving us with a deep sense of pain and loss. No longer will we experience that person's presence, touch, warmth, reassurance, and love.

But what many of us fail to realize is that we need to mourn the losses from any significant relationship. Jimmy and Marla Carlton discovered that truth. Jimmy needed to mourn the fact that he had never felt loved and accepted by his rigid, domineering father. Marla needed to mourn her lack of attention and support from her uninvolved parents. Until Jimmy and Marla confronted those deeply entrenched childhood hurts, they were not free to genuinely love each other.

Because we are all imperfect people born into an imperfect world and grow up in an imperfect environment, we often carry around private bundles of hurts and unmet needs. Every bundle is different. Only you know the hurts you carry from past or ongoing relationships. And, no doubt, the thought has occurred to you, *If only I could discard this bundle of hurts, I could be happy!*

Centuries ago, Christ addressed what it takes to be happy when He delivered His oft-quoted Sermon on the Mount beside the Sea of Galilee. Stating what sounds like a paradox, He declared, "Blessed are those who mourn,/For they shall be comforted" (Matt. 5:4). Granted, this verse doesn't make much sense viewed through the grid of our flawed human wisdom. One wonders what connection there could be between mourning and being happy. The two would seem to cancel each other out.

But Christ understood our dilemma. After all, He's the One who created us with relational intimacy needs designed to be met in relationships with other human beings. He knew there would be times our needs would go unmet and we would be hurt. He knew that sometimes, when we needed attention, we would receive rejection instead; when we needed affection, we'd be met with neglect; when we needed security, we'd be confronted with abuse. He knew we would have reason to mourn, and would need to be comforted.

Christ also recognized an important order in these events—first we mourn, then we receive comfort. He encourages us to *feel* the pain of personal loss—to mourn our hurt. Then, and only then, are we ready to be comforted.

Christ encourages us to mourn our hurt.
Only then are we ready to be comforted.

In previous chapters, you've been urged to look back over your childhood experiences. Undoubtedly, you've found examples of hurt and disappointment. The circumstances that caused the hurt may have occurred long ago, but the feelings may still remain. Therefore, it is important to deal with the hurts you've encountered as a child; face the pain of your past. Then you will be able to grieve your losses and receive the comfort our Lord designed.

For many of us, the idea of facing our pain is tremendously scary. The very thought of examining old, long-buried emotional wounds may send your anxiety level rising sky-high. You are not alone. All of us are reluctant to deal with pain. You can determine your own degree of reluctance by considering whether these statements reflect your thoughts:

- "It happened so long ago, it's not important. I'm over all that now."
- "They'll never change. Why should I even think about it?"
- "It's all in the past, behind me. There's no sense in looking back. I've gone on with my life."

Do any of these statements sound familiar? What thoughts do you have that show a reluctance to look at your past emotional pain? Write down your thoughts, as honestly as you can express them._____

_____

_____

After expressing these thoughts, how are you feeling right now? (For instance: *I feel a sense of relief, like I'm facing something I haven't admit-*

ted before. Or: I'm surprised, I didn't realize all those feelings were there inside me.) _____

_____

_____

Let's suppose you have acknowledged that some emotional pain does exist. You may be asking yourself, "If all this pain has been inside me for so long, why haven't I faced it before?"

It is likely you haven't faced your emotional pain because you haven't had a comforting, supportive environment in which to share your hurts. Until now, no one has urged you to examine and express your pain, so you've kept your feelings bottled up. To determine whether this is true for you, write here about the opportunities you have had (if any) to express emotional pain from your past, including support groups, friends, pastors, counselors, or family members. _____

_____

_____

What feelings do you have about these opportunities or the lack of them? _____

_____

_____

If you've had an opportunity to begin sharing some of your unhealed childhood hurts, you may already be able to identify some of the benefits of addressing these issues. We believe addressing emotional pain from your past can:

1. Give you the freedom to more intimately relate to your spouse, children, and other family members. If you leave behind the anger, fear, guilt, and shame of your past, you will remove many of the hindrances to your intimate relationships.

2. Give you the freedom to trust God to meet many of your needs involving your partner as He desires.

3. Give you the opportunity to enjoy more of an adult-to-adult relationship with your own parents or caregivers. Healing childhood emotional wounds gives you additional freedom to move out of the dependent, care-receiving role.

4. Give you a new appreciation for positive qualities in your family of origin. Unhealed hurts can blind you to many of the strengths in your parents or caregivers.

What thoughts do you have about these benefits you may experience as a result of addressing your emotional pain? _____

_____

_____

How would you feel if you could see changes in your relationship with your spouse and family as a result of resolving your own unhealed hurts?

_____

_____

What do you hope will be different as you address your childhood hurts? I hope_____

_____

What changes do you hope for in yourself? Be specific. _____

_____

_____

What changes do you hope for in your relationship with your spouse?

_____

_____

What changes do you hope for in your relationship with your children?

_____

_____

What changes do you hope for in your relationship(s) with your family of origin? _____

_____

It is important to note that, as we look at the pain of our past, blaming others for our hurt will not bring healing. This healing process is not about placing blame or making accusations. Nevertheless, we must face the truth about our circumstances. Once we acknowledge the hurt and make a truthful assessment about our emotions, then we can hope for healing.

Christ Himself gave us a biblical model for healing our pain, demonstrating these three steps during His crucifixion:

1. Face the Hurt.

Jesus did not deny or minimize His pain. He did not dismiss the hurt or spiritualize it. During His hours in the Garden of Gethsemane, He acknowledged that He had been despised, rejected, ridiculed, and forsaken.

He told His disciples, "My soul is exceedingly sorrowful, even to death" (Matt. 26:38). He even asked them to stay and join Him in the comforting ministry of prayer (notice He wasn't afraid or reluctant to ask for support when He needed it), but His disciples fell asleep, making it still one more "rejection" for our Savior. There is no doubt that Jesus faced His hurt. Isaiah tells us He was "a Man of sorrows and acquainted with grief" (Isa. 53:3).

2. Understand the Truth.

Jesus understood that some of the pain He was enduring was caused by others around Him, but He also understood that His offenders were more than their behavior. They were flawed human beings with needs of their own, blinded to the truth of his identity. Christ's offenders chose to crucify Him, but, in spite of their behavior, *He chose to forgive*.

3. Forgive the Offender.

Jesus made the choice to forgive His offenders. He verbalized this request on the cross: "Father, forgive them, for they do not know what they do" (Luke 23:34). Jesus certainly didn't rely on His feelings for this request; it was an act of His will.

Once again, the order of the steps is essential. If we ignore the step of facing our hurt, we minimize our pain. We can only forgive as deeply as we have felt the pain. Forgiving must be preceded by facing our hurt. Make every effort to complete these steps thoroughly and in the following order.

I. FACING THE HURT

Begin this journey by carefully looking over the following list. In a general way, it describes some of the sources of emotional pain. Read through the list slowly and ask yourself, "Is this true of my life?"

Some sources of pain are a result of early childhood experiences.

- Physical abuse, including violence between parents or toward children
- Sexual abuse, including incest, rape, or even a lack of secure personal privacy in the home
- Emotional or verbal abuse, including rage, ridicule, blame, enmeshment, or criticism
- Parental divorce/death/adoption, causing feelings of rejection and abandonment

- Peer ridicule or rejection, including cruel, humiliating remarks or embarrassing and traumatic failure

Do you think any of these sources of pain are true for you?
_____ Yes _____ No   What feelings do you have right now? Express them freely, spontaneously. _____

_____

_____

Experiences during your adolescent years can also become sources of emotional pain.

- Parental domination, including an overbearing, intolerant home atmosphere
- Parental withdrawal, including a lack of involvement with an adolescent's interests, emotions, and opinions
- Marital discord, including excessive conflict, adultery, separation, and divorce
- Peer rejection or ridicule, including romantic breakups, friendship betrayals, and shame-producing traumas

Do you think any of these sources of pain are true for you?
_____ Yes _____ No   What feelings do you have right now? Write about them freely, honestly. _____

_____

_____

Now, go back to the exercise in the previous chapter where you summarized the needs you missed in your childhood. Reflect on these again. What needs went unmet? What new insights do you have? Write them here. _____

_____

_____

_____

_____

Were your parents available to meet these needs? Explain. _____

_____

_____

_____

_____

Personal Journal

Find a quiet, safe place for this next exercise. Make sure you have plenty of uninterrupted time to complete the assignment. You will be using this time to begin a personal journal. You will need a loose-leaf notebook, a blank book, notepad, or something similar for recording your thoughts and feelings. Don't allow yourself to feel intimidated by the idea of keeping a journal. Your goal isn't perfect grammar, eloquence of language, or a literary masterpiece for the world to read. Your goal is to express yourself as honestly and transparently as you can, in words you feel comfortable with; remember, the process (of writing) is more important than the product (the pages you produced).

Now, begin your journal, writing frankly about your feelings. What do you feel about the unmet needs you have identified? What do you feel about your emotional pain from childhood? Identify each source of pain and what you feel about it. (This list of feelings may be helpful: lonely, sad, afraid, neglected, hurt, unloved, unworthy, bitter, used, rejected, insignificant, unimportant, abandoned.)

For example, you might say, "I missed out on attention from my mom when I was little. She worked nights and was asleep when I left for school every day. I would come home from school and she would give me a list of chores to do as she walked out the door for her job. She didn't even talk to me or ask me about my day. I felt so unimportant, like I was the maid, the hired help."

Therapeutic Letter Writing

After you've spent all the time you need on your personal journal, begin the next exercise. In this exercise, you will write letters to each of your parents (even if one parent was not available) and to any other significant caregivers. Therapeutic letter writing can be helpful in healing hurts from other relationships as well. *However, these letters are not to be mailed.* Use your own paper (or your journal), so you will have plenty of space. Take your time writing these letters; keep writing until you've said everything you need to say. We have included the following "prompts" to help guide you in your letter writing.

Dear Dad/Mom/Stepmom/Grandma/Former Spouse (etc.),

I've been thinking about our relationship—about how I felt and some of the things I missed.

From some of my earliest memories, I have felt . . .

I know I often missed . . .

It hurt me so much when . . .

Now I often feel . . .

It would mean so much to me if . . .

I wish I could hear you say to me . . .

Sincerely,

Your son/daughter/granddaughter (etc.) _____

Sharing Your Hurts Staff Meeting

You and your partner will want to schedule time for a staff meeting before you complete the next steps of the healing process. Sharing your hurts with your spouse is a crucial part of building intimacy.

After both partners have completed their therapeutic letter writing, they will take turns reading their letters. Before you begin reading, tell your partner what you need from him/her:

For example: "Honey, I've been thinking about my childhood and some of the things I felt growing up. I want to read my letters out loud to you. I need you to just listen, and give me time to share my thoughts; then I could really use your comfort and encouragement."

If there are specific behaviors that are comforting to you, you may want to communicate those to your partner as well. Do you need your spouse to sit next to you? With an arm around you? To hold you when you're finished? Or rub your neck as you read? Express your needs. Give your partner the opportunity to comfort you and feel your hurts.

Remember to use the technique of emotional responding. "It hurts me to think of you missing so many things." "It saddens me that you were hurt in those ways because I care about you, I love you, and I'm here for you."

II. UNDERSTANDING THE TRUTH

The next step in the healing process involves understanding the truth about your circumstances and the people involved. It also includes an understanding of Christ's perspective toward people and their behavior.

As you expressed the hurts in the previous exercise, you were able to identify certain "offenders." The next step in healing your pain depends on a willingness to see your "offenders" as more than their offense or behavior. Their actions may have been terribly wrong or negligent, but they are still people for whom Christ chose to die and to whom He has extended His grace and forgiveness. In order to better understand how God views your offenders, complete the following activity.

First, in the spaces below, list all of your offenders' behaviors and the hurt that resulted. Use extra sheets or journal pages if you don't have enough room here. For example:

"I was hurt by Dad's verbal abuse in the following way: I grew up thinking I was worthless and unlovable."

"I was hurt by my stepmom's criticism in the following way: I was constantly anxious because I was always afraid of messing up or doing something wrong."

I was hurt by_____
(offender's behavior)

in the following way(s): _____

_____

_____

I was hurt by _____
(offender's behavior)

in the following way(s): _____

_____

_____

I was hurt by_____
(offender's behavior)

in the following way(s):_____

_____

_____

Look over your offenders' behaviors. What does God say about these behaviors? God says (For instance: *All have sinned; confess your sins, turn from your evil ways and I will forgive you; I will remember your sins no more.*) _____

_____

_____

_____ *Blessed Are Those Who Mourn* **151**

Now, do a personal inventory. What are some of the behaviors for which you've had to ask God's forgiveness? What are some of your offenses against others? Be honest and specific.

Some of my offenses and wrong behaviors include _____

_____

_____

_____

_____

What does God have to say about these behaviors and offenses? God says:

_____

_____

What does God say about His love for you as a person? God says: _____

_____

_____

What does God have to say about His love for your offender? God says:

_____

_____

God makes a distinction between a person's worth to Him and that person's behavior. He extends His love to us in spite of our wrong behaviors. Romans 5:8 tells us, "God demonstrates His own love toward us, in that while we were still sinners, Christ died for us." Our offenders have been offered this same love. Christ died for them, just as He died for us. We need forgiveness for our offenses, just as others need forgiveness for the pain they caused us. We are all both "victims" and "villains," needing God's grace and unconditional love. Seeing our offenders in this light helps us understand how we can choose the next step in the healing process—forgiving our offender.

What thoughts do you have right now? Write them here, being completely honest with yourself and God. _____

_____

_____

III. FORGIVE THE OFFENDER

The next step in healing pain from the past depends on our willingness to choose. Forgiveness is not a feeling; it does not even necessarily mean forgetting. It is a conscious decision on our part to let go of our anger and bitterness—a choice we may make more readily as we recall how generously God has chosen to forgive us. Forgiveness is for our own benefit; it brings healing to our lives, regardless of any change or lack of change in our offender.

Be careful of these internal messages that cause you to resist choosing forgiveness:

- "I'll forgive when my offender asks me."
- "I'll forgive when my offender changes his/her behavior."
- "I can't forgive; they don't deserve it."
- "They deserve punishment for what they did; I'm going to be part of that punishment."
- "It's my right to hold a grudge."
- "I'll forgive when I feel it inside."

For your final exercise, you will seek to verbalize your forgiveness of your offender. To prepare for this choice, write letters, as appropriate, to parents and other significant caregivers. Again, these letters are not to be mailed. This time, however, identify the behaviors that caused your hurt, name the hurt, and then verbalize your choice to forgive. You may also want to include any new guidelines you plan to implement in the relationship in the future.

For example: "Mom, when you threatened to send me away to Dad's, I felt confused, hurt, and scared. I am no longer going to allow myself to be caught in the middle. I am choosing to have a relationship with you, and with Dad. I choose to forgive you, and I am letting go of my fears and anger."

The following prompts may help guide your letter writing:

Dear Mom/Dad/Stepmom/Grandma (etc.),

The behaviors that caused my hurts were . . .

I felt . . .

I am making these choices for my own emotional freedom as I focus on God's promise to meet my needs . . .

I am choosing to forgive you, and I am letting go of . . .

    Sincerely,

    Your son/daughter/granddaughter (etc.)_____

Scripture Journaling—Isaiah 61:1–3

The Spirit of the Lord GOD is upon Me, because the LORD has anointed Me to preach good tidings to the poor; He has sent Me to heal the brokenhearted, to proclaim liberty to the captives, and the opening of the prison to those who are bound; to proclaim the acceptable year of the LORD, and the day of vengeance of our God; to comfort all who mourn, to console those who mourn in Zion, to give them beauty for ashes, the oil of joy for mourning, the garment of praise for the spirit of heaviness; that they may be called trees of righteousness, the planting of the LORD, that He may be glorified.

Christ is clearly presented in these verses. His arms are open to you, offering comfort and grace. What good news do you need to hear from Him? What feelings do you have right now? What do you want to tell God? Bask in His love and mercy. Savor His forgiveness. Experience His undergirding strength. Then write your thoughts and feelings here. _____

_____

_____

Reflect now on Ephesians 4:32, and its message of forgiveness: "And be kind to one another, tenderhearted, forgiving one another, even as God in Christ forgave you."

What feelings do you have about God's forgiveness? What would you like to tell Him about His forgiveness? What would you like to tell God about your forgiveness toward others? Write your thoughts here. _____

_____

_____

MARRIAGE STAFF MEETING _____

Spend this staff meeting, and perhaps one or two others, sharing your therapeutic and forgiveness letters. Both partners should read their letters, taking the opportunity to mourn and receive comfort, and, after they have verbalized the choice to forgive, they should destroy their letters. "Blessed are those who mourn,/ For they shall be comforted" (Matt. 5:4). Destroying the letters helps complete the closure to the hurt and solidifies the decision to forgive.

Please note: This process of journaling about your hurts and forgiveness can be a helpful tool as you move forward in your relationships. You may discover new insights into pain from your past, and you will inevitably encounter hurts from present relationships. This process of facing the hurt, understanding the truth, and forgiving the offender may need to be repeated from time to time in order to keep your "emotional cup" empty of negative feelings.

Rejoice with those who rejoice, and weep with those who weep.
(Rom. 12:15)

———— For Group Discussion ————

Spend most of the session having one or two couples share their genogram with the group. Ask them to highlight conflicts, and talk through their needs that were met as well as needs that went unmet. Place emphasis on who met the needs for attention, affection, empathy, and approval. Give the group the opportunity to ask questions that clarify family relationships, help identify needs, and give compassion and support.

Leaders will want to be particularly sensitive to group members who may gain new insights into their own pain as other persons share their genograms. Check with group members periodically to assess their feelings.

Keep in mind the following principles as you facilitate group discussion:

- What might a young boy or girl have felt growing up in this environment? (Lonely, afraid, confused)
- What do you feel for your fellow group members as you hear of their journey? Can you identify the feeling? Sadness? Compassion? Hurt? Regret?

Sharing the answers to these questions is an integral part of fostering comfort and empathy in your group. You may also want to have couples share their experiences from their Marriage Staff Meetings. Ask questions that will stimulate discussion, such as: "How did you feel while sharing your childhood hurts with your partner? How did it feel after you had shared and received comfort? What new thoughts or feelings do you have about forgiveness?"

Close the session in prayer, thanking God for His love and forgiveness, and inviting Him to stir members' hearts with His Spirit of forgiveness.

Chapter Thirteen

■

BREAK FREE FROM UNHEALTHY THINKING

The honeymoon is over!"

As husbands and wives, we've all gone through the post-honeymoon stage when we are confronted with the reality of who we married. Reality means getting to know your spouse's little quirks or habits, discovering her peculiar preferences and opinions, and coming face to face with his odd, if not sometimes outlandish, thinking patterns.

All of us entered marriage with deeply entrenched patterns of thinking programmed into us since childhood. Have your expectations about marriage included thoughts such as:

- "My husband will have an 8 to 5 job."
- "My wife will have a career and earn a portion of the family income."
- "Husbands always take out the trash."
- "My wife should do the laundry and cleaning."
- "A good marriage means simply staying together."
- "Mothers take care of the children; fathers take care of earning the living."

These messages about marriage and the roles of marriage partners typically reflect the roles modeled by our family of origin. What expectations do you have about marriage and your partner? Complete the following sentences:

A good husband _____

A good wife_____

A good mother _____

A good father _____

A good marriage means _____

All of us entered marriage with deeply entrenched patterns of thinking programmed in us since childhood.

How do these opinions fit with what you saw modeled as a child? _____

_____

You and your partner may have noticed that marriage expectations are exposed most often when they clash. When two people enter marriage with contradictory messages, the result is CONFLICT!

For example, you believe husbands take care of all car repairs. But your husband has no mechanical abilities and believes that whoever has the most time should take the car into the shop.

How might these opposing expectations cause conflict? Can't you just hear the conversation?

"Dear, I thought you were going to fix the car."

"You had the day off. Why didn't you take it to the shop?"

"They charge an arm and a leg. Why can't you take a look at it and see what's wrong?"

"Because when I look under the hood, all I see is a mess of gears and gizmos. That ol' engine could be one of those scrap metal sculptures from the art museum, for all I know."

"I thought all guys tinkered with their cars when they were young."

"Not me. I had better things to do."

"Well, I refuse to spend our hard-earned money on some mechanic who'll tell us we need a new engine when all we need are spark plugs!"

Get the idea? What opposing or conflicting expectations can you identify in your relationship with your partner? Write about them here: _____

_____

_____

How have these expectations affected your marriage? _____

_____

_____

Expectations take center stage most often when they clash.

As you probably already realize, unrealistic expectations about marriage and our spouse can hinder the intimate relationship we long for. Intimacy in marriage is also hindered by other messages we tell ourselves.

As children, we all developed a belief system about ourselves and about life, based on the messages we received in our families and from society—both verbally and by example. In a sense, we tape recorded these messages and stored them in our belief system, and as adults we live them out, whether they were true or not. Some of those messages are very painful; they involve faulty values, impossible goals, or denial of one's significance. Most families never intend to hurt their children, but they often send crippling or destructive messages: *You're stupid. . . . Don't be a child. . . . Don't cry. . . . Don't trust anyone. . . . Don't be close. . . . Act mature. . . . Don't have fun. . . . Get to the top no matter who you hurt. . . . Be serious.*

Jimmy and Marla Carlton had received negative messages like these—messages that were still impacting their adult lives and undermining their marriage. Through counseling, the Carltons began to realize that they no longer had to listen to, or live by, those damaging messages. They could zero in on longstanding negative thoughts and substitute positive truths that would free them to accept themselves and love each other.

"So what you're saying," said Jimmy during a counseling session, "is we've got to identify our faulty thinking and replace it with more realistic beliefs. But that's hard to do. It's like going back and unlearning what you learned as a child."

Marla looked up entreatingly. "So what do we do? How do we break the cycle? How do we start over with the right messages?"

"It comes back to the Scriptures," David Ferguson explained. "God gives us the blueprint. We shouldn't be conformed to this world, but be transformed by the renewing of our minds. We need to take our thoughts captive and cast down our vain imaginations, knowing the truth will set us free . . . because as a man thinks in his heart, so is he."

"But how do we apply that blueprint in our daily lives? Where do we begin?" asked Marla.

"Let's start by taking a look at some of the typical lies we find in our personal lives and marriages."

Listed below are six of the most common unhealthy thinking patterns that contribute to emotional pain. We all seem to fall victim to one or more of these patterns:

- Personalizing
- Magnifying
- Overgeneralizing
- Emotional Reasoning
- Polarizing/Selective Abstraction
- Minimizing

In order to stop the effects of these unhealthy thinking patterns, you must first identify which of these are most common for you. Review the statements below and indicate which are true for you and/or your spouse.

True for Me   **True for My Spouse**

_____ 1. I see things as pretty much black and white.   _____

_____ 2. I tend to make mountains out of molehills.   _____

_____ 3. I often take things personally.   _____

_____ 4. Past disappointments seem to predict the future.   _____

_____ 5. What I'm feeling is more important than the facts.   _____

_____ 6. I often think people make too much out of their
              problems. They should just get over it.   _____

_____ 7. There's a place for everything and everything in
              its place.   _____

_____ 8. I seem to make things a "big deal."   _____

_____ 9. It's very important to sense others' approval.   _____

_____ 10. I just know things won't get any better.   _____

_____ 11. I can't really believe I'm loved unless I feel it.   _____

_____ 12. I can handle almost any problem that comes my way.
               I don't really need much support from anyone.   _____

_____ 13. Being perfect in what I undertake is essential
               to me.   _____

_____ 14. I seem to overreact to relatively small
               irritations.   _____

_____ 15. If someone in my family is upset, I must have   _____
        been part of the reason.

_____ 16. I tend to write people off if they hurt or   _____
        disappoint me.

_____ 17. If I feel unloved, it must be because no one   _____
        loves me.

_____ 18. There's no reason to get so worked up or so   _____
        emotional.

Now look over each of the statements that were true for you. The chart below gives the questions that match the six unhealthy thinking patterns. Find the items that you agreed with, then identify which thinking pattern(s) the statement represents.

	Polarizing	**Magnifying**	**Personalizing**
Questions:	1, 7, 13	2, 8, 14	3, 9, 15

	Generalizing	**Emotional Reasoning**	**Minimizing**
Questions:	4, 10, 16	5, 11, 17	6, 12, 18

Complete these sentences:

According to the exercise above, I have a tendency toward: _____

_____

_____

According to the exercise above, my spouse may have a tendency toward: _____

_____

How Do We Defeat These Unhealthy Thought Patterns?

Before you can begin to correct unhealthy thought patterns, you must clearly identify them. One of the best ways is the ABC Approach, a method requiring you to begin journaling about your life's events, what you *think* about the event, and your *emotional* response. Your journal will have three sections:

- **A** represents the *A*ctivating event that occurs.
- **B** represents your *B*elief system or self-talk—what you mentally tell yourself about the event.

- **C** represents the *C*onsequences—emotional (feeling) or behavioral responses to the situation.

After you've kept your journal for at least a week, analyze your own self-talk. You may be surprised at the insight you gain into your unique style of dealing with life. However, don't be surprised if your self-analysis doesn't instantly change your attitude. Here are two ways to begin working on some new responses.

Before you can begin to correct unhealthy thought patterns, you must clearly identify them.

The first way to defeat unhealthy thinking patterns is to challenge negative thoughts with truthful self-talk. We can extend the ABC approach by adding two new steps, making it the ABCDE approach:

- **D** represents *D*isputing untruths with more rational, truthful thoughts we choose to tell ourselves.
- **E** represents *E*njoying more positive or appropriate responses.

Telling yourself truthful statements over and over in your head, at the time of the event, can put a lid on an emotionally troublesome situation. The process of changing our thinking patterns is not an easy one; it requires patience and a great deal of practice.

A second way to combat the negative impact of unhealthy thinking requires the help of your partner. Marriage partners may not be susceptible to the same unhealthy patterns. This means that as we attempt to confront our belief system and replace distortions with the truth, our partner can be an integral part in helping us hear this truth.

For example, you might say: "Honey, when you see me blaming myself and personalizing, I would appreciate you reminding me that . . ." Or: "Sweetheart, when you see me demanding something really insignificant of the kids, please remind me that . . ."

Discuss your self-talk journal each night before going to sleep. Share the events of the day and your own self-talk about those events. Then give your spouse the opportunity to express the truth about the situation. Sharing your needs and progress in developing truthful thought patterns can be a means of drawing the two of you closer together.

Now, let's take a closer look at the six unhealthy thinking patterns. Pay particular attention to the patterns you seem to battle most often.

THE DESTRUCTIVENESS OF PERSONALIZING: "LIFE EVENTS ARE PERSONAL REJECTIONS AND ATTACKS"

Is this you? You're driving down the highway minding your own business, when suddenly a car swerves over into your lane and cuts you off. Instantly you see red and the adrenaline starts pumping. You lay on the horn and speed up, nearly touching his bumper, all the while spewing a stream of bitter accusations: "You dumb jerk, who taught you to drive? Get that jalopy back in your own lane! I'll show you who's got the right of way!"

Sound familiar? If so, you may be guilty of personalizing—taking external events as personal rejections and attacks. Taking everything personally is a form of distortion in which a person overestimates the extent an event is related to him or her.

"Personalizers" tend to be moody and easily hurt by so-called rejections. Filled with insecurities, they develop low self-esteem and may blame themselves for everything. Others often see them as "fragile," overly sensitive, childish, even hysterical. Frequently "personalizers" felt rejected in childhood or came from highly critical home environments. Whether the rejection was overt and abusive, or more subtle and neglectful, the child grew up with negative self-talk, such as, *What's wrong with me? I can't do anything right. It's my fault. Who cares about me? I'm worthless.*

When we take everything personally in marriage, we run the risk of overreacting to our spouse and causing unnecessary strife. We might do well to remember that what other people say and do says much more about them than about us. But how we react to them says volumes about who we are.

Newlyweds Earl and Anita were entertaining his parents for the first time in their cozy apartment. The table was set with gleaming silverware and fine china, and a vase of fresh flowers graced the linen tablecloth. Anita looked around nervously. A tossed salad was ready and a beef roast was in the oven. Everything had to be perfect for her new in-laws.

But when she removed the roast from the oven, Anita realized it was too done; in fact, it was scorched and stuck to the pan. Near tears, she served it anyway, hoping no one would notice. But, sure enough, as soon as Earl took his first bite, he said, "The roast's a little dry and tough, isn't it, dear?"

Wounded and humiliated, Anita jumped up from the table and threw her napkin in her plate, then ran from the table crying, "I can't do anything right! I'll never please you. I'm a total failure. I hate myself!" She slammed the bedroom door and collapsed on the bed in tears. She refused to come out for the rest of the evening.

Later, when Anita talked about the incident, she claimed that it was the worst night of her life. She had wanted to make such a good impression but ended up making a terrible one, at least in her own mind. She blamed everything on that burned roast.

When Chris Thurman pointed out that the evening might have had a better outcome if her self-talk had been different, Anita was amazed to think that could have made any difference.

"What was your first thought when your husband mentioned that the roast was tough and dry?"

"I thought, *I can't do anything right!*"

"What if, instead, you had thought, *I do most things right, but I'm nervous tonight so the roast got a little overcooked?*"

"I suppose that would have been more accurate," Anita replied. "Earl told me later, that when he cut a little farther into the roast, it was just fine and everyone enjoyed the meal—without me, of course. I was still in the bedroom sulking."

"Tell me more of your self-talk that night," said Chris.

"I thought, *I'll never be able to please my husband.*"

"Can you tell me what a more accurate response would be?"

"If I'd been more objective I would have thought, *Just because Earl mentioned the scorched roast doesn't mean he's displeased with the entire dinner.* In fact, I found out he was very happy with the dinner. It was my temper tantrum that upset him."

"What else did you think that night?"

"I told myself I was a *total failure.*"

"A more accurate belief system would be . . ."

"*I may fail at some things because I'm only human, but I'm good at many things, including cooking. One burned roast doesn't change that fact.*"

"Good thinking, Anita. Did you have any other negative self-talk that evening?"

She lowered her gaze. "I said *I hated myself.*"

"What might you have said instead?"

"I could have thought, *I'm displeased with myself for not catching the roast in time, but the rest of the dinner is fine. I'm an okay person . . . and God likes me!*"

"Excellent, Anita," said Chris. "Now tell me, if you could go back to that evening and react to your husband's remark with your new self-talk, how would things have been different?"

She chuckled. "Well, I wouldn't have run from the table like a little cry-baby. Maybe I'd have laughed it off, or made a joke, or even apologized to Earl's parents for the roast. Then, I would have felt relieved when Earl cut in farther and found that the meat was okay. We probably would have had a very lovely dinner, and I'd have a pleasant memory instead of a humiliating one."

Anita was learning the importance of her self-talk to her marriage. By taking her husband's remark personally and reacting with negative self-talk, she had caused the very consequences she most dreaded. But, by identifying the lies she had told herself and developing more rational and truthful thinking, Anita was eventually able to respond more positively and appropriately to marital and family "crises."

Check Yourself:

Read again the traits of a "personalizer," and answer the following questions: Do you see yourself in any of the comments that describe personalizing? _____ Yes _____ No Do you think your spouse has had occasions of personalizing? _____ Yes _____ No If you answered Yes for either of you, write here about any incidents of personalizing you recall._____

_____

_____

Write here about the effect personalizing has had on you. On your marriage. On your children. _____

_____

_____

Steps to Overcome "Personalizing"

1. Identify Unhealthy Self-talk

Begin by keeping a "self-talk" journal, writing down incidents of personalizing in your own life. This may not be easy at first; you may feel too angry or hurt or upset to write down the details. But making the effort will prove invaluable in overcoming this unhealthy attitude. Whatever the incident, after you've gained your composure, analyze what you were thinking that prompted your response. Your self-talk journal will help you identify "lies" you may often tell yourself. Your journal page should look something like this:

Date	Activating Event	Belief System (Self-talk)	Consequences (My Response)
6/10	husband commented on over-cooked roast at dinner with his parents	I can't do anything right. I'll never please you. I'm a total failure. I hate myself.	angry hurtful words; ran crying from table; slammed bedroom door; sulked alone all night

II. Dispute Faulty Thinking

Practice "taking these thoughts captive" and replacing them with more rational/truthful thinking, like this:

Take thoughts captive—cast them down	Think on those things that are true
2 Corinthians 10:3-5	*Philippians 4:8*
Replace: I can't do anything right.	**With:** I do most things right, but I just over-cooked the meat a bit this time.
Replace: I'll never please you.	**With:** My goal is God's approval, and I hope others will accept that in me.
Replace: I'm a total failure.	**With:** I fail at some things as all humans do, but I'm good at many things and can work to improve anything I wish.
Replace: I hate myself.	**With:** I'm displeased with how I handled this, but I'm really an okay person and God loves me!

III. Enjoy New Responses

By practicing more rational/truthful thinking, Anita's new responses at that family dinner might be:

If husband questions overcooked meat	"Would you like me to cut you another slice? It might be better inside."
If husband is negative	(privately) "It would mean a lot to me if I sensed your appreciation for what is done right; it would encourage me."
If husband is critical	(privately) "It sounds like you've had a hard day. I'd like to hear about it, but it seems like you're taking it out on me, and that's not quite fair."

Read over what you wrote about incidents of personalizing in your own life. Now, write down the healthy self-talk and new responses you might have given in those situations. _____

_____

_____

THE DESTRUCTIVENESS OF MAGNIFYING:
"MAKING MOUNTAINS OUT OF MOLEHILLS"

Teresa Ferguson knows how making mountains out of molehills can affect a marriage. She shares this personal story:

One evening a gentleman visited our home and David asked me to put on a pot of coffee. I did, but it got late and I wanted to go to bed. So I asked David if he would be sure to turn off the coffeepot. He said, "Sure, no problem." So off I went to bed.

The next morning when the alarm went off, David got up and went to the shower. I got up and opened the bedroom door and started for the kitchen to make the coffee. Guess what greeted me the moment I opened the door? Burnt coffee!

This was my self-talk: *What is the very last thing I asked David to do last night? Can't he ever do anything I ask him to? I always do everything he asks ME to do!*

Then, I noticed that the front door had been left unlocked all night. More self-talk: *David left the door open too? We could have been raped, ravaged, and robbed, and he wouldn't even care!*

I looked around, and every light had been left on. My self-talk escalated to new heights of righteous indignation: *I'm the only person who knows how to turn off the lights around here, and I know I'm the only one who knows how to change the empty toilet paper roll!*

I was so furious I wanted to run into the bathroom, rip open the shower curtain, and shout, "Can't you ever do anything I ask you to do?"

But no. I'm a mature woman, and we don't do that. What we do is go and lie on our bed and meditate; we try to figure out how to make our husband look really bad and feel really bad about the things he didn't do last night. But as I was lying there stewing over David's errors of omission, God began countering my self-talk. Here's how it went:

Raped, ravaged, and robbed? Come on, Teresa, that's a little melodramatic.

"Well, yes, I guess it is."

Teresa, you say David never does anything in this house?

"Well, yes, he does help out. He really does." I was beginning to feel a little silly about my outburst.

By the time David stepped out of the shower and returned to the bedroom, I was feeling calm and under control. I didn't say a word, but the first thing he noticed (smelled!) was the burnt coffee.

He looked at me and groaned, "Teresa, I'm sorry! I forgot the coffee! Forgive me?"

I went to him for a hug and said, "Sure. It could happen to anybody."

Privately, I was thinking that I almost missed this special moment with David because of my unhealthy self-talk. I was ready to make a mountain out of a molehill. I would have run in there and shouted and accused David, and ruined our day. But God corrected my self-talk just in time.

Check Yourself:

Many marriages falter because one or both partners suffer from the distortion of "magnifying"—taking life's events and exaggerating them until everything seems like a catastrophe. We take nickel and dime incidents and turn them into million dollar crises. None of us is built to cope with a life that feels that big all the time. Nor can a marriage long endure the constant bombardment of a "magnifying" mate.

Check yourself to see if you're guilty. "Magnifiers" may be volatile with anger, unmerciful with self-condemnation, or "bottomless" with self-pity. Others may consider them self-absorbed, preoccupied with their own crises, whiny, and over-reacting. Their vocabulary often includes words like: *devastated, worst, ruined, terrible, horrible, awful*. Watch for these "trigger" words as you attempt to dispute your own "magnifying" thoughts. "Magnifiers" may have developed this distorted thinking in a home environment where little things were blown out of proportion. Spilled milk merited a character attack; discipline was excessive and out of proportion to the offense; or one parent was preoccupied with loneliness, rejection, or fear, seeing catastrophes in every situation.

A second common childhood pattern is the "overly responsible" child who filled a relational vacuum in his home, seeking to hold the family together by pleasing everyone or meeting one parent's emotional needs due to a breakdown in the marital relationship. Such children often become overwhelmed by life's events.

Do you consider the tendency to magnify to be a problem for you? _____ Yes _____ No Do you recall times your spouse showed a tendency to magnify? _____ Yes _____ No

If you answered yes for either of you, describe here any incidents of magnifying you recall in your marriage. _____

_____

_____

How has this thinking pattern affected you? Your marriage? Your children? _____

_____

_____

Steps to Overcome "Magnifying"

I. Identify Unhealthy Self-talk

How do you overcome the habit of making mountains out of molehills? Listen to your own self-talk.

Begin a "self-talk" journal to record any incidents of magnifying. Pay particular attention to "trigger" words such as *always, every, everyone, no one, never, awful, worst, terrible, horrible.* Whatever the event, after you've gained your composure, analyze what you were thinking that prompted your response. Your self-talk journal will help you identify "lies" you may often tell yourself. Your journal may look like this:

Date	Activating Event	Belief System (Self-talk)	Consequences (My Response)
3/10	Broke coffee cup	This ruins my whole day!	Self-blame; punish myself
3/15	Friend hurts me	I'll never have any friends	Withdraw; angry; depressed
3/20	Teen forgets chore	He's lazy, irresponsible	Reject; bitter; overreact

II. Dispute Faulty Thinking

When you catch yourself overreacting, begin "taking your thoughts captive" and replacing them with more rational, truthful thinking. For example, if you drop and break a cup, don't punish yourself all day; tell yourself, *These things happen. It's only a coffee cup.* If your spouse is late or forgets to call, don't assume he's found someone else or doesn't love you; tell yourself, *Something must have come up, but he loves me and will be in touch as soon as he can.* Note the chart below:

Take thoughts captive—cast them down *2 Corinthians 10:3-5*	Think on those things that are true *Philippians 4:8*
Replace: My whole day is ruined!	**With:** These things happen; it's just a cup.
Replace: I'll never have friends	**With:** This hurts but I know how to handle it.
Replace: This kid's plain lazy!	**With:** I'll emphasize daily responsibilities.

III. Enjoy New Responses

By using more rational/truthful thinking, your new responses to the situations above might be the following:

Broken coffee cup	"Let's clean it up. We can get more cups."
Friend hurts me	"After thinking it over and praying for my friend, I'll

	look for the right time to share my hurt in a loving but honest way."
Teen forgets chore	Review agreed upon chores and discipline consequences; warn, then implement needed discipline.

Read over what you wrote about incidents of magnifying in your own life. Now write down the healthy self-talk and new responses you might have given in those situations. _____

_____

_____

_____

THE DESTRUCTIVENESS OF OVERGENERALIZING: "HISTORY ALWAYS REPEATS ITSELF"

Generalizing—relying on past events to predict the future—can undermine your worth, cast doubts on your adequacy, and prevent you from trusting others or yourself. Couples with this self-defeating style of thinking may conclude, "No matter what we do, we will never get along with each other."

"Overgeneralizers" carry around loads of anxiety, doubt, and fear. They hold on to past hurts, failures, and rejections, and recite them as evidence for their gloomy attitude toward the future. They figure, "Why try? The past will just repeat itself." Other people view generalizers as fearful, untrusting, or unforgiving.

"Generalizers" were often exposed to this way of thinking in their home environment. This generalizing message might come in many different areas:

- One argument with a neighbor means we must never have anything more to do with them
- An embarrassing moment of failure in sports means I'll never be an athlete
- A low grade means I'm not the successful student in the family. Certain negative "labels" from your growing-up years—dumb, clown, fatso, stupid, rebel, weirdo—may have stuck and contributed to negative generalizing about your future. Often these messages are subtle and more likely to develop when children don't receive empathy, comfort, and reassurance at times of inevitable hurt, rejection, or failure.

Check Yourself:

Ask yourself if you've ever uttered any of these overgeneralizations, then take note of the more accurate responses that follow:

"I'll never be able to lose weight."
Just as I chose to eat, I can choose not to eat.
"There's no hope of my ever keeping a job."
If this job doesn't work out, there will be other ones.
"I'll never be genuinely loved by my mate."
With effort, we can grow to love each other.
"Why would anyone want to spend time with me?"
I'm a person of worth with much to give to others.
"I can't count on you to really care about me."
As you express your love to me, I can learn to trust you.
"We'll tolerate each other, but never know real love."
If we are open to each other, feelings of love will grow.

Many of these generalizations may sound familiar to you. Have you experienced this type of faulty thinking?
_____ Yes _____ No   Has your spouse? _____ Yes _____ No

If generalizing has been a problem in your marriage, write about the incidents you remember here: _____
_____
_____

How has this tendency affected you? Your marriage? Your family? _____
_____
_____

Steps to Overcome "Generalizing"

I. Identify Unhealthy Self-talk

Begin by keeping a "self-talk" journal, recording those incidents when you catch yourself generalizing. Analyze what you were thinking that prompted this response. Your journal page may look something like this:

Date	Activating Event	Belief System (Self-talk)	Consequences (My Response)
4/4	Fail at new diet	I'll never lose weight	Stop trying; condemn self
4/6	Husband home late	No man treats me special	Accuse husband of not loving you; bitter; martyr
4/8	Family member disappoints you	I expected to be treated like this. It figures.	Withdraw; depressed; bitter; frustrated

II. Dispute Faulty Thinking

Practice "taking these thoughts captive" and replacing them with more rational/truthful thinking, such as this:

Take thoughts captive—cast them down *2 Corinthians 10:3-5*	**Think on those things that are true** *Philippians 4:8*
Replace: I'll never lose weight.	**With:** As I chose to eat I can choose not to.
Replace: No man treats me special.	**With:** I trust my husband's love and he can help me by calling when he's going to be late.
Replace: I expected to be treated like this.	**With:** This hurts and I'll need to let him/her know how I feel.

III. Enjoy New Responses

With more rational/truthful thinking, your new response to the above situations might be the following:

One day of failure on a new diet	"I'll begin again today!"
Husband home late from work	"I was concerned about you and would appreciate your calling me when you're going to be late."
Disappointed by family member	"I reached out for help and you seemed too busy. I needed you."

History doesn't have to repeat itself. Negative life thinking doesn't have to be a self-fulfilling prophecy. You and your partner—in fact, your entire family—can have a fresh start if you'll wipe the slate clean of generalizations and be open to new opportunities for personal growth and marital intimacy.

Now, read over what you wrote about incidents of overgeneralizing in your own life. Write down the healthy self-talk and new responses you might have given in those situations._____

_____

_____

_____

_____

_____

THE DESTRUCTIVENESS OF EMOTIONAL REASONING: "INTERPRETING FEELINGS AS FACTS"

Allison suffered from "emotional reasoning," confusing feelings with facts. Regardless of the evidence to the contrary, she was convinced that *if she felt it, it must be so*. But her attitude was playing havoc with her marriage. Convinced that her husband, Todd, was having an affair, she hired detectives to follow him and made shrill accusations in front of family and friends. She had no proof, she admitted, only feelings. She felt unloved, so she assumed Todd had a lover; she felt jealous, so she concluded he was being unfaithful. While the logical sequence is to think, then feel, she was reversing the process. No matter how many times Todd assured her of his love, Allison would reply, "No, you don't, because I don't feel it."

Allison's skeptical unbelief may have been role-modeled by fearful parents or evolved out of the pain of broken promises—the "I'll believe it when I see it" mentality. Or she may have suffered some deep emotional trauma during childhood, such as physical or sexual abuse.

Until Allison is willing to take an honest look at her distorted self-talk, her marriage will remain in jeopardy and she'll continue to experience disillusionment and depression. Todd will grow more frustrated with her irrational accusations and may reach the point of actually considering an affair, just to prove Allison right.

Check Yourself:

What about you? Do you see reality through the skewed perspective of your emotions? Are you convinced something is so just because you feel it? Or do you deny the truth because you *don't* feel it? Did you come from a home dominated by fear and mistrust? Did you suffer physical or sexual abuse? Did your parents hurl accusations at you, such as, "I just know you'll go off and get pregnant some day!" Or: "You're going to turn out just like your father if you keep this up!" Did you grow up feeling a nagging sense of worthlessness and betrayal?

Think about your own life and your spouse's and answer the following questions:

Do you see yourself struggling with emotional reasoning? _____ Yes _____ No   Do you think your spouse struggles with emotional reasoning? _____ Yes _____ No   If you marked Yes for either of you, describe the incidents you feel represent emotional reasoning.

_____

_____

_____

How have these events impacted your life? Your marriage? Your children? _____

_____

_____

Steps to Overcome "Emotional Reasoning"

I. Identify Unhealthy Self-talk

Begin by keeping a "self-talk" journal, describing those events in your life that you feel demonstrate emotional reasoning. Analyze what you were thinking that prompted your response. Your journal page may look something like this:

Date	Activating Event	Belief System (Self-talk)	Consequences (My Response)
3/20	Life disappoints me	I know things will never get any better.	Discouragement, disillusionment
3/22	Spouse home late for dinner	I just know he's not where he should be!	Accusing, attacking, angry, resentful
3/24	Relationship hurt	I was right—he doesn't really care about me!	Withdrawal, blame, rejection

II. Dispute Faulty Thinking

Practice taking these negative thoughts captive and replacing them with more rational/truthful thinking, such as:

Take thoughts captive—cast them down
2 Corinthians 10:3-5

Replace: I know things will never get better.

Replace: I just know he's not where he should be!

Replace: I was right—he doesn't really care about me!

Think on those things that are true
Philippians 4:8

With: Things are hard, but as I face them, they seem easier, especially with encouragement from others.

With: I'm concerned and need reassurance.

With: I believe he cares and I need an apology from him.

III. Enjoy New Responses

As you develop more rational/truthful thinking, your new responses might include the following:

Life disappointment	Face difficulties one by one; seek help from others who care
Spouse late for dinner	Kindly express concern and receive your spouse's explanation and reassurance
Relationship hurt	Express your hurt and receive healing through apology and forgiveness; care feelings return

We need to remember that feelings are just that—feelings! They change; they're hard to predict; they may spring from irrational thinking. Feelings have their place, of course, but they can't take the place of truth.

Read over what you wrote about incidents of emotional responding in your own life. Write down the healthy self-talk and new responses you might have given in those situations. _____

_____

_____

THE DESTRUCTIVENESS OF POLARIZING: "SEEING EVERYTHING AS BLACK OR WHITE"

"Polarizing" is a perfectionistic thinking pattern that views life as all-or-nothing, good-or-bad, black-or-white. More than a little difficult to live with, "polarizers" hold to rigid rules for evaluating their life and marriage; they classify events as right or wrong, good or bad; and they judge their performance (or their spouse's) on the basis of their own impossible standards. They feel no satisfaction in modest performance or genuine effort, and there's little joy in success, since it was expected all along. But, when they don't attain their idea of perfection, they're likely to suffer great anger and despair.

Both Marla and Jimmy Carlton suffered from the "polarizing" lie. They cut reality into good or bad, all or nothing extremes. Coming from critical, nit-picking, performance-oriented homes, they saw themselves and their marriage in terms of black or white. Mostly shades of black. Here are samples of their distorted thinking:

Marla: "I'm not a good wife."
          "I can't do anything right to make him happy."
          "Our marriage is a horrible failure. Why even try?"

Jimmy: "I gave up my music. I'm a failure at life."
          "I'm an awful husband and father."
          "Life is a disappointment."

As with the other self-talk lies, Marla and Jimmy had to begin the process of taking their thoughts captive and concentrating instead on those things that were true. Their new belief system included these thoughts: *We love each other and can have a good marriage if we work at it. We don't have to be perfect to make each other happy. We can find new ways to enjoy our music and make it part of our lives again.*

Check Yourself:

Reflect on the possibility of polarizing in your own life and answer the following questions. Have you engaged in the faulty thinking of polarizing? _____ Yes _____ No   Has your spouse shown signs of Polarizing? _____ Yes _____ No   If you answered Yes for either of you, write here about any incidents of polarizing you recall in your marriage: _____

_____

_____

Describe the impact polarizing has on you. . . On your marriage. . . On your children. _____

_____

_____

Steps to Overcome "Polarizing"

I. Identify Unhealthy Self-talk

Begin by keeping a "self-talk" journal, recording those incidents of polarizing in your daily life. Analyze what you were thinking that prompted your response. Your journal page may look something like this:

Date	Activating Event	Belief System (Self-talk)	Consequences (My Response)
4/1	My project criticized	I knew I'd fail at it.	Anger at myself and the critic; depressed for days
4/3	Spouse drives a new way home	This isn't the right way home!	"What are you doing? This isn't the right way!"
4/6	Outdoor party threatened by rain	Another special day is about to be ruined.	My anxiety and anger (not the rain) spoil the day for everyone.

II. Dispute Faulty Thinking

Practice taking these thoughts captive and replacing them with more rational/truthful thinking, as in these examples:

Take thoughts captive—cast them down	Think on those things that are true
2 Corinthians 10:3-5	*Philippians 4:8*

Replace: I knew I'd fail at this.

With: My work wasn't perfect, but it was more than adequate, and I can improve.

Replace: This isn't the right way!

With: There's more than one way to drive home, and I can enjoy this one.

Replace: My day will be ruined!

With: This is a special day because of the occasion. I can plan alternatives if they're needed.

III. Enjoy New Responses

As you employ more rational/truthful thinking, your new responses might include the following:

Criticism of new project	Evaluate criticism, consider changes, and move on
Spouse drives a different way home	Relax; enjoy spouse's company and the new scenery without protesting
Outdoor party threatened by rain	Enjoy the day; alter plans as needed

Now, read over what you wrote about incidents of polarizing in your own life. Write down the healthy self-talk and new responses you might have given in those situations. _____

_____

_____

THE DESTRUCTIVENESS OF SELECTIVE ABSTRACTION: (AN OFFSHOOT OF POLARIZING) "MISSING THE FOREST FOR THE TREES"

Ron and Luella, married nearly eighteen years, had amassed grievances against each other like squirrels hoarding acorns for winter. "She hardly ever fixes home-cooked suppers anymore; I've had it up to here with fast food, microwave meals, and frozen dinners," said Ron, slicing the air with his hand at mid-neck. "And she doesn't iron my shirts like she used to. In fact, half of 'em need buttons sewn on, so they sit there at the back of my closet. Nothing gets done around the house unless I pitch in and help."

"So he's missing a few buttons," argued Luella, twisting a blonde curl around her pinky. "What's he really got to complain about? Nothing! I work hard, but what does it get me? Complaints! I got married for a little romance and roses. If all he wanted was someone to iron and sew buttons, why didn't he hire a maid? It's been three years since he sent me a card, or took me to a fancy restaurant, or brought me flowers. As long as he's got his hot meal and buttons on his shirt, he's happy to sit in his chair and watch TV. What kind of life is that? Where's the excitement? I got married hoping for 'Love Boat' or a Ginger Rogers movie; all I get is 'Monday Night Football' and 'Hogan's Heroes'!"

"Obviously, you'd like a little more romance in your marriage, but how is Ron in other ways?" asked Chris Thurman. "Does he work hard, pay the bills on time, provide a nice home for you?"

"Well, yes. But isn't that what he's supposed to do?"

"Does he help out around the house?"

"Yes, he's pretty good about that."

"Is he faithful?"

"Of course. Ron would never look at another woman!"

"Then he's not all bad, is he?"

"Bad? Who says he's bad? He's a wonderful husband! I just wish he would be a little more romantic."

"How about you, Ron? You feel Luella's neglecting an important area of your marriage. Why do you suppose that is?"

"I don't know. Maybe because she works full time, like me. We're both tired when we get home, so we end up ordering pizza or sticking a TV dinner in the microwave."

"Then Luella isn't ignoring you because she's mean or lazy?"

"Mean? Lazy? No way! She works hard. These days it takes two incomes for a family to get along."

"So, there are many good qualities you love about Luella?"

"I wouldn't have married her if I didn't love her!"

"So you're both saying your mate has many good qualities you admire, but there are a few things that bother you."

"Sounds about right."

"Do you suppose you're both focusing so much on those few negative traits that you've overlooked all the positive ones?"

"Could be."

"Maybe so."

"In other words, looking at the 'big picture,' you'd say your marriage is quite successful, and you're basically happy."

They looked surprised at the idea, but both agreed, relieved they weren't in such bad shape after all.

Ron and Luella were guilty of missing the forest for the trees, of focusing on what was wrong in their marriage rather than on what was right. They spent precious time and energy fussing and fuming over a few minor problems when they could have invested the same time and energy toward positive solutions.

Ron was amazed to realize a few cards and flowers and an occasional "date" would go a long way toward restoring Luella's romantic dreams. Luella was more than willing to prepare some good home-cooked meals on weekends to make up for their fast-food weekdays. And the dry cleaners proved to be the answer for those wrinkled, buttonless shirts. Ron and Luella agreed to stop "majoring on the minors" in their relationship and get on with the business of enjoying a successful marriage.

Check Yourself:

What about you? Have you fallen prey to the lie of selective abstraction? Reflect on your own life and marriage and answer the following questions: Can you think of incidents in your life that reveal this type of faulty thinking? _____ Yes _____ No   Can you recall such incidents in your spouse's life? _____ Yes _____ No   If you answered Yes for either of you, describe the incidents that reveal this area of faulty thinking in your lives or marriage. _____

_____

_____

What impact has the lie of selective abstraction had on your life? . . . On your marriage? . . . Your children? _____

_____

_____

To overcome this faulty thinking pattern in your life, follow the ABCDE approach as already outlined, remembering to journal your life events, your negative self-talk, your emotional responses, followed by the truthful thoughts you should choose and your more positive responses.

THE DESTRUCTIVENESS OF MINIMIZING: "IT REALLY DOESN'T MATTER."

When Jimmy Carlton first began counseling, his response to almost any question was predictable. He minimized everything—denying or discounting any feelings associated with the significant events of his life. For example:

"Jimmy, how did you feel about your dad not showing you affection?"

"I didn't think about it. That's just how men are."

"How did you feel about your parents not attending your ball games in high school?"

"That's life. They were busy people. Were they supposed to drop everything for me?"

"Jimmy, how do you feel about the problems threatening your marriage?"

"What problems? Marla's the one who thinks we've got problems. I don't see what all the fuss is about."

It took Jimmy several months before he began recognizing and validating his own emotions. Since his childhood, he had been denying his emotions so he wouldn't have to feel the hurt. His defensive response was to simply shut down his emotions and shrug his shoulders over life's significant hurts and events. But his protective veneer had a chilling effect on his marriage. To Marla he was a virtual "ice man," without warmth or vulnerability.

Check Yourself:

Minimizers tend to verbalize few emotions themselves and expect the same from others around them, often leaving spouses lonely, frustrated, and feeling deeply wounded. Even during tragic events, minimizers often demonstrate little or no feeling. They deny that anything troubles them, and, when pressed to communicate, they may give facts, opinions, or data instead of vulnerably sharing their needs and feelings.

Often, minimizers come from homes where personal needs are neglected or overlooked. In an effort to avoid the pain of unmet needs, children in these environments will learn to deny their own needs, lose touch with their feelings, and reduce to a minimum their personal sharing.

Can you see yourself falling into a minimizing pattern of thinking? _____ Yes _____ No   Has your spouse displayed minimizing tendencies? _____ Yes _____ No   If you answered Yes for either of you, describe incidents that reveal these minimizing tendencies. _____

_____

_____

_____

How has this pattern of thinking affected you? . . . Your marriage? . . . Your children? _____

_____

_____

_____

_____

To overcome this faulty thinking pattern in your life, begin a journal using the ABCDE approach as outlined previously, remembering to journal your life events, your negative self-talk, your emotional responses, followed by the truthful thoughts you could choose and more positive responses.

Scripture Journaling—2 Corinthians 10:5

. . . and we are taking every thought captive to the obedience of Christ. (NASB)

What thoughts do you need to take captive today? How do your thoughts compare to the truth of Christ? What do you need to tell Him right now? Write your thoughts and feelings here:

_____

_____

_____

_____

_____

_____

_____

_____

MARRIAGE STAFF MEETING

After completing the exercises in this chapter and the journal exercises, share with your partner any of the unhealthy thinking patterns you've discovered in your own life. Begin by saying, "I realize I have a problem with . . ." Talk about some of the childhood experiences that may have contributed to these thinking patterns. How did you observe these patterns in your own family? Ask for your partner's assistance in challenging negative self-talk. Be sure to tell your partner how he/she can best help you. What do you want your spouse to say? How do you want your partner to confront your negative self-talk?

Discuss some of the expectations that were discovered through the beginning exercise. Start this discussion by sharing how these expectations were developed. Then prayerfully consider any changes that need to be made in your own expectations.

Ask group members to come prepared to act out a "favorite" unhealthy thinking pattern. Ask each couple to act out two scenes that reflect both the husband's and the wife's "favorite" thought pattern. Encourage them to put on their best acting skills and have fun with these scenes. A gentle sense of humor can help at a time like this (remember, *gentle, not cutting or sarcastic*). See if the group can guess each pattern that is portrayed.

After each dialogue, invite the group to brainstorm about what the spouse might say to the "unhealthy thinker." Then ask the couple to redo the scene with dialogue that reflects the group's suggestions.

During the group discussion, urge members to share, one by one, the negative patterns they recognize most often in their own lives. Ask each member to share the childhood connections involved in these patterns as well.

Chapter Fourteen

───■───

ESTABLISH A VISION FOR YOUR MARRIAGE AND FAMILY

"Where there is no vision, the people perish."
Proverbs 29:18 (KJV)

Remember Lewis Carroll's delightful story of *Alice in Wonderland?* Alice follows the White Rabbit down the rabbit hole and embarks on an adventure unlike any other. As she wanders through the madcap maze of Wonderland, she encounters an assortment of outrageous, unpredictable creatures—the Dodo, the Caterpillar, the Mad Hatter and March Hare, Tweedledee and Tweedledum. But, perhaps her most telling encounter is with the Cheshire Cat sitting perched on a tree limb above her. As Alice faces a myriad of paths veering off in all directions, she inquires of the cat, "Would you tell me, please, which way I ought to go from here?"

"That depends a good deal on where you want to get to," replies the cat.

"I don't much know or care where—" replies Alice, a bit perturbed.

Then comes the Cheshire's insightful response: "Then it really doesn't matter which way you go, does it?"

Alice's conversation with the Cheshire Cat is, sadly, not only revealing of Alice's situation, but it also captures the dilemma of many marriages and families today. In counseling, we hear the frequent complaint, "We don't seem to be getting anywhere!" "I don't think we're accomplishing anything!" "We just seem to be spinning our wheels!" Such complaints can usually be traced to a deeper concern: individuals, marriages, and families have no idea where they're going, so they don't know how to get there, or whether they've arrived!

The Hebrew word for "perish" in the verse above is also translated "go unrestrained . . . each to his own way." What a tragic but fitting description for many marriages and families. Husbands and wives are each frantically pursuing their own overloaded agendas; children are left to fend for themselves. In fact, in many homes today, children can go through their entire daily routine with only minimal contact with their parents.

Imagine it: The alarm clock rings. Mom and Dad get up and get ready for work while Junior pours himself a cold bowl of cereal. He starts off for school while they head out to work. After school he comes home to an empty house, grabs a snack, watches TV, and does a little homework until Mom comes home exhausted and tosses a couple of TV dinners into the microwave. Junior takes his to his room and eats while watching the "Simpsons"—that inconceivable cartoon catastrophe "lauding" the American family. Dad arrives home too late to say good night; Junior has fallen asleep with his TV still blaring.

An exaggeration, you say? A caricature of today's family? If only that were so!

King Solomon, the writer of Proverbs, was indeed wise when he said that what is needed is a vision. Perhaps today, more than ever, we, as individuals and families, need a sense of direction and destiny, a guiding framework around which we can make our decisions, and distinct objectives toward which we can stretch with all our strength and passions. The contrast is clear: perish or flourish; wander aimlessly or stretch forth purposely.

Perhaps today, more than ever, we, as individuals and families, need a sense of direction and destiny, a guiding framework around which we can make our decisions, and distinct objectives toward which we can stretch with all our strength and passions.

BENEFITS AND BLESSINGS FROM GOAL SETTING

Vision is not without cost. Time must be allocated, and considerable thought given. Sacrifices must be made if goals are to be realized, but there are great "payoffs":

Goal setting is a basis for marriage and family oneness

Amos 3:3 poses the question, "Can two walk together, unless they are agreed?" Agreeing on where you're going is essential to oneness in relationships. You can start with a simple agreement that neither husband nor wife makes a time commitment involving the other without first discussing and agreeing on the matter. Goals can involve family nights, household plans, vacation ideas, or anything with the potential to encourage "walking together" as a couple or a family.

Take time now to reflect on the benefits of goal setting in your home; then answer the following questions:

I remember how important it was to me when my spouse and I came to a mutual understanding and agreement concerning _____

_____

One particular area I hope we can come to supportive agreement on is

_____

_____

Goal setting offers a framework for decision-making

Life consists of endless pressing decisions: where to invest your time, attention, effort, and money. Without established goals, confusion, contradiction, and conflict will abound. By setting goals, a family faced with a decision can simply ask, "Will this choice further accomplish our family goals, or hinder them?" Depending on the answer, you can then proceed, or decline.

Share your thoughts on this possible benefit of goal-setting by completing the following statements:

I remember our family experiencing confusion, disagreement, or disappointment when we were confronted with the decision to _____

_____

As I think about the many decisions our family will face in the future, I most hope we will discuss _____

_____

Goal setting is a reminder of important priorities

"Good" things are the worst enemies of the "best" things. Goal setting serves as a frequent reminder of our accountability to priorities that matter to us. Clearly defined goals will help us give our relationships with God and family the significance they deserve in our daily lives.

Reflecting on this possible benefit of goal setting, complete the following statements:

I often go overboard in giving too much attention or concern to (For instance: *job, kids, finances, hobbies, shopping, others*)_____

_____

I would like to consistently give more priority to_____

_____

Goal setting provides a sense of accomplishment and security

Remember the positive feeling when you've checked off everything on your "things-to-do" list? As you set goals and see them accomplished, you experience the secure feeling that your life is not haplessly out of control, but that you've taken charge of your destiny.

Seeing marriage and family goals completed brings a deep and meaningful sense of accomplishment to each family member.

Think about your past accomplishments and successes and finish the statements below:

I remember how important it was when I completed or accomplished (For instance: *getting my degree, learning to paint, getting that promotion*) _____

_____

When I do finish an important project or goal, I feel_____

_____

Goal setting is an example and witness to others

Our generation lives in a "leadership vacuum," with everyone looking for individuals or families who know where they're headed. Christian families can be a witness and an example by establishing goal-directed homes with a "vision."

Reflect on your example to others as you answer the questions below.

How have you seen God use an area of family strength in your home to encourage or challenge others? _____

_____

In what area of your life would you like to see your family become a better example? _____

_____

Often in our Intimacy Therapy sessions we ask couples questions like these (check the ones for which you personally have an answer):

_____ What's the next special "date" I have planned to look forward to with my spouse?

_____ What particular character qualities are we now emphasizing as we "train up our children"?

_____ What's the next major household expenditure we've agreed on making?

_____ What are our financial plans for eliminating credit card debt? For saving toward our children's college education?

_____ Which married couple friends are we purposefully developing close relationships with?

_____ What ministry dreams and plans do we share together as a couple?

_____ What spiritual goals are we sharing through our prayer times, devotionals, or Bible study?

_____ What plans do I have for personal development through education, self study, or career enhancement?

For how many of the above items do you and your partner have answers? Each one addresses your family's future and your sense of vision. The special emphasis on goal setting in this chapter is designed to be explored during a "get-away" goal setting retreat for husbands and wives. We will guide you in making plans for your own get-away retreat.

Preparing for your own Goal Setting Retreat

Select a weekend when both of you are free. It may take some effort to coordinate your schedules, but keep in mind that this weekend will be an investment in your marriage, an opportunity to keep your marriage fresh and vital as you tap into all you've learned about the pursuit of intimacy in your relationship.

DIRECTIONS FOR YOUR GOAL SETTING RETREAT

1. This is a weekend for the *couple only*. Don't take your children. Trade off baby-sitting with another couple, send the kids to Grandma's, or whatever it takes to be alone!

2. Together, *plan a time* in your schedule for a weekend, starting Friday in the early afternoon and ending on Sunday afternoon. (Weekdays can work as well, but you will need about three days.)

3. Together, *plan a place* to go. You'll want to consider cost, travel time, and recreational opportunities. Even if there's no budget for this getaway, trade off baby-sitting with another couple and stay home—ALONE in your own home!

4. A possible schedule is included below. If you adhere to it closely, you'll be able to complete all the materials. Please understand the purpose of this weekend: communication and planning, not simply a relaxing weekend.

5. The Goal Setting Retreat is organized into a Preliminary Session on *Personal Vision*, followed by eight sections concerning key areas of personal and family life.

6. Each section allows for Personal Reflection, followed by Couple Sharing.

7. Many couples find it helpful to pray together as they begin or conclude each section. Begin with silent prayer if it feels more comfortable to you.

8. The questions do NOT have right or wrong answers. They are designed to help you learn more about each other and gain a sense of how God can involve you in mutual support.

9. Listen attentively as your partner shares, gaining insight into *who* he/she is and *how* God can deepen your journey together toward oneness.

10. After each of the eight sections, you'll have an opportunity to reflect on a few specific goals that evolve out of your sharing. At the conclusion of your Goal Setting Retreat, you'll summarize these goals.

Goal Setting Retreat Typical Schedule

FIRST EVENING

2:00   Check in/Relax

5:30   Dinner

7:00   Personal Vision

8:30   Break

9:00   Section I:
            Spiritual Goals

10:30   Enjoy Yourselves

SECOND MORNING

7:00   Rise and Shine

7:30   Breakfast/Quiet
            Time/Relax

8:30   Section II: Marriage

9:45   Break

10:15   Section III: Family

11:30   Lunch/Break/Relax

SECOND AFTERNOON

2:00   Section IV: Household

3:15   Break/Relax

4:00   Section V: Finances

5:45   Dinner/Break/Relax

SECOND EVENING

7:00   Section VI: Career/
            Domestic
            Responsibilities

8:15   Break/Relax

8:45   Section VII:
            Personal/Social

10:00   Enjoy Yourselves

THIRD MORNING

7:00   Rise and Shine

7:30   Breakfast/Quiet
            Time/Relax

8:45   Section VIII:
            Ministry

10:00   Break

10:30   Goal Setting
            Worksheets for
            Spiritual Goals,
            Marriage, Family,
            and Household

12:00   Lunch

THIRD AFTERNOON

1:00   Goal Setting
            Worksheets for
            Financial, Career,
            Personal/Social,
            and Ministry

2:00   Break/Relax

2:30   Discuss Follow-up
            Plan

3:30   Relax/Return Home

YOUR PERSONAL VISION

*"God causes all things to work together for good
to those who love God . . ."*—*Romans 8:28* (NASB)

Take several minutes to reflect on God's role in your past, present, and future. Then, share your responses with your spouse.

Remembrances from the Past

1. "What" and "who" has God used in your life to give you your perspective about marriage, family, and homelife?_____

_____

_____

2. What personal attitudes, habits, and priorities have been changed within you in the last few years? Did God use specific people? Any particular events? Any specific Scripture passages? _____

_____

_____

3. Describe the background and events surrounding how you came to establish a personal relationship with Christ. If this is something you're still considering, describe where you are in this journey. _____

_____

_____

4. What were some of the things you first learned as a new Christian?

_____

_____

5. Take a few moments to consider any other significant events or turning points in your Christian life. Pause to thank God for His working thus far in your life. _____

_____

_____

Reflections on the Present

1. In what ways are you now making marriage and family a key priority in your life? _____

_____

_____

2. In what ways and areas are you now growing spiritually? _____

_____

_____

3. What circumstances does God seem to be using in your life to per-

fect a Christ-like character? What changes do you sense God desires to make in you?_____

_____

_____

4. In what ways and areas are you now developing as a "total," more well-rounded person? _____

_____

_____

5. Do you know what your mate's "vision" is? How can you complement that vision? _____

_____

_____

Dreams for the Future

1. What dreams do you have for your personal, spiritual, and business life? _____

_____

_____

2. What dreams do you have for your marriage and family life?_____

_____

_____

3. What financial dreams and goals do you have? _____

_____

_____

4. What avenue of ministry for you, your marriage, and your family do you dream about?_____

_____

_____

5. Write out your answer to the following DREAM: "If all my dreams for the future could come true today, here's what my life, marriage, and family would be like": _____

_____

_____

After you and your spouse have individually completed these sections on the past, present, and future, return to "Remembrances from the Past" and take turns sharing your answers. Continue through the present and future sections as well. LISTEN to each other's words and HEART as you share!

You're now ready to embark on a journey of reflection and discussion through eight key areas of your life. The following questions and Bible study material will help focus your understanding of yourself and your spouse, providing opportunities for setting specific goals. Each section is designed for Personal Reflection followed by Couple Sharing.

SECTION I—SPIRITUAL GOALS

1. Draw a line graph beginning with your birth up to the present time. Chart your spiritual growth, showing your salvation experience, times of rapid growth, "backsliding," plateaus, and so forth, right up to the present time. Now show where you'd like to be "spiritually" at the end of the next year.

2. Would you enjoy seeing improvement in the areas of prayer, your devotional life, or studying Scripture? Explain._____

_____

_____

3. Would you benefit from additional involvement with other Christians in Bible study, home groups, worship? Explain. _____

_____

_____

4. What specific character qualities (patience, honesty, faith, compassion, helpfulness, and so forth) do you feel God might desire to work on in your life? _____

_____

_____

5. Do particular Scripture passages come to mind regarding the charac-

ter qualities noted in the question above? (Your Bible or concordance might help.) These verses would make excellent memorization projects.

_____

_____

6. What good Christian books or tapes would you like to invest in? ____

_____

_____

After completing and sharing this first section with your partner, spend some time discussing three to five specific goals you might focus on for the next several months. (It will help to keep your goals relatively "short term"; set goals to be accomplished during the next year.) Before writing down your own goals in the space below, read these "sample" goals to help prompt your thinking:

- Read Proverbs each month, one chapter a day.
- Read through the Bible in a year.
- Memorize one Scripture verse per week.
- Read the biographies of four Christian leaders.
- Spend thirty minutes a day in devotions, using *INTIMATE MO-MENTS* daily devotions for couples (Nashville: Thomas Nelson Publishers, 1993).
- Listen to teaching tapes on the way to work.
- Attend worship services weekly.
- Study topical material on patience and forgiveness.
- Attend a spiritual renewal conference.

Specific goals we would like to undertake in our SPIRITUAL LIFE during the next year:

1. _____

_____

_____

2. _____

_____

_____

3. _____

_____

_____

4. _____

_____

_____

5. _____

_____

_____

SECTION II—MARRIAGE GOALS

Read the following Scripture passage and list the characteristics or responsibilities stated for the husband and the wife:

Passage	Husband	Wife
(Eph. 5:15-33)	_____	_____
	_____	_____
	_____	_____
	_____	_____
	_____	_____

1. Do you believe your marriage is maturing and that you are becoming "one"? Give examples. _____

_____

_____

_____

2. As you think of the roles and responsibilities in your family, do you have specific personal needs your spouse could help with? List them here: _____

_____

_____

_____

3. What improvements or changes could you make that would help your marriage communication? Write them down here. _____

_____

_____

_____

4. Think about and then write down your answers to the following

questions. Then, during your sharing time, make note of your partner's responses.

My Thoughts	Questions	My Partner's Thoughts
_____ _____ _____	a. Do I express my love for you verbally in satisfying ways? How can I improve?	_____ _____ _____
_____ _____ _____ _____ _____	b. Could I improve in areas such as manners, impatience, complaining, getting ready on time, selfishness, and so forth?	_____ _____ _____ _____ _____
_____ _____ _____	c. What can I do when we're out in public to make you feel more special and secure?	_____ _____ _____
_____ _____ _____ _____	d. Should we go out on more "dates" together? Where? Do we need more get-away weekends? Where?	_____ _____ _____ _____
_____ _____ _____	e. What can I do to make our sexual relationship more intimate and fulfilling?	_____ _____ _____

After completing and sharing this second section with your spouse, spend time discussing three to five specific goals you might focus on during the next several months. (Again, keep your goals "short term," to be accomplished during the next year.)

Some "sample" goals to prompt your thinking include:

- Consistent weekly times for talk (Staff Meetings).
- Complete "Love Map" exercise, Chapter 16, page 253.
- Participate in a seminar on marriage.
- Read *Communication Keys to Your Marriage*.
- Express daily praise and appreciation of my spouse.
- Schedule quarterly "Get-Away" times without the kids.
- Read *Solomon on Sex* (Nashville: Thomas Nelson, 1977) together.
- Schedule "dates" together, alone, twice monthly.

- Identify and enjoy two new hobbies or interests together.
- Join a marriage support group for deepening intimacy.

Specific goals we would like to undertake in our MARRIAGE during the next year:

1. _____
2. _____
3. _____
4. _____
5. _____

SECTION III—FAMILY GOALS

What guidelines and principles concerning children and parents do you see in the following passages? How do these apply to your own parenting experiences? For example, after reading Psalm 127:3, you might ask yourself, "How do I treat a 'precious' gift? I should cherish, value, praise, and protect it. How am I accomplishing this with my own children? In what ways do I cherish, value, praise, and protect them?"

Psalm 127:3_____

_____

Deuteronomy 6:4-9 _____

_____

Proverbs 3:11-12 _____

_____

Proverbs 22:6 _____

_____

2 Timothy 3:14-17 _____

_____

1. How do you feel you could better fulfill your responsibilities as a parent?_____

_____

_____

2. Are there particular burdens you have about establishing a better re-

lationship with your family of origin? With your in-laws? Are there specific steps you could take to help? _____

_____

_____

3. Could your children benefit from more of your undivided attention in "fun" activities? At meal times? During special outings with each child? Explain. _____

_____

_____

4. Think about and write down your answers to the following questions. Then, during your sharing time, make note of your partner's responses.

My Thoughts		Questions	My Partner's Thoughts
_____	a.	Could we benefit from more time together, planning our parenting approach? When? To discuss what?	_____
_____			_____
_____			_____
_____			_____
_____	b.	What additional family time activities would you like to see planned?	_____
_____			_____
_____			_____
_____	c.	What additional support would you like to have from your spouse in parenting?	_____
_____			_____
_____			_____
_____	d.	What specific goals would you have for each of your children in their training? Discipline? Character?	_____
_____			_____
_____			_____
_____			_____

After completing and sharing this section with your spouse, spend time discussing three to five specific goals you might focus on during the next several months. (It will help to keep your goals relatively "short term"; focus on things you can accomplish during the next year.)

Here are some examples of family goals to help prompt your thinking for your own family:

- Begin weekly family nights for fun and conversation.
- Plan together a family summer vacation.
- Eat five meals per week together at home without TV.
- Have weekly staff meeting talks with spouse about rules, discipline, and parenting ideas.
- Father take daughter on annual "date."
- Plan a mother/son cooking/craft/hobby project.
- Maintain family prayer together at meals.
- Establish monthly contact with a "distant" relative.
- Teach teenagers how to change tires and use jumper cables.

Specific goals we would like to undertake in our family during the next year:

1. _____
2. _____
3. _____
4. _____
5. _____

SECTION IV—HOUSEHOLD GOALS

In considering how well your family handles home responsibilities, answer the following questions and then share your answers with your spouse:

1. Do we make good use of our time around the house? For example, do we watch too much TV? Should we read more or spend more time on hobbies or just relaxing? _____
_____

2. Should we improve our eating habits, with more nutritional foods, fewer sweets, and more meals together at home? _____
_____

3. What home improvement projects would I like to see done this next year?_____
_____
_____

4. Which things in item #3 above might we each take primary responsibility for? Which could we do together? _____
_____
_____

5. Could I or other family members help more by picking things up around the house? Cleaning up? Helping out? _____

_____

_____

6. What chores have been assigned to each family member? Which new chores might it be helpful to assign? _____

_____

_____

After completing and sharing this section with your spouse, spend time discussing three to five specific goals you might focus on during the next several months. (Remember, keep your goals "short term," to be accomplished during the next year.)

The following examples of goals in this area may prompt your own thinking:

- Do family meal planning at weekly staff meetings.
- Wallpaper bathrooms and kitchen.
- Select and purchase a new living room lamp.
- Install deadbolt locks on all exterior doors.
- Develop a landscape plan for the front yard.
- Develop and agree on a list of household chores.
- Refinish the children's furniture as a family project.
- Install lock on bedroom door for privacy.
- Establish one night a week for reading, games, or hobbies.
- Clean out the garage or attic for a garage sale.

Now list the specific goals you would like to undertake in your household during the next year:

1. _____

2. _____

3. _____

4. _____

5. _____

SECTION V—FINANCIAL GOALS

Write down the guidelines and principles for finances you find in the following Scripture verses.

Passage	Notes
1 Timothy 5:8	_____
	_____
	_____
1 Timothy 6:9–11, 17–19	_____
	_____
Romans 13:7–8	_____
	_____
1 Corinthians 16:1–3	_____
	_____

1. What could you do to help or improve your family's financial situation? _____

_____

_____

2. Do you feel your family is spending money where you should be? Do you have any suggestions for a change in priorities?_____

_____

_____

3. Would it be helpful to establish a family budget your family would follow? How might it be done? _____

_____

_____

4. Do you feel you are giving enough to your church, other ministries, or those in need? Any suggestions for increasing your giving?_____

_____

_____

5. Do you feel you should be saving or investing some (or more) money on a consistent basis? Any suggestions for accomplishing this? ___

_____

_____

6. Do you feel you should buy things now and make monthly payments, or save the money first and pay cash? Do you have any suggestions for improvement in this area?_____

_____

_____

7. If something suddenly happened to your spouse and he/she went to be with the Lord, how would you answer the following questions:

- Do you have life insurance? How much? With whom?
- What would you do about funeral arrangements?
- Do you know if and where you (and your spouse) have a savings account, bonds, stocks, property, or other sources of income?

8. Do you know if and to whom you and your spouse owe money?
   a. auto payments
   b. house payments
   c. installment payments
   d. personal loans
   e. bank loans
   f. credit cards
   g. college loans

After completing and sharing this section with your spouse, spend some time discussing three to five specific goals you might focus on during the next several months. (Remember to keep your goals relatively "short term," so they can be accomplished during the next year.)

The following are examples of financial goals that might spur your own ideas:

- Read two books on Christian financial principles.
- Develop a family financial statement.
- Establish a family budget and tracking system.
- Begin systematic giving to our church and special ministries.
- Save 10 percent of your annual household income.
- Attend a "financial freedom" seminar.
- Eliminate all credit card debt by the end of the year.
- Complete work on a family will and/or Living Trust.
- Establish a centralized place for all financial records, deeds, and other important papers.

Now, list the goals you would like to establish for your household finances during the next year.

1. _____

2. _____

3. _____

4. _____

5. _____

You may wish to use the following forms to help you in figuring your family's financial status and indebtedness.

SECTION VI—CAREER/DOMESTIC RESPONSIBILITIES

Answer the following questions as honestly as you can and then share your answers with your spouse:

1. How do you feel about the amount of time each of you gives to your own personal career and/or domestic responsibilities? _____
_____

_____

2. Do you feel pushed constantly, or given so many responsibilities you must neglect your family? Who or what pushes you? How could your spouse help? _____
_____

_____

3. Can you say "no" when you begin to feel over-extended? Can your mate? How could you be more supportive of each other? _____
_____

_____

4. In what ways do you encourage and support your mate in his or her career/domestic responsibilities? How could you improve? _____
_____

_____

5. What can you and your spouse do to continue developing your vocational growth and goals, such as reading, seminars, adult education, projects, and so forth? _____
_____

_____

6. What are three specific things you would like to see accomplished this coming year in your vocation/domestic responsibilities? _____
_____

_____

MONTHLY INCOME & EXPENSES

INCOME PER MONTH _____
  Salary
  Interest _____
  Dividends _____
  Notes _____
  Rents _____

TOTAL GROSS INCOME _____

LESS:
  1. Tithe _____
  2. Tax _____
NET SPENDABLE INCOME _____

  3. Housing _____
    Mortgage _____
    Insurance _____
    Taxes _____
    Electricity _____
    Gas _____
    Water _____
    Sanitation _____
    Telephone _____
    Maintenance _____
    Other _____

  4. Food _____

  5. Automobile _____
    Payments _____
    Gas & Oil _____
    Insurance _____
    License _____
    Taxes _____
    Maint./Repair
      Replacement _____

  6. Insurance _____
    Life _____
    Medical _____
    Other _____

7. Debts _____
  Credit Card
  Loans & Notes _____
  Taxes _____

8. Entertainment & Recreation _____
  Eating Out
  Trips _____
  Baby-sitters _____
  Activities _____
  Vacation _____
  Other _____

9. Clothing _____

10. Savings _____

11. Medical Expenses _____
  Doctor _____
  Dentist _____
  Drugs _____
  Other _____

12. Miscellaneous _____
  Toiletry, cosmetics _____
  Beauty, barber _____
  Laundry, cleaning _____
  Allowances,
    lunches _____
  Subscriptions _____
  Gifts
    (incl. Christmas) _____
  Special Education _____
  Cash _____
  Other _____

TOTAL EXPENSES _____

INCOME VS. EXPENSE _____

Net Spendable Income _____

Less Expenses _____

LIST OF DEBTS

TO WHOM OWED	CONTACT NAME PHONE NUMBER	PAY OFF	PAYMENTS LEFT	MONTHLY PAYMENT	DATE DUE

After completing and sharing this section with your spouse, spend some time discussing three to five specific goals you might set for your family during the next several months. (Remember, make them short-term, to be accomplished during the next year.)

Some examples to prod your thinking include:

- Join a professional organization in your field.
- Participate in a "Parents' Day Out" program.
- Attend a time management seminar.
- Apply for a job transfer or a new job.
- Reorganize your home or office work space for efficiency.
- Participate in career guidance testing.
- Write an article for a professional journal.
- Learn a computer program for home or work use.
- Read helpful articles on delegation or biblical assertiveness to help you say "no."
- Don't bring work home!

Now, indicate the goals you would like to establish in your home concerning career and domestic responsibilities this coming year:

1. _____
2. _____
3. _____
4. _____
5. _____

SECTION VII–PERSONAL/SOCIAL GOALS

1. What areas in your personal life do you feel "strong and secure" in? What areas do you feel need attention, such as physical fitness, social life, intellectual pursuits, or self-discipline? _____

_____

_____

2. What improvements in your physical fitness or appearance would you like to make? _____

_____

_____

3. What couples would you like to see you and your spouse get closer to as friends? _____

_____

_____

4. What could your mate do to make you more at ease in your social life? (For example: *Talk less, talk more, dress better, be on time, not embarrass you with jokes or sarcasm*)_____

_____

_____

5. What do you do to keep your intellectual life sharp? What more could you do?_____

_____

_____

6. Should you be more informed on current events? Improve your eating habits? Cultivate new areas of interest? Get more recreation? _____

_____

_____

After completing and sharing this section with your partner, spend time discussing three to five specific, short-term goals you might implement in your home during the next several months.

These examples of personal/social goals might motivate your thinking along these lines:

- Read six nonfiction books this year.
- Lose a specific amount of weight.
- Develop three new sets of couple friends.
- Exercise fifteen minutes each day.
- Learn to play tennis, golf, or racquetball.
- Read two news-related periodicals weekly.
- Study for and take GRE.
- Learn a foreign language or how to play piano.
- Join a civic club for recreation and new friends.
- Eliminate one irritating habit.

Now list the personal/social goals you would like to establish for your family or yourself during the next year:

1. _____

2. _____

3. _____

4. _____

5. _____

SECTION VIII—MINISTRY GOALS

What guidelines and principles for ministry do you find in the following verses?

Passage	Notes
1 Timothy 2:1-7	_____
	_____
1 Timothy 4:1-16	_____
	_____
Matthew 28:18-20	_____
	_____
Romans 15:1-6	_____
	_____

1. Based on your life journey so far, what are some dreams you have about how God might want to involve you in ministry to others? _____

_____

_____

2. Are there particular aspects of church involvement you might enjoy, such as choir, Bible study, children's activities, or being an usher, teaching a class, or serving on a committee? _____

_____

_____

3. What ideas do you have for ministry together as a couple? _____

_____

_____

4. What special talents, gifts, training, or life experiences do you see in your spouse that could be a blessing to others? _____

_____

_____

5. How might your home become a place of ministry to other couples, families, children, or teenagers? _____

_____

_____

6. How could God now involve you in helping other couples with their own "pursuit of intimacy" journeys? _____

_____

_____

After completing and sharing this section with your spouse, spend time discussing three to five specific goals you might implement during the next several months (short-term, of course, to be accomplished during the next year).

Read the following examples of ministry goals to spur your own thinking:

- Become a "mentor" couple for troubled marriages or engaged couples.
- Volunteer as a Sunday school worker.
- Spend a week of vacation doing mission work.
- Begin a couple's "Pursuit of Intimacy" study at home or church.
- Join the church choir, prayer ministry, or other program.
- Start a Christmas "praise" letter to family and friends.
- Start a once-a-month dinner for neighborhood couples.
- Memorize verses for a gospel presentation.

PLANNING FOR ACTION

Now that you've completed the eight sections on setting specific goals for yourself and your family, you're ready to develop an "Action Plan." Take one category at a time, and, on the Goal Setting Worksheet on the next page, restate your three to five goals in the "What" (Objective) column.

Next, discuss the Plan ("How"), to determine how you will accomplish each goal. Finally, discuss a Schedule ("When"), that is, a deadline for implementing or completing the project (for example, finish wallpapering the bath-

GOAL SETTING WORKSHEET
"Where there is no Vision, People Perish"—Proverbs 29:18 (KJV)

Period covered ———— to ———— Prepared by ————————————

Goal Setting Areas	What (Objectives)	How (Plan)	When (Schedule)
Spiritual			
Marriage			
Family			
Household			
Financial			
Career			
Personal/Social			
Ministry			

room by March 1), or establish a recurring time commitment (for example, Marriage Staff Meetings weekly on Thursdays for lunch, 11:30–1:00 P.M.).

Work your way through each of the eight sections in this same manner, remembering that a goal needs these three key elements in order to stir vision and give purposeful direction:

WHAT—do I want to see accomplished? Being as specific as possible makes a goal "measurable" and "observable" (in other words, "becoming more spiritual" is too vague and undefined; "establishing a morning devotional time" is more defined and workable).

HOW—will I go about accomplishing the "what"? Deciding on a specific plan or method gives additional definition to my goal, so I know when I've accomplished it (for example, I'll have weekday devotions using the *Intimate Moments* devotional guide).

WHEN—will this "how" be done? If it's a daily or weekly goal, time must be allocated in my schedule (for example, devotional time using *Intimate Moments* scheduled Monday–Friday from 7:00–7:30 A.M.). If your goal is not a recurring one, then a completion date needs to be set for the task (for example, I'll finish painting the kitchen by August 4).

As a last step in helping you organize your goals that have weekly time commitments, we suggest developing a weekly planning schedule, possibly one for the husband and one for the wife. Your schedules might look something like this:

Husband's Weekly Planning Schedule

Time	Sun	Mon	Tues	Wed	Thurs	Fri	Sat
6:00 A.M.							
7:00 A.M.	Couple devotions using *Intimate Moments* book						
8:00 A.M.							
	Church						
Noon			Career Development Lunch Meeting		Marriage Staff Meeting		
6:00 P.M.		Exercise		Exercise		Exercise	
7:00 P.M.		Weekdays—Family Evening Meals Together					
8:00 P.M.		Family Night Activities with Kids				Couple Date or Social Time with Other Couple	

Wife's Weekly Planning Schedule

Time	Sun	Mon	Tues	Wed	Thurs	Fri	Sat
6:00 A.M.							
7:00 A.M.		Couple devotions using *Intimate Moments* book					
8:00 A.M.				Parents' Day Out Program			
	Church						
Noon			Volunteer Work at Church or Local Hospital		Marriage Staff Meeting		
6:00 P.M.		Exercise		Exercise		Exercise	
7:00 P.M.		Weekdays—Family Evening Meals Together					
8:00 P.M.		Family Night Activities with Kids				Couple Date or Social Time with Other Couple	

You may wish to use the following WEEKLY PLANNING SCHEDULE Sheet, or you may wish to purchase or devise one of your own. What is important is having some method to keep track of commitments so your family doesn't lose sight of their newly established goals.

FOLLOW-UP PLAN

Annual Goal Setting.

Usually, we recommend a series of one-year goals. Longer range goals, such as buying a house or a wife quitting work at some future date, should be addressed but then broken down into what can be accomplished this year. Many couples use the week between Christmas and New Year's as their goal-setting time. Some couples use the school year as their annual time frame and begin their new goals each September. You might schedule your goal-setting time over a weekend without the children or schedule some time over several days. The important issue is to begin!

Quarterly "Check-ups."

Once you've written your annual goals, plan a few hours quarterly to review and do some "fine-tuning." An extended, leisurely breakfast or dinner for the two of you works well, giving you time to review completed goals

WEEKLY PLANNING SCHEDULE

Prepared by: _____
Date: _____

	Sunday	Monday	Tuesday	Wednesday	Thursday	Friday	Saturday
5							
6							
7							
8							
9							
10							
11							
Noon							
1							
2							
3							
4							
5							
6							
7							
8							
9							
10							
11							
12							

and discuss the next quarter's emphasis. Focus positively on the progress you've made, not on what hasn't been done.

Weekly Staff Meeting Reviews/Family Nights.

With your written goals in hand and time frames established for their implementation, you have a considerable amount of material for your weekly marriage staff meetings. Whenever appropriate, you might also focus on specific goals during your Family Night time to involve your older children and teenagers in establishing a "vision" for your family.

Scripture Journaling—Amos 3:3

Can two walk together, unless they are agreed?

Implied in this "walk together" is agreeing on where you're going. Do you recall a time when you and your partner had real agreement about a goal you were working toward? Do you remember the emotional involvement you felt, the excitement, perhaps even the sense that this project was "bigger than both of you?" Perhaps you were preparing for your first child, or helping your partner finish college, or building your own home, or starting a business together. How did it feel to see that goal accomplished? How did you feel toward your spouse? Write about that experience here. _____

_____

_____

Think about what's different in accomplishing a goal "alone" versus sharing in its accomplishment with your spouse. Do you recall an incident when you felt you were struggling alone to meet a goal? Write about how you felt then compared with the feeling you had when you and your spouse shared an important goal. _____

_____

This blessing of not being alone in your struggles and journey is part of God's extraordinary plan for marriage. Tell God how you feel about His unique plan for your marriage and the special spouse He has provided for you.

Heavenly Father,
When I think about my marriage and the partner You've given me, I feel

_____

_____

_____

_____

MARRIAGE STAFF MEETING _____

Use this staff meeting to incorporate your discussion of goals into your weekly sessions. Discuss practical details, such as 1) Will we both bring our goals to our meetings? 2) Shall we review each major category each week? 3) Will we divide the eight categories so that each of us "monitors" progress on four of them and initiates discussion as appropriate?

Be careful not to use these times to be *critical* of the progress or *lack* of progress made on specific goals. Keep a positive, upbeat attitude; focus on the positives of what you have accomplished, not the negatives. You can't overdo expressing appreciation for what has been accomplished. Make it a point to put your gratitude into words. Be as specific as possible. For example: "Having our morning devotions has been really special to me." "I'm excited about paying off our credit card debt." "I'm looking forward to our scheduled get-away weekend."

—— *For Group Discussion* ——

Continue to have couples share their genograms during your group sessions. Encourage members to comfort one another for childhood losses that need to be mourned (Matt. 5:4). The group leader might create an atmosphere of increased emotional awareness by asking questions such as these: "What do you feel for John and Nancy as you hear about their pain? What would you like to say to them?" Give members an opportunity to express their empathy and understanding. Have spouses share their empathy last, offering reassuring words and hugs as appropriate.

As couples complete their marriage goal-setting weekends, urge them to give testimonies about what they learned about each other, their relationship, and the direction of their marriage. You might begin by asking them these questions: "What one particular goal are you most excited about pursuing? What new insight did you gain about your spouse? How does it feel to have a sense of common direction? In what specific goal are you looking forward to being of support to your spouse?"

Chapter Fifteen

— ■ —

WALK TOGETHER THROUGH THE STAGES OF MARRIAGE INTIMACY

Bill and Mindy had been married nearly ten years and still didn't have the slightest idea what their intimate journey was all about. When they reluctantly began counseling, there was little joy in their faces. Worse, they made constant digs at each other, barely suppressing their mutual animosity. Obviously, the romance had gone out of their marriage years ago.

"No matter what I do, she makes me feel mad or guilty," said Bill, a large man with beefy arms, who settled into his chair like a sea captain ready to steer his vessel. A thatch of red hair tumbled over his ruddy forehead as he nervously tweaked his bulbous, W. C. Fields nose. His eyes squinting out from little pockets of flesh might have been merry if his mouth weren't turned down in a hangdog grimace.

"Guilty? How?" David Ferguson queried.

"How? I dunno. She doesn't like anything I do. If I settle down to watch TV, she's on my case. If I fix myself a snack, she says I'm too fat. If I hang out with the neighbors, she says I'm wasting time. I can't win, no matter what I do."

"How would you like Mindy to react?"

He gave her a quick glance, weighing his words. "I guess I'd like her to let me be. Stop making me feel guilty. Let me watch TV, fix a snack, or hang out with the neighbors without making me feel like I'm a bad person."

"What do you say about that, Mindy?"

"I say, practice what you preach!" Mindy sat primly in her chair, her purse in her lap, her torso arched forward slightly, as if she were ready to bolt should the conversation become too uncomfortable. A slim woman with features a bit too chiseled, she wore a tailored suit and her hair upswept in a classic style. In every way, she and Bill couldn't have been more unalike.

"Bill says I nag him about everything, but, believe me, he has his own way of expressing his displeasure," she declared, lifting her chin indignantly. "When I want him to take me somewhere he grunts and groans and makes my life miserable, so I end up wishing I'd left him home. But, when I want to go to my painting classes or see a concert with my friends from church, he acts like an old wounded dog. Mopes around, his chin dragging the ground, muttering to himself. He just infuriates me!"

"Is there anything you enjoy doing together?"

"Well, yes," said Bill. "We enjoy going to church. That's the only time we seem to get along."

"Only because we're good at pretending," countered Mindy. "If folks knew what we were really like, the way we bicker and quarrel, they'd probably turn their backs on us for good."

"Tell me," said David. "Is that how you see God too?"

"I guess so," Mindy admitted. "Everything I do, I think, *This will make Bill mad at me*, or *this will make God mad at me*. And just thinking that makes me mad. Stupid, huh?"

"No. Just human," said David with a little smile.

"I guess that describes me too," said Bill. "I figure nothing I do will make Mindy happy, and probably nothing I do will make God happy either. So why try? So, I get my shots in first, complaining about Mindy before she nags at me. And I try to keep God from getting on my case by going to church. But I suspect He sees through all that."

"So you'd have to say you don't get much joy out of your relationship with Mindy or your relationship with God?"

Bill shrugged. "The idea of joy never really entered my mind in either case."

Mindy nodded. "Joy is the last word I'd use to describe our relationship. And as for God . . ."

"What word would describe your relationship with Him?"

"Duty, maybe. Or obligation. I suppose that sounds very shallow. I don't mean it to. I do love God and want to serve Him, just as I suppose, down deep, I really love Bill. Only, somehow, we've gotten into this awful rut . . ."

"Would you like to get out of that rut?" asked David.

"Sure," said Bill. "Only how?"

"It begins with telling yourself the truth. Seeing things from God's perspective. Learning His design for each stage of your marriage. Christ wants to walk you through it, step by step. He wants to make your lives—and your marriage—abundant. He offers you the joy of being loved unconditionally, accepted completely, and forgiven freely. Let yourselves feel the freedom of His love on an emotional level and you'll experience real joy. Gradually, the joy Christ pours into your emotional cup will spill over to your mate, and you'll begin to experience what love and marriage were meant to be. Does that make sense?"

Bill rubbed his bulbous nose. "Man, it's worth a try."

Mindy smiled for the first time. "I don't know if the word *joy* is in my vocabulary, but it would be good to feel loved and accepted the way you described."

A few months later Bill and Mindy came in grinning like the proverbial Cheshire Cat. Like awkward, self-conscious youngsters, they were spilling over with enthusiasm, both eager to share the events of the past months.

"I can't say it's perfect—no marriage is—but things are definitely different," Mindy said, her face flushed. "Bill and I used to nag each other without even thinking about it, like we were on automatic-pilot or something. Now, when I start to say something, I catch myself, and so does he."

"She's more like the woman I married—a woman I can live with," said Bill, his eyes twinkling like merry half-moons. "We used to concentrate on the bad stuff, and I guess it blinded us to the good stuff. Now, we're seeing things more realistically."

"We're concentrating more on God and His love, too," said Mindy. "Always before, I knew in my head that God loved me, but I never let myself feel His love."

"In the past, our whole marriage was based on giving each other a hard time," said Bill. "I'm not saying we don't still get angry with each other, but we're defusing the hot buttons. We don't need to raise the red flags over every little slight or difference of opinion anymore. In fact, we even find ourselves wanting to do nice things for each other." Bill laughed heartily. "And that's a first in both our books!"

Bill and Mindy are just beginning to learn the truth of what God designed marriage to be—a life of "serving one another, as good stewards of the manifold grace of God" (1 Peter 4:10 NASB). Serving others—looking past our own needs to the needs of another—is characteristically Christ-like (Phil. 2:4). It requires looking beyond their faults to see their need—a Christ-like miracle Bill and Mindy are now experiencing in their own marriage. As husbands and wives, we've all been called to just such a life of caring and serving, beginning first at home with our families, and then extending outward to others.

In this chapter, we will walk you through the four stages of your marriage—beginning with New Love, then Shared Love, to Mature Love, and finally, Renewed Love. We will help you to 1) explore and resolve unfinished business from the *past*, 2) maximize *present* enjoyment, and 3) plan ahead for *future* challenges.

As you think about what lies ahead for you in your marriage journey, complete the following statements:

I'm particularly looking forward to _____

_____

_____

I can imagine that my spouse and I will face real challenges concerning

_____

_____

What insights do these Scripture passages offer as they relate to your marriage and family journey?

Proverbs 18:22

_____

_____

Proverbs 31:10–12

_____

_____

Psalm 127:3–5

_____

_____

THE STAGES OF A MARRIAGE

Marriages go through several typical stages—first growing, then contracting. A couple marries and soon children are born and grow older, then mature and leave the nest to begin their own adult lives. The parents are alone again, until eventually one spouse dies, leaving the other alone, thus completing the cycle.

The concept of family life cycles provides more than a descriptive identification of families at different periods of their married lives. It is a frame of reference that allows us to identify key "stages" that have an important effect on individual behavior and interaction within the family.

As the cycle shifts, for example, from newly married to the child-rearing stage, couples are required to modify their roles. Whereas once they were only husband and wife, now they're both mates and parents. As their lives undergo significant changes, they must face different demands, learn new skills, and develop new attitudes.

Family life-cycle stages help explain the constantly changing demands and expectations of family interaction. Being aware of these stages helps us to be prepared for the inevitable challenges and stresses accompanying them. We use the following four stages to help couples prepare for life's inevitable stresses:

Stage I	**NEW LOVE**	The honeymoon begins, and two individuals start blending their lives together.
Stage II	**SHARED LOVE**	The first child arrives, and love must now be shared.
Stage III	**MATURE LOVE**	The first child becomes a teen, and love had better be mature!
Stage IV	**RENEWED LOVE**	The last child is launched into the real world, and love can now be renewed!

Reflect on your thoughts and feelings considering these four stages and complete the following statements:

Stage I: Some of the challenges I would expect (or have experienced) moving from a courtship into a committed marriage relationship include

_____

_____

Stage II: Adding school-age children to the family system would tend to create additional stress, such as _____

_____

Stage III: The arrival of teenagers might add (or DID add!) the extra pressures of_____

_____

Stage IV: Being "alone" together as a couple in an "empty nest" could bring the additional challenges of _____

_____

Remembering that because of divorce, remarriage, blended families, and other unique circumstances, few families move through the family life cycle in ways that are "typical," take note of the *average* periods of time designated to each cycle in the chart below:

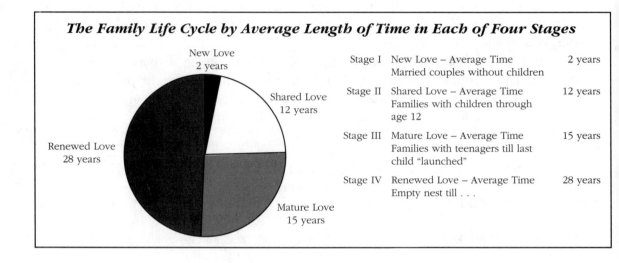

The Family Life Cycle by Average Length of Time in Each of Four Stages

New Love
2 years

Shared Love
12 years

Renewed Love
28 years

Mature Love
15 years

Stage I	New Love – Average Time Married couples without children	2 years
Stage II	Shared Love – Average Time Families with children through age 12	12 years
Stage III	Mature Love – Average Time Families with teenagers till last child "launched"	15 years
Stage IV	Renewed Love – Average Time Empty nest till . . .	28 years

Realizing that no family fits into these stages and time frames perfectly, think about your marriage in a general sense and reflect on both your past and future. Then answer the questions below.

	Challenges we faced (or expect to face)	**Positive benefits we experienced (or hope to experience)**

Stage I—New Love
How long do you expect to be (or were you) in this stage?
_____ Years

Stage II—Shared Love
How long have you been (or were you) in this stage, i.e., with pre-school and elementary-age children?
_____ Years

Stage III—Mature Love _____

How long will you   _____
be (or were you)   _____
in this stage,   _____
i.e., with   _____
teenagers or   _____
young adults   _____
at home?   _____
_____ Years   _____

Stage IV—Renewed Love _____

How long have you   _____
been (or hope to   _____
be) in this stage,   _____
i.e., empty nest?   _____
_____ Years   _____

The "Teachable Moment"

Individuals and families have "critical" moments when they are ready to face new challenges. Any sooner and they're ill-prepared; any later and the "unfinished business" hinders them. It is the same in your developmental journey as a couple. As you experience healing from past hurts and establish present ongoing disciplines (such as confession/forgiveness, prayer, and regular "dates"), you will be ready to face the challenges of an abundant future together.

However, it is important to realize that intimacy needs are greatest at the moments of transition from one stage to another. For example, at Stage I, when a couple has their first child and enters Stage II, the new mother may feel overwhelmed and need extra support and appreciation from her husband, while he may feel rejected and need extra attention and reassurance from his wife.

Each developmental stage requires that a couple adapt, face new challenges, and take on added responsibilities while also seizing unique opportunities. This is the time for couples to draw together and focus on giving to each other in four special ways, elaborated in Chapter 5, that we call "Intimacy Ingredients":

Affectionate Caregiving—emotional caring that reassures a hurting spouse or initiates verbal or physical affection.

Vulnerable Communication—risking openness about feelings, needs, and hurts, secure that I won't be ignored, rejected, or hurt even more.

Joint Accomplishment—closeness that comes from feeling "we" did it! This includes sharing common interests, setting joint goals, or feeling mutual excitement over an event, such as a baby's birth, a son's graduation, or a daughter's wedding.

Mutual Giving—two people thinking more highly of the other than of himself/herself, giving to meet each other's needs, and showing love in ways especially meaningful to the other.

Let's look at an example of how these Intimacy Ingredients might be utilized as a couple moves from Stage I to Stage II in their marriage:

Affectionate Caregiving:	After the arrival of a new baby, the couple returns to affectionately caring for each other as they prioritize their marriage.
Vulnerable Communication:	The couple vulnerably communicates with each other about child-raising issues.
Joint Accomplishment:	The couple jointly accomplishes new divisions of labor brought on by child-raising.
Mutual Giving:	The couple now is free to mutually give to each other in supportive, caring ways in their new role as parents.

In the following pages, we will present practical steps to nurture these ingredients through each developmental stage. Regardless of what stage you are in, you'll find it helpful to work through the material on all four stages, since the effort you put into these challenges now will pay off in the long run.

AN OVERVIEW OF STAGE I—NEW LOVE

When a couple marries, things change. Before, they were together because they loved each other. Now, they are also together because they're *married!* The knowledge that there is a legal and moral tie binding them to each other may create uncertainty over how much they "romantically" love each other. The more a spouse thinks about this "obligation" of marriage, the less likely one thinks of love for his or her partner. Some couples focus so strongly on this sense of obligation, they kill romance and begin to feel trapped in the marriage. Other couples undervalue their commitment and wind up divorced because one or both become romantically displeased with the other.

The tension between romantic attraction and permanent commitment remains throughout marriage. The enduring and fulfilling marriage maintains a balance affirming both truths—underlying love and undying commitment under God.

After the wedding ceremony, newlyweds try desperately to get along, but they come from two different family backgrounds. Sooner or later, one or both will expect the other to do something that is not in line with what he had modeled in his family. During this "honeymoon" phase, both partners will usually give in to appease the other, putting aside their feelings to maintain harmony in the relationship.

The enduring and fulfilling marriage maintains a balance affirming both underlying love and undying commitment under God.

But, as differences become more apparent, tension mounts, conflicts grow, and disillusionment may abound. As disagreements become more frequent, a couple gradually realizes they must meld the rules of two separate families of origin into the rules of their unique marriage. The honeymoon is over, and the challenges of Stage I are underway!

Self-assessment

Check those statements that are "true."

☐ In-laws don't control our schedule, finances, or decisions.

☐ We don't have recurring power struggles over who "wins" in daily decisions.

☐ I am not repeatedly hurt by my spouse not measuring up to my expectations.

☐ We have established our "couple" identity with common interests, couple friends, and our own traditions.

☐ We tend to quickly confess and genuinely forgive each other over inevitable hurts.

☐ We have established a mutually satisfying sexual relationship.

Total: 0–2 checked = major concern
3–4 checked = needs improvement
5–6 checked = good

What steps could you take to correct any of the above that are not yet "true"? _____

_____

What help might you need from your spouse to make each of the above statements "true"? _____

_____

Noted below are practical ideas for maintaining and deepening intimacy during the common challenges in Stage I—New Love:

Affectionate Caregiving—I Care About You

- It is tempting to "let down" on the little expressions of love now that you're married. Review some of your dating habits that you may wish to revive, and recall loving expressions you have neglected to use since your marriage.
- When your partner is upset, anxious, or hurt, don't try to "fix it"; rather, just listen and offer comfort.
- Resist waiting for your partner to take the initiative in verbalizing love or showing affection. You move first!
- Tell your spouse you're sad when he's been hurt or disappointed, because you care . . . because you love him.

Now reflect on your own marriage and complete this statement: I realize I could give more attention and effort to_____

_____

Vulnerable Communication—I Trust You

- Practice open-ended questions—"Share with me something about your day," is better than "How was your day?"
- Make priority time for quiet talks—or the tyranny of other things will crowd them out.
- If you turn first to other family members or friends for advice or comfort, your spouse will feel hurt and left out.
- Encourage conversation about feelings, fears, dreams, and hurts— just listen and care!

In reflecting on my marriage, I realize I could give additional attention and effort to _____

_____

_____

Joint Accomplishment—I Need You

- Develop common interests, hobbies, and fun diversions; don't wait for your partner to come up with ideas; take the initiative!
- Face the challenge of developing a common budget and joint finances.
- Read together a good book on goal setting for the Christian home.
- Creatively share specific areas of appreciation with your spouse, each one of you boldly declaring, "I need you!"

In reflecting on my marriage, I realize I could give additional attention and effort to _____

_____

_____

Mutual Giving—I Love You

- Focus often on the blessings and benefits of God; let gratefulness well up inside and a desire to give will overflow; begin writing down a list of all you are grateful for.
- Resist giving to your partner in ways you would enjoy; give to meet her needs, not yours.
- Review your partner's growing-up years in terms of what he missed out on—appreciation, affection, empathy, among others—and make it your priority to give him what he missed.
- Encourage your partner to share her needs; probe as necessary to discern how you can best demonstrate your love.

In reflecting on my marriage, I realize I could give more attention and effort to _____

_____

_____

AN OVERVIEW OF STAGE II—SHARED LOVE

As newborns arrive and begin to grow, they fortify their parents' belief in the inherent "fallenness" of human beings! Usually, during the child's second year, the couple realizes that the child has a will of his own which differs vastly from the will of his parents. Decisions must be made about when and how to discipline the child.

We humans dislike discipline. It is an emotional issue with a family history—actually, *two* family histories. As a child, each partner was disciplined differently, for different reasons, and each one has strong feelings about the way his parents disciplined.

Thus, the terrible two's are more likely to be terrible for the parents than for the child. New and highly emotional decisions about child rearing intensify conflict over who makes the rules, and may even destroy the previous balance of power.

When the child is five or six, he enters school, and suddenly the family, through the child, is on public display. How the child behaves reflects on the parents, and negative reports from school authorities may rekindle open conflict between the parents.

When a child enters school, time schedules change and adjustments must be made. Both husband and wife may be heavily involved in their careers while juggling too many family responsibilities. Often, lonely and hungry for closeness but with little time for intimacy, they may be ripe for an affair.

Self-assessment

Check those statements that are "true."

☐ We have recognized and overcome some of the hidden agendas or "expectations" we each brought from our childhood.

☐ Neither work pressures nor the children's needs hinder us from routinely setting aside special times just for us.

☐ I've ceased any doubting over my spouse being God's special provision just for me.

☐ My partner's peculiar imperfections are not stealing my joy in marriage.

☐ We seem to focus more on giving to each other than being preoccupied with what we're "getting."

☐ I've come to see many of my shortcomings and how my spouse balances me with his strengths.

Total: 0–2 checked = major concern
         3–4 checked = needs improvement
         5–6 checked = good

What steps could you take to correct any of the above that are not yet "true"? _____

_____

What help might you need from your spouse to make each of the above statements "true"? _____

_____

Noted below are practical ideas for maintaining and deepening intimacy during the common challenges in Stage II—Shared Love:

Affectionate Caregiving—I Care About You

- Prioritize couple "dates" for special romantic times alone, meaning no kids, no friends, just the two of you!
- Express empathy and compassion when your partner has had a rough day.
- Don't forget special gifts, love notes, and "I was thinking of you" phone calls.
- Be ready and willing to "help out" with expanded responsibilities, even if they are not on your "list."

In reflecting on my marriage, I realize I could give more attention and effort to _____

_____

_____

Vulnerable Communication—I Trust You

- Take time to share together the joys of watching your child grow up; make family times a priority in your lives.
- Be vulnerable in expressing needs for affection and sexual intimacy.
- Save any criticisms or concerns about parenting decisions until you can deal with them privately, maybe at a weekly staff meeting.

- Affirm each other openly with appreciation and support in front of your children, such as, "We have a special dad, kids."

In reflecting on my marriage, I realize I could give more attention and effort to _____

_____

_____

Joint Accomplishment—I Need You

- Take time privately to develop an attitude of oneness about parenting goals and discipline plans.
- Read together good books on parenting and discuss them. We recommend *The Father Book* by Frank Minirth, Brian Newman, & Paul Warren (Nashville: Thomas Nelson, 1992), or *Things That Go Bump in the Night* by Paul Warren & Frank Minirth (Nashville: Thomas Nelson, 1992).
- Develop family friendships with positive influences for your children.
- Develop new common interests or hobbies to encourage time together as a couple.

In reflecting on my marriage, I realize I could give more attention and effort to _____

_____

_____

Mutual Giving—I Love You

- Share parenting responsibilities in order to have some individual relaxation time or favorite diversions.
- Creatively plan for romantic times ALONE in your own home.
- Always have a fun get-away time scheduled to look forward to.
- Don't sweat the small stuff; give in to each other in the minor parenting decisions.

In reflecting on my marriage, I realize I could give more attention and effort to _____

_____

_____

AN OVERVIEW OF STAGE III—MATURE LOVE

"Mature love" describes this stage based on the maturity you'll need to successfully navigate the countless competing demands and challenges. The arrival of teenagers highlights the beginning of this stage. Be prepared for your love to be tested as those once lovable youngsters change overnight into moody, uncommunicative strangers who don't want to be hugged and are anything but appreciative.

During this stage, parents are often at a crossroad in their own careers, and struggling to make ends meet just as college expenses loom on the horizon. Many mothers are reentering the work force, sometimes leaving teens or other family members to care for the household.

In short, adolescence is a time when family rules are challenged, family structure is changed, intimacy patterns are disrupted, and individual concerns over sexual identity and work identity are paramount for both children and adults. No wonder adolescence is a time of lower marriage satisfaction for both husbands and wives. With several children in the home, this stage can be extended for a long period of time, often compounding the stress.

Self-assessment

Check those statements that are "true."

- [ ] Each of us has established a fulfilling life through our unique gifts, talents, hobbies, and skills.
- [ ] We work well together as a team in dealing with our kids, so they are not able to manipulate us against one another.
- [ ] I have come to recognize the imperfections in my growing-up years, have felt the feelings accompanying those years, and have received understanding and comfort from my spouse.
- [ ] We freely give priority time to our marriage without complaining.
- [ ] Our kids are becoming our friends as we release them to live their own lives.
- [ ] We have addressed the pending loss of our children, jobs, and parents by deepening our couple relationships and new dreams with each other.

Total: 0–2 checked = major concern
3–4 checked = needs improvement
5–6 checked = good

What steps could you take to correct any of the above that are not yet "true"? _____

_____

_____

What help might you need from your spouse to make each of the above statements "true"? _____

_____

_____

Noted below are practical ideas for maintaining and deepening intimacy during the common challenges in Stage III—Mature Love:

Affectionate Caregiving—I Care About You

- Set aside time for weekend get-aways for just the two of you, to rekindle romance and refocus your goals.
- Connect with each other emotionally, spiritually, physically, as you part in the morning and reunite in the evening.
- Role-model open affection to your adolescents, as you sit together, hold hands, cuddle, and embrace.
- Practice open apologies when you've clearly been impatient, intolerant, or insensitive to your spouse or children.

In reflecting on my marriage, I realize I could give more attention and effort to _____

_____

_____

Vulnerable Communication—I Trust You

- Don't keep your seemingly "little" joys and blessings to yourself; share them with your partner. Each of you will benefit from positive remembrances.
- As you mentally begin your "mid-life" evaluation of goals, dreams, and disappointments, set aside quality time for sharing them with an attentive, supportive spouse.
- Begin talking about life "beyond the children," beginning to develop goals and plans for the empty nest.
- Together as a couple, seek the input and counsel of other families

who have "survived" this stage; the value of their perspective and mentoring can be tremendous.

In reflecting on my marriage, I realize I could give more attention and effort to _____

_____

_____

Joint Accomplishment—I Need You

- Continue Marriage Staff Meetings to plan your parenting strategies, developing oneness and resolving problems as they arise.
- Because adolescents can drain your emotional and physical resources without showing much appreciation, don't worry about "overdosing" your spouse with lots of expressed appreciation.
- From time to time, involve one another in your favorite activities, hobbies, or diversions; watch out for self-reliant, independent living!
- Support each other empathetically; as your spouse reflects on regrets and disappointments, express comfort, such as, "Honey, I hurt for you that you're so discouraged today. I love you."

In reflecting on my marriage, I realize I could give more attention and effort to _____

_____

_____

Mutual Giving—I Love You

- Review your partner's unique intimacy needs and determine to meet those needs.
- Stay attuned to your partner's particular "down" cycles, focusing on God to meet your needs so you can be supportive during these difficult times.
- Pray together often during critical times of decision and discipline, trusting your children to the Lord.
- Be especially caring and empathetic toward your partner's childhood reflections, since pain and regrets may surface as parents age and die.

In reflecting on my marriage, I realize I could give more attention and effort to _____

_____

_____

AN OVERVIEW OF STAGE IV—RENEWED LOVE

In Stage IV, the longest of all stages, couples return to where they began twenty or thirty years earlier. The nest is empty and, for better or worse, they are alone together again. Now, over the next decades, they work to readjust their relationship, see their adult children marry, and most become grandparents.

As adolescents become adults and leave the nest, some parents may find their offspring's move away from home traumatic, especially if that child has been the emotional focus of one or both parents. Once all the children have left home, most couples spend twenty-plus years together. Some divorce, explaining that they only stayed together for the children.

When a couple's children marry and have children, the couple must accept changes in the structure of their own family. For some parents who have already "let their child go," the transition to being a grandparent is easy. However, grandparents who have kept tight control of a child, even after he's married, often find themselves caught up in the affairs of their child's family. They need to accept their status as advisors and peers to their children, rather than try to run their adult child's life. It is especially dangerous when grandparents form a coalition with the grandchild against the parent.

One of the biggest struggles of this stage is satisfying needs for a "new vision," or purpose, in living. Stage IV couples need a fresh vision (Prov. 29:18)!

In a social system that works against age, and with standards of living eroding drastically as retirement savings dwindle, retired couples need to gain a sense of mastery over their lives, and a feeling that they are meaningfully contributing to their world.

Self-assessment

Check those statements that are "true."

☐ Are you free from a preoccupation with age and health that would keep you from enjoying life?

☐ Is your marriage close so that your children leaving the nest won't pose a threat to your happiness?

□ Are you careful not to lead separate, overly self-reliant lives that would hinder your intimacy?

□ Are you able to experience the simple joy of being alive today?

□ Are you able to mutually share what it means to be a friend with your grown children?

□ Are you able to wake up to a fresh vision and goals for the rest of your life together?

Total: 0–2 checked = major concern
3–4 checked = needs improvement
5–6 checked = good

What steps could you take to correct any of the above that are not yet "true"? _____

_____

What help might you need from your spouse to make each of the above statements "true"? _____

_____

Noted below are practical ideas for maintaining and deepening intimacy during the common challenges in Stage IV—Renewed Love:

Affectionate Caregiving—I Care About You

- Begin discussion and planning for a "second honeymoon" trip to rekindle romance and celebrate your new freedom!
- Creatively expressing your love and appreciation never grows old, so send a card, leave a note, buy a gift, or send flowers.
- Read together Christian books on renewing romance and sexual intimacy. We recommend *Love Life for Every Married Couple* by Ed Wheat (Grand Rapids: Zondervan, 1980).
- Respectful, appreciative comments in public about your spouse help communicate a powerful message that he or she is special.

In reflecting on my marriage, I realize I could give more attention and effort to _____

_____

_____

Vulnerable Communication—I Trust You

- Expressing empathetic concern to your spouse encourages him to share his anxieties and fears. For example: "You seem a little anxious about something, sweetheart. I'd sure like to listen and understand and give whatever support I can."
- During quiet times together, reflect on fond memories and your gratitude for what you have; it helps avoid becoming negative and seeing life as "half empty."
- Dream together about things you would still like to do and mutually support each other in accomplishing them.
- Openly sharing your spiritual journey and devotional life creates important opportunities for closeness, prayer, and emotional support.

In reflecting on my marriage, I realize I could give more attention and effort to _____

_____

_____

Joint Accomplishment—I Need You

- Explore together new opportunities for ministry to others, making your experience, time, talents, and gifts available for God's use and direction.
- Discuss together and finalize financial and other plans related to your future, retirement, aging, and death.
- Rekindle some common interests or hobbies you used to share.
- Cultivate two or three new couple friendships each year to expand your horizons and keep life interesting.

In reflecting on my marriage, I realize I could give more attention and effort to _____

_____

_____

Mutual Giving—I Love You

- Give your partner time, encouragement, and "permission" to pursue individual interests, hobbies, or goals.
- Supporting each other in family traditions, holidays, and grandparenting times will draw you together. Don't "delegate" this role to your spouse!
- Gently comforting your spouse during times of life's inevitable losses will deepen your closeness.
- Continue giving to meet your partner's unique intimacy needs, including attention, acceptance, affection, appreciation, and respect.

In reflecting on my marriage, I realize I could give more attention and effort to _____

_____

_____

Scripture Journaling—I Chronicles 12:32

. . . of the sons of Issachar who had understanding of the times, to know what Israel ought to do . . .

The sons of Issachar, as part of David's mighty men of Hebron, understood the times, so they would know what Israel should do. What did David's men need to understand about their times? How does looking around to understand the times help prepare us to know what to do? Discuss how the absolutes of God's Word have a timeless relevance. How are the principles of God's Word relevant as we seek to understand our own times? How does "understanding the times" fit the concept of marriage stages? Express your thoughts here:_____

_____

_____

_____

MARRIAGE STAFF MEETING

Review together your initial reflections on which of these four stages you and your spouse fit in. Discuss such questions as these:

- Do we seem to have some "catching up" to do in resolving issues we missed in previous stages?
- What positive feelings do you have and what opportunities do you see as we anticipate this intimate journey?

Now, go through your materials on each stage and share them with each other. Then discuss these questions:

- What are some specific follow-up steps you could take to help address each challenge? (Stress "ownership" of your own responsibilities, such as: "I realize I could make more effort to creatively express my love for you through notes, gifts, and endearing words.")
- What specific areas of help would you appreciate your spouse considering? (Emphasize "speaking the truth in love"—Eph. 4:15. For example: "I'd sure enjoy it if we could plan some fun romantic times to look forward to.")

As you go through each stage, identify definite follow-up goals that will become a part of your marriage goal-setting plan.

Lifestyle Discipline:

The discipline of vision is crucial to marriage closeness. We each tend to look back at the negative factors in our lives—what we missed, what went wrong, where we failed. Or we look at the future with anxiety and fear.

Having clear-cut, positive goals to look forward to spurs HOPE, which prompts FAITH ("Faith is the substance of things hoped for"—Heb. 11:1). You can't have faith if you're not hoping for something! So, maintain your goal-setting habit!

—— For Group Discussion ——

Groups will often include couples at all different stages. After identifying where each couple is in their journey, have them relate key challenges they faced in Stages I, II, III, and IV. Discuss the benefits of "looking ahead," so couples can plan to attack the challenges that inevitably come.

You might wish to have a time of vulnerable sharing of significant issues each member wants to assume responsibility for. For example: "I realize I need to express my love for my spouse more often." "I realize I need to listen more to what my partner is really saying." "I realize I need to confess the anger I've been feeling toward my mate and ask forgiveness."

You may want to give couples time to pray together and simply tell God, in the presence of their spouse, what they've just told the group. (For instance: "Dear God, I want to confess the anger I've had toward my spouse, and I ask You to forgive me. Free me of a critical spirit. Help me to be more loving and understanding. Amen.")

One other option may be to have men pray together and women pray together, especially as members become accountable to one another.

Close the session by having each member reflect on some positive aspect of the future, and then complete this statement: "When I think about the stages of my marriage, I'm really looking forward to_____

_____

_____

_____

_____

Chapter Sixteen

———— ■ ————

BECOME FRIENDS, LOVERS, AND SAINTS THROUGH INTIMACY DISCIPLINES

Today, after completing their Intimacy Therapy session, Marla and Jimmy Carlton know what it means to enjoy a healthy, nurturing, intimate relationship. Of course, they're still as different as night and day—Marla a bit too quick to verbalize her opinions, and Jimmy a bit too reticent to express his feelings. But they are growing closer every day.

And while their marriage isn't perfect or trouble-free, they have learned how to heal their hurts, express their neediness, and give to meet each other's needs. As they consistently practice Intimacy Disciplines, they are becoming the friends, lovers, and saints God desires them to be.

What they've learned, you can learn. No matter how troubled your marriage has been, no matter how alienated you may have felt, there is hope. Believe it. You can experience new levels of intimacy in your relationship. We have seen it happen in the lives of hundreds of couples over the years. It can happen for you too.

But, as you might expect, it doesn't happen simply by reading one book, or even doing exercises in a workbook. To truly transform a marriage into the relationship God designed it to be, a couple must put into practice the Intimacy Disciplines we've noted throughout this book. So, come. Let's complete our journey.

FRIENDS, LOVERS, AND SAINTS

It shouldn't surprise us that the Triune God who manifests Himself as Father, Son, and Holy Spirit would also create people with that same triune complexity. We recall that God formed man's BODY out of the dust of the ground, and breathed into him the SPIRIT of life and man became a living SOUL (Gen. 2:7 paraphrased).

In order for us to relate intimately with our spouse, we must do so on all three levels. That means friends sharing friendship, bonding together in common interests and goals as we cherish and support each other. It also means lovers sharing passion and enjoying each other physically as we "become one flesh." And it means saints sharing fellowship as we bask in the awe and wonder of Christ's transforming grace.

Let's look more closely at each of these three areas and the lifestyle behaviors you can adopt to accomplish each one in your own marriage.

FRIENDS

FRIENDS make time for each other.

You build closeness by enjoying memorable times together. Review some of the activities below that help you build friendship with your mate:

- **Date Again**—return to the "little things" you enjoyed while dating—a special restaurant, "our" song, favorite perfume, romantic walks, sitting together, holding hands, talking by a cozy fire until midnight.

- **Develop Common Interests**—take turns picking out fun things to do—sports, hobbies, cultural events; just enjoy being together!

- **30 Second Phone Calls**—telephone occasionally and just say, "Hi, honey, I was thinking about you and just wanted to say I love you and am looking forward to seeing you tonight."

- **Initiate-Initiate-Initiate!**—touch, caress, give hugs, express appreciation, verbalize your love, send notes, share sexually.

- **Creative Dating**—"capture" your spouse for a surprise picnic, or overnight stay at a romantic hotel, or a candlelight dinner at home alone.

- **Welcome Home**—always greet your spouse eagerly when you arrive home; touch, smile, and speak, communicating "I'm glad to see you!"

As friends, an important aspect of nurturing intimacy in your relationship will be regular Marriage Staff Meetings. Unless you deliberately set aside time for each other each week, you'll discover that work, child-raising, carpools, and a myriad other disruptions and distractions will keep you apart. Plan to spend about two hours together each week. Schedule a time; don't leave it to chance. Write it on your calendar, and make it a priority; protect your time together from phone calls, visitors, and other inevitable interruptions.

Here's a typical agenda. Fill in the blanks to make it fit your own marital needs and circumstances.

MARRIAGE "STAFF MEETINGS"

Calendar Coordination—for the coming week. *(What's planned? Who's going where? What activities are scheduled? When's our next couple date? How about calendaring in some of our lovemaking times?)*

Our schedule for this coming week includes _____

_____

_____

_____

_____

Discuss Family Goals—monitoring progress and working together. *(Written annual goals should be broken down into quarterly/monthly target dates. How can we ease a tight budget? What's our next major household expenditure? Shall we schedule vacation plans? How are our personal goals progressing—diet, exercise, reading, making new friends?)*

Goals we should discuss this week as a family include _____

_____

_____

Parenting Plans—Plan and be united, or the kids will divide and conquer. *(Discuss discipline issues, what's working, what isn't. Plan family times together, plus quality times with each child. Review schedules, responsibilities—who needs help or a break? Set goals for your children's behavior, attitudes, and responsibilities.)*

Some of the issues we need to discuss, schedules we need to plan, and goals we need to set for our children include _____

_____

_____

Listening Times—one or the other may just need to talk. *(Share stresses involving work or friends, hopes and dreams, feelings and insights, concerns and fears. Don't argue; give undivided attention, empathy, support, and eye contact.)*

(Wife) Some of the things I'd just like to talk about and have you listen to include _____

_____

(Husband) Some of the things I'd just like to talk about and have you listen to include _____

_____

Productive "Criticism"—lovingly sharing hopes for the future. *(Avoid "you" statements and generalities, such as, "You never spend time with me" or "You always take the kids' side against me!" Use "I" and "me" statements positively, such as, "I sure miss being alone with you," or, "It would mean a lot to me if we could agree in front of the kids.")*

(Wife) Some of my hopes for the future I'd like to share include _____

_____

_____

(Husband) Some of my hopes for the future I'd like to share include ___

_____

_____

Appreciation—for "who" each of you is, and "what" you've done. *(Use these weekly meetings to remind yourself that your spouse is a blessing to you. Give sincere compliments to each other: "Thanks for your help with the kids." "I appreciate your patience when I was out of sorts.")*

(Wife) This week I especially appreciate my husband for _____

_____

_____

(Husband) This week I especially appreciate my wife for _____

_____

_____

FRIENDS Heal Inevitable Hurts

Romance cannot co-exist with resentment, yet marital conflict is inevitable. Every marriage has its share of hurtful words, misunderstandings, dashed expectations, and unmet needs. If these hurts aren't properly resolved, they will accumulate into bitterness, then resentment. We have talked in previous chapters about your emotional cup; the only way to keep it from overflowing with negative emotions is to empty it regularly through confession and forgiveness. Review, with your spouse, the chart on the next page showing the process for healing family emotional hurts, then complete the statements that follow.

Some of the ways I have hurt my spouse and my family this week include _____

_____

_____

After you and your spouse have each completed this statement, spend some time prayerfully confessing and forgiving each other.

FRIENDS Share the Truth in Love

Ask yourself these questions:

- Can I openly and lovingly communicate my needs to my spouse as well as to others?
- Can I honestly discuss my hurts?
- Can I expect God to meet my needs and still vulnerably share them with my spouse?
- Can I "[speak] the truth in love"? (Eph. 4:15)

Frankly, speaking the truth in love can be rather tricky. You may have a tendency to hide your feelings, to pretend that nothing is wrong, while you silently brood over perceived wrongs.

The other extreme is to share the truth . . . but not in love. More like venom, in fact. There may be nuggets of truth in the attacks you level, but

HEALING FAMILY EMOTIONAL HURTS

"Put away all bitterness and anger — and be kind, tender-hearted,
forgiving each other . . . " Ephesians 4:31–32

IDENTIFY HURT

I. ALONE list ways in which I have hurt my spouse and our marriage (or my parents/child).
   Examples: *selfish, critical/negative, insensitive, disrespectful, verbally abusive,*
   unsupportive, ungrateful, unfaithful, wrong priorities, rejecting, unforgiving
   (specific hurtful events, fights, arguments or "scenes" may need confession—use extra
   paper as needed!)

GAIN GOD'S FORGIVENESS

II. CONFESS to God and receive His forgiveness.
   1 John 1:9 "If we confess our sins, He [God] is faithful and just to forgive us our sins and to cleanse us
   from all unrighteousness."
   Example: *God, I have deeply hurt You and my spouse (child or parent) by my (from Item I).*
   These are very wrong and I ask You to forgive me. Thank You for doing so
   and I ask You to change me into the kind of person I need to be.

CONFESS HURT

III. TOGETHER share your lists and request forgiveness.
   James 5:16 "Confess your trespasses to one another, and pray for one another, that you may be healed."
   Example: *(At husband's or father's initiative) I've seen that I've hurt you deeply by being (from Item I).*
   I have been very wrong. Will you forgive me? ("Wrong" is much better than "sorry" since
   confess means "to agree with God" and God has said these things are wrong.)

   Response: "I forgive you."

   Remember: Forgiveness is a <u>choice</u>, not primarily a feeling! The question is not "do you <u>feel</u>
   like forgiving, but <u>will</u> you?" Will you release (drop) the hurt? . . . and then new
   feelings will come!

CHOOSE TO FORGIVE

   Other: *It might be important to ask, "Are there other major hurts that I've not seen that need my apology?*
   Please share them with me so I can confess them now and seek your forgiveness."

   Next: Wife shares her list (followed by children sharing theirs if this is a family session).

HEAL WITH NEW MEMORIES

IV. EXCHANGE LISTS and tear them up!
   Philippians 3:13 " . . . forgetting those things which are behind and reaching forward to those things
   which are ahead."

   Start the "forgetting" process with a focus on this new memory of forgiveness as lists are exchanged and
   destroyed. (Some people burn or bury them!)

   Additional suggestion: Hold hands and pray (even silently), thanking God for His forgiving you,
   changing you and healing your marriage and family.

CONTINUE

V. A NEW HABIT! " . . . *do not let the sun go down on your wrath.*"— Ephesians 4:26
   <u>Confession</u> to God and others we hurt, along with <u>forgiving</u> others who have hurt us, must become a
   daily habit if intimacy is to be maintained; otherwise your "Emotional Capacity" begins to fill again with
   hurtful emotions.

Become Friends, Lovers, and Saints Through Intimacy Disciplines **243** if the truth is hurled like a weapon, it wounds. Like poison darts. No love is evident in those slings and arrows.

Neither of these extremes will produce closeness in a relationship. Only as we share honestly and openly about what we need and what hurts us can we begin to develop closeness with our mate.

If you find your tendency is to speak the truth, but *not* in love, you may want to keep these principles in mind before you utter a word.

Think before you speak—just because you think something, you don't have to say it!

Take wrong thoughts "captive" as you share them with God, and allow Him to empower you to "cast them down" (2 Cor. 10:5). Sharing them with God helps get them out of your system and gives Him time to remind you of the truth.

Replace these thoughts with new ones which more adequately represent the truth. For example, "My wife is probably tired or needing time to relax. I know she loves me and I can use the time alone to think through some personal priorities."

Choose to speak edifying words—now that new thoughts have replaced the old ones. For example, "While I take a walk, why don't you relax or do something you enjoy? I'll look forward to us spending some time together when I get back."

During your next Marriage Staff Meeting, discuss what it means to "speak the truth in love," and tell your spouse, "I'd like to be more sensitive to you when we talk, so would you share with me some recent time when I've hurt you by something I said, or by the way I said it? I'd really like to know, so I can work at changing."

Then listen to what your spouse has to say, without arguing or being defensive. During the week, share it with God so He can work in you to change it.

Spend some time reviewing the worksheet, SPEAKING WORDS THAT EDIFY, then follow the steps that help you identify your complaints, re-think your concerns, and re-word them into positive sharing. When you've finished this worksheet, complete the statements below:

In considering the biblical admonition concerning an "unbridled tongue" (James 1:26), I realize I need to _____

_____

_____

SPEAKING WORDS THAT EDIFY

— Essential to Productive Criticism —

A "bridled" tongue, the Bible says, is a sign of maturity (James 3:2) and when it comes to criticism there's not a more difficult area of communication to "bridle." "Wholesome" words, the Bible says, are those that "edify" . . . build up and encourage (Ephesians 4:29). Miraculously even my "criticism" has the power to edify if I learn the three principles below of taking negative thoughts "captive" and re-wording them **before** I speak.

Steps	Examples	
I. Identify Your Negative/General Complaints *You never care what I think!* *You always forget what's important to me!* *You're just selfish!* Write recent complaints you've had:	*You're a jerk for ignoring your kids.* ● ● ● ●	*You seem to greet the dog better than you do me.* ● ● ●
II. Re-Think What Your Specific Concerns/Needs Are *I just need his undivided attention occasionally.* *I miss hearing from her that she loves me.* *I'm feeling a little left out and need some quality time.* Re-write your complaints from Step I into specific needs you have:	*I'm really fearing the impact on the kids of so little time with Dad.* ● ● ●	*One way I feel loved is through affection and I'm feeling rejected without it.* ● ● ●
III. Re-Word into Positive/Vulnerable Sharing *I've really missed our having some time alone; could we look at our schedules tonight and plan some? I really miss you.* *It would really mean a lot to me if we could visit soon about some discipline guidelines for the kids; I'm really needing your input.* Re-word your needs from Step II into positive/vulnerable expressions of your needs: (See "Thanks"/"Wish" List).	*Honey, what can I do to help free some of your time so you could be with the boys? They really enjoy being with you.* ● ● ● ●	*Sweetheart, I'm really looking forward to when you're more comfortable initiating affection. That means so much to me. I love you.* ● ● ●

"THANKS"/"WISH" LIST

I. BACKGROUND — This exercise is designed for couples and families to promote communication—especially concerning "sensitive" topics. A major benefit is to learn to share your wishes in a **positive** way.

II. BEGIN BY LISTING AT LEAST SIX AREAS OF GENUINE "THANKS"—you have about this relationship, i.e., husband and wife prepare lists or parents and children prepare lists. (Be specific, looking particularly for things you may have come to take for granted.)

> *Examples:*   *I'm grateful for your diligence as a provider for our family.*
> *I'm thankful for your faithfulness and loyalty as a wife.*
> *I'm thankful for the way you show you care with words and touch.*
> *I appreciate your sensitivity to others feelings.*

"Thanks" List

1.   4.

2.   5.

3.   6.

III. NEXT, LIST UP TO SIX "WISHES"—you might like to see concerning improvements and changes in this relationship. (Be specific and **positive** as you look for major items of importance to you.)

> *Examples:*   *I'm hoping you can become more comfortable initiating affection.*
> *I'd like to see all cursing and abusive language stop.*
> *I wish we would not criticize one another in front of others—particularly our children.*
> *I'd hope that you might speak respectfully to those in authority.*

"Wish" List

1.   4.

2.   5.

3.   6.

IV. SHARE YOUR LISTS WITH ONE ANOTHER—Take time together which is private and un-rushed
  – In sharing your "Thanks" lists be genuine, showing interest, emotion, and good eye contact.
  – In sharing your "Wish" lists be positive, encouraging, and looking to the future with hope.

> *Examples:*   *It would be important to me if* _____
>
> *It would mean a lot to me if* _____
>
> *I'm looking forward to the time when* _____

  – This sharing of "wishes" helps avoid the destructive cycle of:
  • Having expectations and anticipations (i.e. wishes) of another person.
  • Not communicating these wishes.
  • But, becoming hurt or angry when these expectations aren't met! This isn't fair to either of the parties.
  – Exchange lists if it will help you remember some of your partner's "Wishes."

V. PRACTICE PRAISE—Not Nagging—for the Next Month
  – Make no further mention of the "Wishes" during the next month (to do so would be to approach "nagging" and actually hinder progress.)
  – Make consistent effort to share praise for your "Thanks" List—plus other appreciations that come to mind.
  – Look for opportunities to share praise and appreciation
  • Privately with one another during daily conversations and private times
  • Publicly when in the company of others—like family members, children, or friends
  • In writing with special notes, cards, or gifts

Someone I've hurt recently with my words is _____
when I _____

_____

Now I realize what I should have said is _____

_____

_____

After you've completed the exercise above, spend some time going over the worksheet "THANKS"/"WISH" LIST and make your own lists of what you're thankful for in your spouse, as well as those improvements and changes you would like to see accomplished in your relationship. Encourage your spouse to complete a "THANKS"/"WISH" LIST as well. Then, during a special private time together, lovingly, prayerfully go over your lists. Plan to make this exercise a regular part of your lifelong Intimacy Disciplines.

FRIENDS Need to Express Appreciation

You and your spouse may appreciate each other for:

What You Do

The emphasis is on behavior, accomplishments, and other externals: "The dinner was great!" "I'm proud of your grades." "You look terrific in that outfit." "I appreciate your help with the lawn."

Who You Are

This emphasis is on character qualities and internal strengths. You may find it more difficult to compliment, but expressing appreciation in this area can have a significant impact on your spouse. (For example: "Your sensitivity to others is a real encouragement to me." "I don't tell you often enough, but I really appreciate your diligence as a provider for our family." "When I think of all the ways I've let you down, I'm so thankful God gave you such a forgiving spirit.")

You can express your appreciation in public or private, verbally or in a hundred creative ways. Spend a few minutes contemplating some of the ways you can express or demonstrate your appreciation for your partner, then complete these sentences:

Some of the creative ways I can express my appreciation for my spouse are _____

_____

_____

I wish my spouse would express appreciation for me by _____

_____

_____

FRIENDS Practice Emotional Responding

Did you ever stop to think that God is emotional? Scripture is filled with references to God expressing emotions, such as joy, compassion, grief, and anger. (Check out John 15:11, Neh. 9:17, and Eph. 4:30.) In fact, God *is* LOVE (1 John 4:8)! Thus, to be created in the image of God involves the capacity to experience and express emotion.

Moreover, all deep and intimate relationships must include an emotional element. Emotional closeness is a major factor in being "best friends" with your spouse, and it's a significant ingredient in sexual intimacy as well.

To create emotional closeness, you must develop a "vocabulary" of what you feel. Next, you must have open and supportive relationships in which feelings can be expressed and reassurance given. Remember, when your spouse shares emotions, don't reply with logic, reasons, facts, criticism, complaints, or neglect. Instead, learn the art of emotional responding.

Study the charts on page 249 to help you distinguish between the classic "productive" and "unproductive" responses to emotional need. Then complete the following statements.

Recent times when I gave my spouse unproductive responses include

_____

_____

Recent times when I used emotional responding include_____

_____

_____

Comparing these two approaches, I would have to say_____

_____

_____

The emotional response that would make me feel most like "best friends" with my spouse is _____

_____

_____

UNPRODUCTIVE RESPONSES

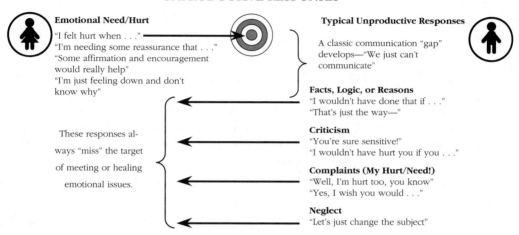

Emotional Need/Hurt

"I felt hurt when . . ."
"I'm needing some reassurance that . . ."
"Some affirmation and encouragement
would really help"
"I'm just feeling down and don't
know why"

These responses al-
ways "miss" the target
of meeting or healing
emotional issues.

Typical Unproductive Responses

A classic communication "gap"
develops—"We just can't
communicate"

Facts, Logic, or Reasons
"I wouldn't have done that if . . ."
"That's just the way—"

Criticism
"You're sure sensitive!"
"I wouldn't have hurt you if you . . ."

Complaints (My Hurt/Need!)
"Well, I'm hurt too, you know"
"Yes, I wish you would . . ."

Neglect
"Let's just change the subject"

EMOTIONAL RESPONDING

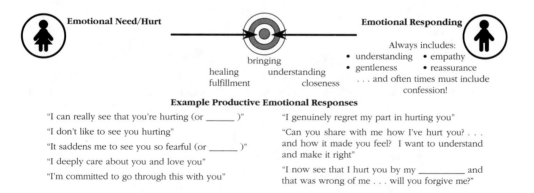

Emotional Need/Hurt

bringing
healing   understanding
fulfillment   closeness

Emotional Responding

Always includes:
• understanding   • empathy
• gentleness   • reassurance
. . . and often times must include
confession!

Example Productive Emotional Responses

"I can really see that you're hurting (or _____)"

"I don't like to see you hurting"

"It saddens me to see you so fearful (or _____)"

"I deeply care about you and love you"

"I'm committed to go through this with you"

"I genuinely regret my part in hurting you"

"Can you share with me how I've hurt you? . . .
and how it made you feel? I want to understand
and make it right"

"I now see that I hurt you by my _____ and
that was wrong of me . . . will you forgive me?"

I think the emotional response my spouse needs most from me is _____

_____

_____

LOVERS

LOVERS Make Time for Being Together Sexually

Only by better understanding where we *are* can we ever hope to get where we want to go! This age-old proverb is nowhere more true than in your journey toward more fulfilling sexual oneness. Let's look at "where you are" in your physical intimacy.

Our Intimacy Therapy work with couples employs classification systems which focus on sex as:

1. Something you DO . . . like other activities. (This hinders intimacy!)
2. Something you HAVE . . . like other possessions. (This hinders intimacy!)
3. BEING TOGETHER . . . to share another's presence. (This promotes intimacy!)

If sex is merely something you DO, then you'll evaluate it like other activities, such as tennis or golf:

- how often?
- how long?
- how adept?

Conflicts naturally follow over these and related variables.

If sex is simply something you HAVE, then you tend to view it as something to negotiate, trade, and conditionally share, like money or other possessions:

- not now
- maybe later
- maybe, if you would just . . .

Conflicts logically follow over manipulations, bargaining, and partners who go on strike!

As sex becomes more BEING TOGETHER, you begin to emphasize sharing and affirming each other's presence. Each feels cherished and valued as an important and meaningful person.

LOVERS Cultivate Romance

Keep in mind that sex is among the top four problems couples bring to a marriage counselor. "Quantity" is the most frequent complaint. Tragically, couples often define their sexual relationship in terms of numbers! How often do we have sex? How many times did one or the other reach orgasm? How much foreplay was there? How long did it last?

How tragic to take the God-designed plan for "two becoming one flesh" and reduce it to numbers. Some of us compound the problem by attempting to "negotiate" these numbers, comparing our sexual frequency with the "average" couple, whatever that is, or agreeing to "trade" two more sexual encounters per week for twenty minutes of foreplay (or a dinner date and cleaning the garage!).

The following approach is much more successful:

Improve lovemaking quality, and quantity resolves itself!

Begin your acts of tenderness when you part in the morning, expressing your desire to be together that night, so that throughout the day you can both anticipate the pleasurable evening ahead.

Add variety to your lovemaking. Vary the atmosphere by changing locations or times of day; change the lighting or use candles; change lingerie or sexy nightwear; change powders, perfumes, or aftershave. Play your favorite music.

Vary your routine by changing sexual positions; change who initiates (trade off pleasuring each other). Add a full body massage with baby oil or lotion; be together creatively somewhere other than the bed.

Communicate more openly. Don't let sexual intimacy be a guessing game. Two physically different people with differing personalities, backgrounds, preferences, and hang-ups must learn to talk openly about their sexual preferences. Don't make the mistake of assuming your partner should automatically know your wishes if he/she truly loved you. Having to verbalize what you need doesn't discount the deed!

Increase sexual desire. Remember, sex isn't all in your head, but a great deal of it is! Your thoughts can help put you in the right mood, and your mental appreciation of your spouse helps make your times together more meaningful and pleasurable. Many couples enhance their passion by letting their minds wander over pleasurable thoughts of their spouse throughout the day. By stimulating yourself mentally, your desire can be heightened even before the two of you touch. A vividly imagined "undress rehearsal" of how you'd like the encounter to unfold can be very stimulating.

David Ferguson has some special advice for husbands. He says: The three most important things in dealing with a wife sexually are:

1) Sex must become something you give to your wife and not something you take. Nothing quenches a wife's sexual feelings faster than feeling she has been taken from. Most guys have a locker room mindset that sex is something you take: "How far did you get with that girl?" "Does she make out?" Those are typical male attitudes.

2) You will improve your sexual intimacy immensely if you learn to give first to your wife emotionally. For a woman, sex is first emotional and then physical. For men, it tends to be just the opposite. When a couple has a fight, sometimes a man thinks, *I know what will fix this. We'll just make love!* The woman thinks, *Are you kidding? Not now, and maybe not ever!* How does a husband give emotionally? By spending time with his wife, vulnerably sharing his feelings, talking about things that are meaningful to her, and praising her character qualities.

3) Increase your nonsexual touching. Often, the only time a man touches his wife is when he wants to have sex. A woman begins to fear that if her husband touches her, she knows where they're headed, so she begins avoiding all touch. Make a point of occasionally holding hands (especially when praying together), putting your arm around her shoulder, embracing, or touching in other affectionate but nonsexual ways. A wife will feel cherished—and more responsive—when she knows her husband is touching her because he loves her, not because he wants to have sex.

LOVERS Share All of Themselves

The most fulfilling relationships are those in which there is freedom and openness to give and receive touch. But, there must be a balance to include all three dimensions—spiritual touching (for instance, embracing or touching while praying), soul touching (for instance, walking arm in arm, sitting close together), and sexual touching (for instance, soft skin touching, or brushing kisses on the back or the neck). One of the best ways to share all of yourselves is to regularly review, share, and anticipate the following "LOVE MAP" exercise. As you depict your own "ideal" intimate encounter, you can virtually "self-talk" your way to a more passionate love life!

Both you and your spouse should plan to spend some time before your next Marriage Staff Meeting filling out the LOVE MAP below to reflect your personal preferences and desires for sexual intimacy. Then, schedule a private "date" where you can spend an evening alone and take turns going over your LOVE MAPS. Have fun, and repeat this exercise as often as you wish!

LOVE MAP
". . . and they shall become one flesh"—Genesis 2:24

I. BACKGROUND—Four of the major hindrances to sexual intimacy are addressed in this exercise. These major hindrances are as follows:

1. **Lack of Openness/Communication**—Sex is <u>not</u> an easy subject to discuss for most couples; little experience or role-modeling, plus learned avoidance of the topic, leaves many couples in a cycle of little openness, resentments, and frustrations.

2. **Unhealthy Preoccupation with "Getting" Rather than "Giving"**—tragically many of us (especially men) grew up with a mind-set that sex was something to be taken, earned, or manipulated; the art of giving oneself to another person is therefore foreign to us and awkward.

3. **Boredom—Lack of Creativity/Freshness**—"Sameness" produces complacency and feelings of obligation and duty while creativity communicates initiative, desire, and anticipation.

4. **Lack of Anticipation and Expectancy**—as a man (or woman) THINKS, so is he (or she)!—Proverbs 23. Your mind is your most important sexual resource; learning to mentally anticipate times of being together with your spouse builds excitement, creativity, and desire.

II. COMPLETING YOUR "LOVE MAP"—Each spouse completes the chart below in answer to this question: "From my point of view, a perfect sexually intimate time with my spouse would include the following":

1.   7.

2.   8.

3.   9.

4.   10.

5.   11.

6.   12.

(Include personally meaningful items related to timing, location, clothing, and romantic preparations.)

(You might want to consider personal preferences related to initiative, foreplay, positions, and "afterplay".)

III. MARRIAGE INTIMACY—the Freedom to SHARE all of Oneself with Another Person . . . Body, Soul, and Spirit
- Exchange your "Love Maps"—pick a private time and place
- Discuss them as much as you are comfortable—(You'll grow more comfortable as you repeat the exercise.)
- Clarify and answer questions as appropriate
- "Free" your spouse to fulfill as much of your love map as he/she is now comfortable with . . . don't "insist," get pushy, or love conditionally!

IV. GIVE TO ONE ANOTHER—Schedule two times of intimacy to fulfill both Love Maps
- Husband (as the leader) should first "Give" in fulfilling his wife's Love Map—with a subsequent time for the wife to "Give"
- Schedule (plan a time for this so you can both anticipate it)
- Throughout the day, spend moments anticipating the pleasures of the two of you "becoming one"
- Freely share all of yourself with one another

V. REFLECT/EXPERIMENT/REPEAT THE EXERCISE—Have Fun!
- Return to Step II above and repeat this exercise!

SAINTS

SAINTS Make Spending Time with God a Priority in Their Lives, Both Individually and Together.

When it comes to spiritual intimacy, many couples wonder where to start. They find physical oneness (sex) relatively easy to "assess" or "count," while emotional oneness is more difficult to grasp, and spiritual oneness is almost too vague even to discuss. They wonder, *Does spiritual closeness mean attending the same church, or having identical beliefs, or using the same Bible?*

Sadly, for many couples, their individual spiritual life may be maturing, but their spiritual closeness as a couple is more a myth than reality. We suggest these principles for improving your spiritual closeness both personally and as a couple.

Where to start personally—commit to one new spiritual goal.

Couple closeness is based on two individuals each getting closer to God, only to find they feel closer to each other as well. You might try one of these goals or select one of your own:

- Read through the entire New Testament this year (one chapter a day will more than do it).
- Memorize ten Scripture passages on communications (Eph. 4:29, Prov. 10:19, 12:18, 12:25, 15:1, 15:28, 16:23, 17:27, 18:13, and 25:24).
- Establish a daily devotional time.
- Apply yourself to consistent topical Bible study.

Where to start as a couple—begin occasional silent prayer together. One of our recent surveys indicated fewer than 15 percent of church-going couples prayed together. The reasons may be obvious:

- I'm not sure what to say.
- I'd feel embarrassed or inhibited.
- I wouldn't pray as "good" as the minister.
- I might get corrected by my spouse.
  . . . and the list of excuses goes on.

Our simple recommendation is this: Spend a few minutes talking about things that matter—concerns, hopes, dreams, or fears. Talk about kids or work or money or feelings or future events. Then reach over and take your spouse's hand, and pray silently for two or three minutes. Later, if you become comfortable with praying out loud, fine. If not, that's fine too.

As you spend these times together, you'll sense an important spiritual closeness you hadn't felt before. You may find that a new emotional and physical closeness will follow as well.

In Matthew 18:19, Christ tells us, "Again I say to you that if two of you agree on earth concerning anything that they ask, it shall be done for them by My Father in heaven." Can you think of any more powerful "two" praying together than a husband and wife who, in God's eyes, are already one?

SAINTS Practice Praise and Worship for God's Unbounded GRACE!

For all of us, our only hope for a truly successful marriage lies outside ourselves and beyond our limited human resources. We cannot do it alone. You see, to sustain a genuinely intimate relationship, we would need an unending source of love, acceptance, comfort, and forgiveness. None of us can manage that on our own. But there is good news. Such a source is available. His name is Jesus . . . and He calls His divine contribution . . . GRACE.

Grace Initiates

"For by grace you have been saved"—Ephesians 2:8

It begins with grace. Divine grace initiates us into an intimate relationship with God. It was Christ who humbled Himself, took on the form of a servant, and became obedient to the point of death (Phil. 2:8) that we might become "partakers of the divine nature" (2 Peter 1:4). Noted Bible scholar Donald Barnhouse describes our undeserved gift of grace this way: "Love that goes upward is worship; love that goes outward is affection; love that stoops is grace." Christ stooped down from heaven, entered into our world, and gave Himself for us. What an example!

Grace Liberates

"It was for freedom that Christ set us free"—(Galatians 5:1 NASB)

It is grace that frees us from the penalty of sin and grants us eternal life so that one day we will be free from the presence of sin (Titus 3:5). But, much more, it is grace that liberates us from the power of sin.

- There's liberty from selfishness . . . freeing us to see and give to meet the needs of others.
- There's liberty from criticism . . . freeing us from judging others.

In other words, in our intimate relationships we have freedom to resist judging another's behaviors and freedom instead to give unselfishly to meet their deepest intimacy needs (Phil. 2:3).

Grace Motivates

"As good stewards of the manifold grace of God"—1 Peter 4:10

Living in the "awe and wonder" of all that we "have" and "are" in Christ motivates our own stewardship of grace. It goes like this: If God can bestow His grace on us, by His grace we can show His grace to one another. As we respond to His love, we feel welling up within us such a joyful gratefulness and humble appreciation that our giving to a spouse, child, friend, or even an enemy becomes spontaneous, almost beyond our control. Out of our innermost being flow such rivers of living water that they nourish intimacy in all our relationships (John 7:38). Grace is infectious, contagious, compelling, and irresistible!

Grace Lubricates

". . . be filled with the Spirit . . . giving thanks . . . submitting to one another"—Ephesians 5:18–21

Chuck Swindoll, in his excellent book *The Grace Awakening*, speaks of the marriage "oiled by grace." Grace lubricates the inevitable "rough edges" of our humanness. The demands and closeness of marriage and family inevitably bring our flaws and rough spots to the surface, but the truly intimate relationship ministers the oil of God's grace:

- As acceptance is granted . . . in spite of "performance"—Romans 15:7.
- As uplifting words are shared to build up and encourage—Ephesians 4:29.
- As personal responsibility is emphasized in our walk with our Savior—Romans 14:12.

As couples, we often miss the obvious. Couples miss the obvious fact that the closer we feel to God, the closer we will feel to each other; the

JOURNAL OF GRATEFULNESS

—an ongoing family project—

"Bless the Lord, O my soul, and forget not all His benefits" – Psalm 103:2

The Benefits of Gratefulness

Multiplied blessings are ours as we pause to "forget not all His benefits" toward us (Psalm 103:2). Among the numerous benefits of a grateful heart are the following:

- Gratefulness guards us from a critical, negative attitude.
- Gratefulness guards us from a judgmental spirit.
- Gratefulness, when expressed to others, can motivate them to continue in "good deeds."
- Gratefulness, when acknowledged to God, is an important element of worship.

The Search for Blessings

Regularly involve family members in a blessing search as each member names a recent blessing and assumes responsibility for sharing appreciation. Where to "look":

- Loved ones, who you've recently been reminded of in a special way.
- Character qualities in family or friends which are challenging.
- Often overlooked blessings of life, health, provision, creation.
- Specific answers to prayer.
- Spiritual realities like the Scriptures, salvation, Holy Spirit, etc.

The Expression of Appreciation

Appreciation helps seal in my heart the reality of the blessing as well as bless and encourage others. Appreciation can be shared:

- Verbally with a simple "thanks."
- In writing, with a note of appreciation.
- Publicly as testimony is given of our genuine gratitude.

Note: Especially as God has blessed us, our verbal thanks and testimony to others are of major importance.

Date	Family Member	How We Have Been Blessed *. . . look for God's interventions, expressions of family member love, answered prayers, and special people, events, and happenings*	How We Shared Our Appreciation *. . . say "thanks"; write a note; take a gift; give testimony*

more in tune we are with God, the more in tune we are with each other. And the more thankful we are to God for all He has given us, the more grateful we will feel for our spouse and family.

Spend some time before your next Marriage Staff Meeting going over the worksheet, JOURNAL OF GRATEFULNESS. Begin your own journal of gratefulness, writing down each day the people and events that have blessed you. Then share what you've written with those who have blessed you.

SAINTS Nourish Themselves with Scripture

Why is it so important that we immerse ourselves in the Scriptures? Perhaps Philippians 3:10 says it best: "That I may know Him and the power of His resurrection, and the fellowship of His sufferings, being conformed to His death." Let's look at that verse phrase by phrase, and use it as a springboard to other verses that help us glimpse a clearer picture of Christ.

That I May Know Him (Identifies Who He Is):

"Hearing Christ during quiet, reflective times allows me to "be still and know that He is God" (Ps. 46:10).

Time "with" Christ is important; our intimacy grows as I invest my time in praise of His working and in worship of His character (Mark 3:14).

Being alone with Christ in prayer and meditation is important to me, reminding me of my dependence on Him, especially as I see His dependence on the Father (Mark 1:35).

Seeing Christ in His humanness with compassion and tears gives me insight into how He will live through me (Luke 19:37–41).

That I May Know the Fellowship of His Sufferings (Identifies Him with Me):

Christ understands our struggles, trials, and pain; therefore, we're not without support (Heb. 4:15).

Christ ministers as one who has received compassion; therefore, we're not without comfort (Isa. 53:3).

Christ identifies with our loneliness and distress; therefore, we're not alone (Matt. 26:38).

Christ comprehends our anger that rises from a grieved heart; therefore, we're not judged or condemned (Mark 3:5).

That I May Know the Power of His Resurrection (Identifies Me with Him):

Because He died and rose again . . . I can live IN Him, drawing on His strength, wisdom, and love (Gal. 2:20).

Because He died and rose again . . . I can live AS Him, extending His presence into my world by the power of His Spirit (1 John 4:17).

Because He died and rose again . . . I can live FOR Him, living as His ambassador, sharing His life and love (2 Cor. 5:20).

Because He died and rose again . . . I can live TO GLORIFY Him, responding in gratefulness and wonder at the grace He's given me (1 Cor. 6:20).

Do you see how it works? How Christ becomes more real as you plunge into the depths of His Word, as you taste and are filled by the Living Waters? Read and savor. Drink, and let your thirst be quenched. Eat, and be filled.

During your next devotional time, read over and complete the worksheet on the next page, DISCOVER THE POWER AND POTENTIAL OF MEDITATION. Spend as much time as necessary reflecting on those "battles" you are fighting today, or those areas of personal need that threaten to overwhelm you this very moment.

Follow the three steps of Meditation: Memorize, Personalize, and Visualize. Then, during a quiet moment with your spouse, or during a future Marriage Staff Meeting, share those battles and how God worked in your life to ease the burden.

SAINTS Experience Intimacy in God's Family.

Read over the worksheet on page 261 titled, "Intimacy Ingredients from the Upper Room."

After spending some time in silent prayer and meditation, write in the space below about how your relationship with God and your relationship with your spouse has changed since you began this study.

My relationship with God has changed as _____

_____

_____

My relationship with my spouse has changed as _____

_____

_____

Write from your heart about how the two relationships are connected and how one impacts the other._____

_____

_____

DISCOVER THE POWER AND POTENTIAL OF MEDITATION

"In humility receive the word implanted, which is able to save your souls" (James 1:21 NASB)

Humility speaks of "teachableness" and submission; dependence rather than independence. The Word "receive" means literally to "embrace" as in a strong WELCOME. The dependence and welcome are focused on the Word.

Christ-likeness for the Christian comes forth as the Spirit within us ministers the Word through our "soul" (mind, emotions, and will) – to empower our lives. This is the spirit-controlled life that God provides and Satan resists!

Noted below are key ingredients in the principles of meditation:

In humility "welcome" the Word!

SPIRIT

SOUL
MIND
EMOTIONS
WILL

BODY

Allow God to show you areas of personal need and find passages of Scripture relating to them. Then, take these Scripture passages through the following steps:

"MEDITATION" INVOLVES
ALL THREE OF THESE STEPS

This Book of the Law shall not depart from your mouth, but you shall meditate in it day and night . . . and then you will have good success.—(Joshua 1:8)

But his delight is in the Law of the LORD and in His Law he meditates day and night . . . And whatever he does shall prosper.— (Psalm 1:2–3)

1. MEMORIZE —
   The entrance of Your words gives light—(Psalm 119:130). *It is a pleasant thing if you keep them within you.*— (Proverbs 22:18)

2. PERSONALIZE —
   Put Scripture into the first-person and quote it back to God. *If you abide in Me, and My words abide in you, you will ask what you desire and it shall be done for you.*—(John 15:7)

3. VISUALIZE —
   Picture or "visualize" key words. *If you cry out for discernment, And lift up your voice for understanding, If you seek her as silver, and search for her as for hidden treasures; then you will understand the fear of the LORD and find the knowledge of God.*— (Proverbs 2:3–5)

LIST SOME AREAS OF PERSONAL NEED OR AREAS OF
"BATTLE" YOU ARE NOW "FIGHTING" IN YOUR LIFE

1. _____   4. _____

2. _____   5. _____

INTIMACY INGREDIENTS FROM THE UPPER ROOM

Topical Study from John's Gospel, Chapters 13–17

INTIMACY INGREDIENTS	RELEVANT SCRIPTURE PASSAGES
I CARE ABOUT YOU *Casting all your anxiety upon Him because He **cares** for you* (1 Peter 5:7 NASB)	• "Then He poured water into the basin, and began to wash the disciples' feet" (John 13:5 NASB) • "I will come again, and receive you to Myself" (John 14:3 NASB) • "But the Helper, the Holy Spirit . . . He will teach you all things" (John 14:26 NASB) • "Peace I leave with you, My peace I give to you" (John 14:27 NASB) • "These things I have spoken to you, that My joy may be in you" (John 15:11 NASB) • "Your sorrow will be turned to joy" (John 16:20 NASB) • "Your heart will rejoice, and no one takes your joy away" (John 16:22 NASB)
I TRUST YOU *Let a man regard us in this manner, as servants of Christ, and stewards of the mysteries of God. In this case, moreover, it is required of stewards that one be found trustworthy* (1 Corinthians 4:1–2 NASB)	• "I have called you friends, for all things that I have heard from My Father I have made known to you" (John 15:15 NASB) • "From now on you know [my father] and have seen Him" (John 14:7 NASB) • "I will love him, and disclose Myself to him" (John 14:21 NASB) • "When He, the Spirit of truth, comes . . . He will disclose to you what is to come" (John 16:13 NASB) • "The words which Thou gavest Me I have given to them; and they received them" (John 17:8 NASB) • "And the glory which Thou hast given Me I have given to them" (John 17:22)
I NEED YOU *I am the vine, you are the branches; he who abides in Me and I in him, he bears much fruit; for apart from Me you can do nothing* (John 15:5 NASB)	• "You also ought to wash one another's feet, for I gave you an example" (John 13:14–15 NASB) • "He who believes in Me . . . greater works than these shall he do" (John 14:12 NASB) • "I chose you . . . that you should go and bear fruit" (John 15:16 NASB) • "And you will bear witness also, because you have been with Me" (John 15:27 NASB) • "As Thou didst send Me into the world, I also have sent them into the world" (John 17:18 NASB) • "That they also may be in Us, that the world may believe that thou didst send Me" (John 17:21 NASB)
I LOVE YOU *A new commandment I give to you, that you **love** one another, even as I have **loved** you* (John 13:34 NASB)	• "Greater love has no one than this, that one lay down his life for his friends" (John 15:13 NASB) • "I will ask the Father, and He will give you another Helper" (John 14:16 NASB) • "I will not leave you as orphans; I will come to you" (John 14:18) • "Because I live, you shall live also" (John 14:19 NASB) • "Just as the Father has loved Me, I have also loved you; abide in My love" (John 15:9 NASB) • "While I was with them, I was keeping them . . . and I guarded them" (John 17:12 NASB) • "I desire that they also, whom Thou hast given Me, be with Me where I am" (John 17:24 NASB)

I do no ask in behalf of these alone, but for those also who
believe in Me through their word . . ." John 17:20

Write about what you feel you have gained from this study—special insights into your marriage, or any new sensitivity you've developed toward God and your spouse. _____

_____

_____

Write about any changes you've noticed in your perception and understanding of yourself since beginning this study. _____

_____

_____

Our hope is that, as you and your spouse implement these Intimacy Disciplines into the fabric of your lives, the *three* of you will share a most intimate, loving, and rewarding journey—you, your spouse, and your Creator!

Appendix 1

---■---

PRINCIPLES OF INTIMACY THERAPY

1. Intimacy Therapy views man from a Judeo-Christian world view as being created in God's image and having existence in three dimensions—spirit, soul, and body. These dimensions give rise to various human functions, namely: The Body functions through the five senses and we are "world conscious"; the Soul functions through our thoughts, feelings, and choices and we are "self-conscious"; the Spirit functions through conscience, intuition, and worship and we are "God conscious."

2. Intimacy Therapy sees man as separated from God, by nature, and as being motivated out of a need for intimacy with God and intimacy through meaningful relationships ordained by God, i.e marriage, the family, and the church (the body of Christ).

3. Intimacy Therapy views fulfillment and abundance in life from a biblical perspective as coming by grace through faith in personal intimacy with Jesus Christ and in intimate relationships with meaningful others as ordained by Him.

4. Intimacy Therapy views problems in living (i.e., pathology) and marital and family conflict from an object-relations/developmental framework, in the context of unmet intimacy needs which result in unhealthy thinking, unhealed emotions, and unproductive behaviors.

5. Intimacy Therapy views this pattern of unmet needs, unhealthy thinking, unhealed emotions, and unproductive behaviors as the

major hindrances to intimacy and thus the focus of therapeutic intervention.

6. Intimacy Therapy includes a systems perspective which seeks to address, in marriage and family counseling, the personal, relational, and intergenerational origins of the intimacy hindrances noted above. Thus, in marriage counseling, a premise of Genesis 2:24 would be to "leave father and mother, cleave to one another, and the two shall become one flesh." In other words, since "leaving" precedes "cleaving," one would expect intergenerational issues to hinder the relational issues involved in marital "cleaving."

7. Intimacy Therapy seeks to address enhancing intimacy through meeting intimacy needs in the spectrum of four major ingredients or intimacy processes, namely: Affectionate caring, vulnerable communication, joint accomplishment, and mutual giving for intimacy to be maintained; these intimacy processes become linked to one another in a repeated spiral over the family life cycle.

8. Intimacy Therapy views the family life cycle as bringing predictable challenges to relational intimacy, and thus the need to repeat the "spiral" of intimacy ingredients, beginning with affectionate caring; thus, the marital stage of mutual giving is challenged by the addition of children to return to affectionate caring, followed by vulnerable communication, joint accomplishment, and, again, mutual giving.

9. Intimacy Therapy draws on emotionally focused therapies as an addition to cognitive and behavioral techniques. The "empathetic comforting of identified hurts and needs" is a pivotal element in the affectionate-caring ingredient of intimacy. Because a fundamental breakdown or hindrance to intimacy results from a lack of empathetic comfort, this connection serves as the beginning point of Intimacy Therapy.

10. Intimacy Therapy, in a "staged" approach to marriage counseling, seeks to address in Stage 1: Initial Assessment (or self-inventory) of the individuals, the marriage relationship, and intergenerational dynamics; in Stage 2: Increased Stability of the marriage relationship as a basis for improved functioning and additional therapeutic intervention; in Stage 3: the Leave-Cleave issues of intergenerational significance which contribute to personal problems in living and marital

discord; in Stage 4: the Becoming One Disciplines which help ensure relational intimacy, personal maturity, and positive mental health.

11. Intimacy Therapy views the Christian counselor (layperson, pastor, or mental health practitioner) as playing a God-intended role within the Body of Christ to assist and encourage others along a journey toward experiencing "life and life abundant" (John 10:10). Specifically, the counselor's role is fourfold within the framework of eliminating hindrances and enhancing intimacy. He is to assist the couple in their need for intimacy with God and with one another by:

Eliminating Hindrances	Enhancing Intimacy
a. Identifying and Interrupting Unproductive Behaviors	Modeling and Reinforcing Productive Behaviors
b. Resolving Unhealed Emotions	Experiencing Positive Emotions
c. Identifying and Countering Unhealthy Thinking	Internalizing Healthy Thinking
d. Identifying Unmet Intimacy Needs	Modeling and Encouraging the Meeting of Intimacy Needs

Appendix 2

■

IMPLEMENTING A MARRIAGE INTIMACY MINISTRY

Designed to be used as part of a comprehensive ministry to marriages and families, we hope that this workbook will provide you with practical tools and helpful information as you serve the Lord.

There are at least four ways to use Intimate Encounters as a marriage enrichment tool, along with supportive material from *The Pursuit of Intimacy* and *Intimate Moments*. These four uses are summarized below with detailed explanations in the pages to come. Feel free to adapt these concepts to fit your church, organization, or ministry needs.

USES FOR INTIMATE ENCOUNTERS

1. Marriage Intimacy Teaching Series. This class might be of any size and would be sponsored by your church or organization. In the context of a sixteen week series, the principles of Intimacy Therapy would be introduced through large and small group formats. *Intimate Encounters* would serve as the textbook for these teaching sessions along with supportive material from *The Pursuit of Intimacy* and *Intimate Moments*.

2. Marriage Intimacy Support Group. This group would provide mutual encouragement and accountability in the context of a small group environment (eight to ten people). Such a group might focus on engaged partners, newlyweds, individuals in mid-life, or those needing support because of a broken relationship. *Intimate Encounters* would be used as a guide for sixteen weeks of interaction and discussion.

3. Mentoring Ministry. This approach has a discipleship focus, where a mentor couple would come alongside another couple or individual for the purpose of role-modeling, counseling, and support. Using *Intimate Encounters*, a mentor couple might meet with an engaged couple, a couple needing marriage counsel, or an individual struggling with the pain of a broken relationship.

4. Marriage Intimacy Counseling Sessions. There may be situations when a couple needs an individualized relationship with a minister or counselor. The caregiver may want to use *Intimate Encounters* as a guide for homework assignments, counseling topics, and discussion questions.

A complete curriculum guide, as well as information about training opportunities are available through the Center for Marriage and Family Intimacy, P. O. Box 201808, Austin, TX 78720 (800-881-8008).

The Pursuit of Intimacy: What Falling in Love Was Meant to Be, by David & Teresa Ferguson and Chris & Holly Thurman, provides a detailed study of the ten "action verbs" of Intimacy Therapy.

Intimate Moments, by David & Teresa Ferguson and Chris & Holly Thurman, provides daily devotions for couples with a particular focus on Intimacy needs.

BENEFITS OF A TEACHING SERIES DEDICATED TO MARRIAGE INTIMACY

A teaching ministry dedicated to marriage intimacy will provide the most comfortable environment for those who may be reluctant to address marriage issues, or individuals who may be new to the church environment.

The format detailed in *Intimate Encounters* can be easily adapted to regular Sunday morning or Wednesday evening church schedules. Church leaders may want to begin a new class that is open to members from any age group. Other churches may want to implement the *Intimate Encounters* material into existing adult classes.

A marriage class provides an important accountability connection with other Christians. Church leaders may find that this class is an excellent resource for couples who want to enrich their marriage relationship, and a vehicle for community outreach. Additionally, if a minister determines that a couple has counseling needs that require significant attention, a marriage class can serve as a point of stabilization. Ministers can refer couples to a marriage class and then make referrals to support groups or mentors as they become available.

Suggested Roles and Responsibilities of the Teaching Leader

A good teaching leader:

- is committed to the Scriptures. He/she is not necessarily a scholar, but has reverence for God's Word, and believes in the power of applied Scripture to change marriages.
- works with other leaders. He/she coordinates with other class leaders to set ministry goals and define teaching topics each week.
- guides the study during both the small and large group sessions.
- gives sincere attention to class members, building a relationship of trust and support.
- is sensitive to the needs of non-churched class members and helps them feel welcomed and appreciated.
- implements the teaching series on marriage and relationships.

Suggestions for a Marriage Intimacy Teaching Ministry

Teachers will want to schedule the marriage and family series at least once a year. Our suggested curriculum plan follows a thirteen to sixteen week schedule.

Each marriage class will have different needs, but we have found that using a combination of large and small groups effectively communicates the principles of Intimacy Therapy. Teachers will want to dedicate the large group (opening) session to presentation of key principles in each workbook chapter. Then by using discussion questions and group activities from *Intimate Encounters*, encourage practical application of the key concepts.

Teaching leaders will want to be especially sensitive to the needs of class members during small group activities because their needs will not always match the planned agenda. Sometimes you will want the group to visit and get better acquainted; sometimes you will want to pool knowledge and help the group find answers to situations or apply scriptural teachings. At other times, you will want to provide a safe atmosphere where class members can share pressing needs. It will be up to the teaching leader to be aware of these needs and be prepared to cope with various situations should they arise.

Lastly, do not be anxious about finishing *Intimate Encounters*. Again consider the needs of the class members and tailor each lesson accordingly. Relax and enjoy being involved in the Lord's ministry to marriages.

BENEFITS OF A MARRIAGE INTIMACY SUPPORT GROUP MINISTRY

By establishing marriage support groups the church or organization provides an opportunity for growth and change for many individuals. The support group provides a place to refer hurting people; the entire congregation can be affected by the renewed focus on meeting intimacy needs and group leaders realize new skills and abilities.

Support groups offer refuge and strength as they:

- share unconditional love and acceptance.
- offer a safe, trusted place to share feelings.
- encourage members to express needs and receive God's healing.
- provide a gentle framework for challenging unhealthy behaviors.
- offer true fellowship and community.

Roles and Responsibilities of the Support Group Leader

A good support group leader is one who:

- feels a strong desire to provide a place where hurting people can gather for the purpose of experiencing God's healing.
- prayerfully considers his own time commitments, life experiences, and personal health before beginning this journey.
- is able to create an accepting, nonjudgemental environment for those around them.
- has a firm commitment to confidentiality and to God's Word.
- can be transparent and vulnerable about his own struggles without using the group as a sounding board.
- is able to empathize with various age groups and life stages.
- has a compassion and grace oriented spirit rather than someone who may try to fix others.

How to Begin a Support Group Ministry

1. Identify leadership. Leaders and co-leaders should work through *Intimate Encounters* individually, with a spouse, or in a group prior to leading a marriage support group.

2. Obtain pastoral support. A church staff person should be enlisted to provide accountability and support for group leaders.

3. Establish a referral base. Occasionally outside help or professional counseling may be necessary in order to help a person get beyond a particular struggle. It will be appropriate to encourage professional help if an individual is suicidal, homicidal, unable to interpret reality, extremely depressed, fearful or anxious, abusing alcohol or other chemicals, or presenting issues that are beyond your ability to help.

4. Set goals for the group. Prayerfully consider the purpose for the support group and the kind of environment that will bring the most healing.

5. Determine a starting date.

6. Select an appropriate time. Support group meetings are usually one and a half to two hours in length. Be sure to set specific starting and ending times and make a commitment to respect these times.

7. **Reserve a location to meet.** You will want to meet in a quiet atmosphere so as to limit interruptions. Meet in a room that will accommodate the size of the group. Also, be sure that the chairs can be arranged to facilitate discussion (i.e. circle, semi-circle).

8. **Decide how to advertise.** This group might consist of couples referred by ministers and the church staff or you may want to consider some of the following:

- church bulletins and newsletters
- Sign-up Sundays
- pulpit announcements
- community newspapers
- testimony by group member
- contact therapists/hospitals

9. **Determine how to finance the group.** Expenses for the workbooks and supplies can be covered by group members, by the sponsoring organization, or a combination thereof.

10. **Consider supplies needed.** In addition to *Intimate Encounters*, secure other items such as markerboard, markers, Kleenex, beverages, etc.

Walking Through a Meeting

The following outline represents the basic components of a typical Marriage Intimacy Support Group.

- The group gathers and prays.
- Sometimes the group may participate in group building activities.
- Each member briefly shares an accountability report and/or a meaningful intimacy encounter which he/she shares with his/her spouse.
- The group leader(s) present(s) new material to be discussed.
- Sometimes the group leader(s) may choose to discuss an urgent need of one of the group members rather than the topic set aside for that meeting.
- The group leader(s) bring some closure to the discussion.
- The group leader(s) share any assignments or reading that will be discussed next week.
- The group closes with prayer.

Suggestions for the Support Group Leader

Intimate Encounters is designed to be used in small group settings. The information included in the gray sections of this workbook will reflect most of the essentials in leading marriage support groups.

It will be important for all support group leaders to take advantage of any training opportunities available in their community. Make sure you have a support system of your own, a place where you can share your own needs and receive comfort.

Because of the sensitive issues that will be discussed in these marriage support groups you will want to make this group a closed group. Invite members to join the group for a period of three weeks. Than after the three weeks, no new members are invited to join. Any new members will need to wait until the sixteen weeks have been completed.

A copy of the following Support Group Commitment should be provided for each member to read. This should be discussed at the first meeting and other discussions included as necessary.

SUPPORT GROUP MEMBER COMMITMENT

Our support group is a family of individuals who meet to share their thoughts and feelings concerning struggles, pain, strengths, and hope. We acknowledge that God is present with us and is our source of hope. We encourage each other to seek Him through their journey of healing.

As a Christ-centered support group, we seek to meet the following needs of the individual:

Attention	to enter into other members' lives through interest, concern, and caring. (1 Cor. 12:25)
Acceptance	to treat others as Jesus treats us with a kind, positive reception. (Rom. 15:7)
Appreciation	to communicate gratefulness and praise for others. (1 Cor. 11:2)
Comfort	to offer consolation through words, feelings, and touch. (1 Thess. 5:18)
Encouragement	to urge and persuade others toward health and wholeness. (1 Thess. 5:11)
Respect	to demonstrate honorable consideration and courtesy for others through words and actions. (Rom. 12:19)
Security	to convey the feeling to others that they are safe and free from danger. (Mark 9:50)
Support	to practically assist in helping others with their problems or burdens. (Gal. 6:2)

As a Christ-centered support group we seek to maintain the unity and health of the group by:

- maintaining confidentiality (all names, words, actions, observations, and impressions are not repeated outside the group).
- promoting community by not talking about members not currently present.
- seeking to participate in both the giving and receiving of support and care.

- honoring the leadership by accepting their direction of the group and reserving leadership concerns until after the group time.
- seeking Christian counseling outside the group time when one's emotional intensity requires more time and care than the group is able and equipped to handle.
- understanding that our greatest gift to each other is to listen and encourage rather than to fix, advise, or attempt to solve others' problems as we see them.
- offering constructive feedback and brainstorming when invited by members.
- acknowledging and respecting differences in stages of growth and healing and refraining from comparison.
- acknowledging that we are affected by both past and present circumstances but will focus on current life situations and relationships.

In order to maintain and care for the support group, the church-based group leader:

- understands that this is a non-professional group under the leadership of the local church, or ministry, which sponsors it.
- seeks guidance and support from his pastor and/or local professional.
- offers continuing education opportunities during group time from outside professionals.

BENEFITS OF A MENTORING MINISTRY

In a mentoring ministry a two-on-two relationship is established between a mentor couple and a discipled couple. Impact could be made in three areas:

1. Premarital. Mentor couples could supplement a minister's efforts with engaged couples.

2. Extension of marriage counseling. Mentor couples could be helpful as an addition to marriage counseling or in some cases instead of marriage counseling.

3. Ministry to one spouse. Mentor couples may find it appropriate to minister to one spouse who expresses a desire to restore a broken or separated relationship.

Church leaders may find that there will be a fewer number of couples who need a mentor relationship. However, this option may be most appropriate if:

- the couples' needs require more than a sixteen week commitment.
- one or both partners exhibit an extreme level of anger or anxiety.
- the couple presents issues of immorality or infidelity inappropriate to group settings.
- the couple would benefit from additional accountability, apart from a support group or marriage class.